A Trolleybus
to the
Punch Bowl

The Trolleybuses and Routes of the
South Lancashire Transport Co. Ltd.
1930 to 1958

by
Phillip J. Taylor

TRIANGLE

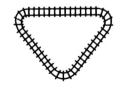

PUBLISHING

Copyright © Phillip J. Taylor 2002
First published 2002 by Triangle Publishing.
British Library Cataloguing Data.
Taylor P.J.
A Trolleybus to the Punch Bowl.
ISBN 0-92529333-7-3
Printed in England by
The Amadeus Press Ltd.,
Cleckheaton.
Text by Phillip J.Taylor.
Maps by A.Palmer.
Compiled and edited for publication
by D.J.Sweeney.
Cover design by Scene, Print & Design Ltd.,
Leigh, Lancs.
Designed and published by
Triangle Publishing,
509, Wigan Road,
Leigh, Lancs. WN7 5HN.
Tel: 01942/677919
www.trianglepublishing.co.uk

Front Cover.

Roe bodied Guy BT No.31, rebuilt with a new front, turns from Market Street, Atherton, into Wigan Road on a Farnworth route service on 27th February 1956.

Rear cover, upper.

Bolton's town hall provides the backdrop to Weymann bodied Sunbeam MS2 No.66, awaiting departure to Leigh from a deserted Howell Croft bus station on 19th February 1956.

Rear Cover, Lower. Roe bodied Guy BT No.35, having unloaded alongside Atherton Savoy cinema, pauses before making a right hand turn into Wigan Road to the Farnworth route boarding point on 27th February 1956.

Photos, the late J.Batty.

Plate 1. The most modern trolleybuses operated by South Lancashire Transport were six three axle Sunbeam MS2s delivered in 1948. Being 30ft in length with stylish highbridge Weymann bodywork they were impressive machines and quite a contrast to the lowbridge Roe bodied Guys which were in many ways synonymous with the SLT. Sunbeam No.67 stands at Bolton's Howell Croft terminus beneath the town hall clock in the company of a Bolton Corporation Crossley DD42/3 in July 1956.

Photo, J.C.Gillham.

CONTENTS

ACKNOWLEDGEMENTS

The final ceremonial run of trolleybus No.71 on 1st September 1958 took place when I was 9 years old. At that age I was travelling to Bolton School on my own using the Leigh to Bolton trolley as part of my journey. Whilst I was old enough to retain vivid memories and absorb much of the detail of the system, it will be no surprise that I can claim just one photograph as my own concerning anything to do with the SLT. Ironically I took this in 1985, photographing the redundant tram tracks in Templeton Road on the St. Helens route just before they finally succumbed to tarmac, in truth more to do with the trams than the trolleybuses which had replaced them 55 years earlier!

A book such as this requires both the seeds of inspiration to be cultivated and the material to support it. As far as the former is concerned my thanks go, not only to an inner sanctum of 'knowledgeable persons' on SLT matters whom I have known individually for many years, but also to those whom I have come to know on the way whom have offered their assistance and encouragement as the book progressed.

My thanks go to all those who made available their photographic records, artefacts and maps of the SLT whether privately or corporately and to librarians and local historians who gave their time to provide material for inclusion. My apologies are offered for any errors or omissions regarding accreditation.

Mention must be made of the 'anonymous many' who contributed by way of odd snippets including those in public houses as far apart as Haydock and Farnworth who were able to recall the SLT as if the red trolleybuses would still be their transport home. The SLT served mining communities and those same persons were moved to remind me of the disaster of December 1910 at the Pretoria Pit at Chequerbent when an underground gas explosion claimed the lives of 344 men and boys.

The staff of Worsley village library provided me with a copy of 'The Worsley Village Heritage Trail' and directed me to the booklet's researcher and author Ann Monaghan, Life Times Outreach Officer, City of Salford Education and Leisure. My thanks go to Ann for making available some excellent photographs of Walkden Memorial in the latter days of the trolleybuses.

My appreciation goes to the landlord of the *Black Horse* public house in Farnworth for the loan from his lounge wall of the print of Higher Market Street showing the Farnworth trolley loop running towards Brackley Street.

This book would be much the less were it not for the considerable input, both photographically and factually, from Jack Batty who sadly passed away during 2000. Jack, who had an extensive knowledge of the system, lived for many years at Four Lane Ends and viewed the SLT with great affection. He was active in photographing and filming the system in colour just before the first closures and it seems wholly appropriate to dedicate the colour spread to a selection of his work.

Another member of the inner sanctum is Peter Thompson whom I thank for both his photographic contribution and for proof reading and providing a critique of the manuscript. Peter, who frequently visited the SLT from 1956 onwards until its closure, as if tending an elderly aunt, had the presence of mind to commit to notes much of what he observed, insignificant at the time perhaps, but a valuable source of corroborating evidence for the purpose of this book. Using only basic photographic equipment, Peter succeeded in capturing the flavour and character of the SLT, ingredients that contribute significantly to this nostalgic reflection.

Another who holds the SLT close to his heart is Jim Saunders. I always knew Jim to be the owner of infinite detail concerning the SLT infrastructure and its operation. The creation of a book about the SLT, so long after the system closed, was bound to expose conflicting evidence, knowledge gaps, and apparent anachronisms. Jim's assistance in the research and detective work which ensured that facts eventually prevailed over fiction has been invaluable. Thanks also go to Jim for his recommendations regarding photographic selection and suggested changes and additions to the text.

Support and recommendations from Dennis Sweeney of Triangle Publishing have been invaluable. My thanks go to him and to Brian Hughes for access to his comprehensive ticket collection.

Finally, in my case, such a book could not have come into existence without the support and encouragement of my wife Susan and her tolerance of a house full of books and photographs. My thanks go to her and to my two sons Richard and Edward who ensured that I was not deprived of 'windows of opportunity' at the computer.

INTRODUCTION

On 24th March 1972 the last trolleybus ran in public service in Britain on the once extensive Bradford system. Thus ended a chapter of public transport in this country which, over a period of some 60 years, has seen around 50 undertakings commit to the trolleybus at various times.

This mode of operation had its zenith just before the second world war. However, post war austerity, the high cost of equipment renewal and, in due course, fuel price politics all weighed in favour of the more flexible motor bus.

The South Lancashire Transport Company, with its headquarters at Howe Bridge, Atherton, and Mr. E.H. Edwardes as General Manager, commenced the introduction of trolleybuses to replace trams in 1930. The fleet reached a maximum strength of 71 vehicles, the oldest of which had achieved a venerable age of 28 when the system finally closed on 31st August 1958.

To the casual observer, the SLT trolleybus system was a curious affair with red trolleybuses often of quite antique appearance playing hide and seek over an apparently large area to the west of the City of Manchester.

The hub of the system was Atherton from where the wiring of just over thirty one route miles radiated in four directions including Leigh to the south, Bolton to the north and Farnworth to the north east, but not before one had been taken on a considerable detour en route via Worsley and Swinton. Finally to the west was the joint operation with St. Helens Corporation's red and cream trolleybuses via Hindley and Ashton in Makerfield to St. Helens. Such was the uniquely interurban nature of the SLT.

Had the politics of the day been different, the early post war years may have seen extensions to the system, perhaps in conjunction with Bolton Corporation, to Walkden and Pendlebury via Farnworth, also to Westhoughton via Deane.

Part of the charm of the system was its ability to pop up when least expected, crossing the busy A 580 East Lancashire Road, joining and suddenly leaving the main A6 at Little Hulton and Swinton, or even diverting onto unmetalled roads with tram track still in situ on the way to St. Helens.

The overall route mileage gave a hint to the meandering nature of some routes such as that between Atherton and Farnworth. Indeed the SLT is no example to the students of today studying integrated transport policy. The SLT, along with the Manchester and Ashton-under-Lyne trolleybus systems, formed the last vestige of a once extensive electric road passenger transport network serving South Lancashire that had enabled travel under wire by tram and trolleybus from Liverpool's Pier Head to the foothills of the Pennines near Saddleworth and as far into Cheshire as Hazel Grove and Altrincham.

I vividly recall travelling from Manchester along the A6, arriving at the traffic lights at Swinton to be met by the overhead wires accompanying the broad dual carriageway portion of Partington Lane joining from the left. The loosely suspended overhead followed the corner at Swinton church to join the A6 as part of the Atherton to Farnworth route. If one was lucky, since some services were not too frequent, a venerable red lowbridge trolleybus, silently negotiating the bend, proved a sight to ponder.

This was the best of the SLT, yet as suddenly as it came upon you at Swinton, it took its leave at Little Hulton, disappearing to the right at traffic lights to climb Cleggs Lane, along which the wires were suspended over one side of the road from the bracket arms of former trampoles; testimony to SLT economy. Further along the A6 trolleywires reappeared, this time as the Leigh to Bolton route crossed at Four Lane Ends.

Few would have boarded at Atherton with the aim of travelling all the way to Farnworth. This route, whilst having a through trolleybus service via Swinton, was indirect and better considered as providing overlapping or 'end on' services sharing common wiring and connecting Atherton, Mosley Common, Worsley, Swinton and Farnworth, often with light patronage.

The only route that could be described as arterial and consistently well patronised was that from Leigh to Bolton. The Atherton to St. Helens route was relatively direct although abounding with short workings or 'jiggers' as they were known shuttling colliers, factory workers and shoppers.

Industrial landscape and terraced rows along the way were the order of the day, though genteel suburbia around Over Hulton and Worsley, the latter with its waterways and sylvan settings, provided welcome interludes.

If the routes were not varied enough then the trolleybuses surely were. When the system closed in 1958 several of the original vehicles introduced in 1930 were still in service including number 1.

Their varied appearance was thanks to a policy of make do and mend and a series of rebuilding programmes. Even as late as 1958, the last year of operation, it was possible to see trolleybuses in almost original condition and in four variations of the basic red livery.

So much was the variety of the SLT, it was too easy to forget that for 28 years its red trolleybuses played their part in carrying cotton and coal workers, office and factory workers, mothers, toddlers, schoolchildren and shoppers to their daily places. Their doing this for 28 years was in no small way thanks to the unstinting efforts of those for whom the SLT was their livelihood, in the offices, on the buses, in the depots all of whom kept the system operational.

The reader is taken on a photographic trip along each of routes recalling with an anecdotal flavour some of the occurrences along the way which made the SLT what it was. All seventy one trolleybuses are included illustrating the often innovative alterations made to the fleet over the years.

This book thus attempts to capture the 'flavour' of the SLT rather than be descriptive of the politics of South Lancashire public transport of the time. I lived on the Leigh to Bolton route and was nine years old when the system closed; just old enough to retain vivid memories. It was the sheer presence of the system with each trolleybus having its own character that captured my imagination. I was not alone and remain grateful to many others, somewhat my senior, who took the trouble to photograph the SLT thus making this nostalgic appreciation possible.

Phillip J. Taylor,
Oakham, Rutland, 2002.

Plate 2. Trolleybus No.59, a highbridge Roe bodied Leyland TTB stands at Spinning Jenny Street terminus, Leigh, in 1950. The original drop windows have been replaced with sliding ventilators and the trolleybus carries the attractive first post war livery of red with a grey roof and two white bands together with an advertisement for Belle Vue 'Showground of the World' commonly applied to SLT trolleybuses in the early 1950s.

Photo, the late Reg Wilson.

A JOURNEY ALONG THE ROUTES:
1. ATHERTON TO ST. HELENS.

Atherton, the St. Helens route terminus.

Plate 3. Atherton, Wigan Road, No.9. Trolleybus No.9, one of the original batch of 10 Guy BTX 3-axle Roe bodied lowbridge trolleybuses introduced in 1930, is seen in 1956 having arrived from St. Helens and about to reverse into Lambeth Street, Atherton. The bus remains little altered from original condition and carries the final livery of red with a single cream band that was also applied to the Lancashire United motor buses. The conductor, having already set the destination blind for the return journey to St. Helens, signals to the driver that it is clear to reverse. In the distance the wires follow Wigan Road to St. Helens whilst to the right is Mealhouse Lane. Bus stops for Bolton, Mosley Common and Swinton services were behind the photographer and provided the ideal vantage point from which to witness the St. Helens route terminus manoeuvres.

Photo, Dennis Gill.

Plate 4. Wigan Road /Lambeth Street. Little remains on 17th August 1998 to remind us of the St. Helens route trolleybus terminus. However, close inspection reveals that the car in Lambeth Street is resting on the same setts upon which the trolleybuses once stood. The turn from Wigan Road into Mealhouse Lane is less severe following demolition of the corner property but the attractive little 'cottage' style house with its two tall chimneys on Wigan Road bend remains as witness to 26 years of trolleybus activity.

Photo, Author.

Plate 5. Atherton, St. Helens No.310. Atherton was the most easterly point reached by St. Helens trolleybuses. No SLT trolleybuses ever carried route numbers apart from a short period during the war. However, St. Helens designated the joint service with SLT to Atherton as route 1, ultimately becoming Merseyside PTE service 1. Renumbered 651 after deregulation in 1986, the service from Atherton became hourly operating to Ashton only until 26th April 1999 when Blue Bus reintroduced a through service to St. Helens. Gently backing into Lambeth Street is St. Helens No.310, a 1945 Sunbeam W with Roe utility lowbridge bodywork. This view illustrates the complexity of the overhead wiring at this location, often considered the masterpiece of the overhead line department! Trolleybuses from St. Helens had to stop with their trolley heads just beyond the trailing frog without overshooting the spacer bar and insulators seen at the top of the picture. These wires, providing a 'head shunt' for the reverser, were suspended over the Bolton/Swinton route wires leading around to the right into Mealhouse Lane. Seen to the bus's left is wiring providing

a connection between the St. Helens route and the rest of the system used only when transferring trolleybuses from Platt Bridge to Atherton Howe Bridge depot. The Wigan Road wires crossing the reverser wires above No.310's trolley heads to join the St. Helens route wires terminated at a traction pole to the left of camera. As a consequence transfers from Howe Bridge to Platt Bridge depots necessitated halting the vehicle in Wigan Road and transferring the booms to the St. Helens route wires.

Photo, Dennis Gill.

Plate 6. Atherton, No.17. No.17 waits in Lambeth Street Atherton before returning to St. Helens on 10th July 1956. The setts upon which the trolleybus stands remain today as do the terraces in Mealhouse Lane but the factory chimney and alas the wiring and trolleybuses have long since disappeared, the last to St. Helens running just 4 months later on 11th November. Trolleybuses reversed onto the right hand side in Lambeth Street in order to better negotiate the sharp left turn back into Wigan Road. No.17, a Guy BTX of the 11 to 30 batch delivered in 1931, originally resembled the earlier batch. However it was one of several vehicles to undergo partial rebuilding in the early 1950s receiving deepened side panels, a reconstructed back end around the platform and a completely new front.

Photo, J. C. Gillham.

A stranger visits Atherton.

Plate 7. Atherton, St. Helens No.380. The Atherton to St. Helens route was invariably worked using lowbridge trolleybuses because of railway bridge height restrictions at Platt Bridge, Redgate and Dangerous Corner, the last, with a 14ft. 6 ins. clearance, necessitating the overhead's placement to one side of the road to prevent the trolleybooms fouling the parking hooks. Dangerous Corner bridge was removed in 1953 but lowbridge buses still operated this route except for one occasion on 19th June 1956 when St. Helens East Lancs highbridge bodied Sunbeam F4 No.380 arrived at Atherton. An amazed SLT timekeeper on duty could not help but say "How the Hell did you get here?" Built in 1951, No.380 became the most modern trolleybus to operate a service in Atherton, quite a distance from its more normal St. Helens /Rainhill /Prescot circular services 7 and 8.

Photo, the late E.K. Stretch..

Plate 8. Atherton, St. Helens No.111. Some time before the June 1955 St. Helens Corporation renumbering scheme, No.111, later No.311, is seen making the left turn onto the setts in Wigan Road to return to St. Helens. The SLT traction pole mounted reverser light wired into the 600 Volt DC overhead is augmented by a somewhat more powerful mercury vapour street lamp mounted on the nearest traction pole. The wiring connecting the St. Helens route with the rest of the system permitting depot transfers leads left into Mealhouse Lane. Occasionally, when the reverser trailing frog became damaged, St. Helens route buses turned at Atherton by using this wiring and taking a rectangular route by way of right turns into Bag Lane, Market Street and at the Savoy Cinema back into Wigan Road. The trolley booms would be swung back onto the St. Helens route spur tied off to the traction pole just visible by the bus shelter in the background.

Photo, C. Carter.

Plate 9. Atherton, No.17. Waiting in Wigan Road to move forward and reverse into Lambeth Street is No.17. A trio of passengers passes the advertising hoardings proclaiming messages concerning mustard, chocolate and washing powder which remain unchanged today. Cigarette advertising was many years away from health proclamations and subsequent banning. Belle Vue Manchester was widely advertised in the area, and on the trolleybuses for that matter, as 'The Showground of the World'. The attractions there together with the zoo provided me as a young boy with the opportunity to travel from Piccadilly, Manchester, along Hyde Road on that city's 12XX class Crossley trolleybuses which, introduced in 1950 with modern appearance and curved bases to the windscreens, could have been SLT's inspiration when undertaking the rebuilding of certain of the older trolleys. Compare this view with that of unrebuilt No.9 as in **Plate No.3.** *Photo, C. Carter.*

Plate 10. Atherton, St. Helens No.311. Leaving Atherton terminus around the corner, St. Helens Sunbeam No.311 passes 'The Hollow' having crossed Collier Brook bridge, widened in 1932. Today, an island behind the bus gives traffic easy access to Gloucester Street and on to Bolton Road thereby avoiding Mealhouse Lane. These trolleybuses, registered DJ 9183 to DJ 9192 introduced in 1945 were regulars on this route. They had Roe UL24/26R bodies and were originally numbered 105 to 114, later becoming 305 to 314. All but two were withdrawn after closure of the St. Helens route in November 1956, No.311 lasting until August 1957 and 312 until April 1958. *Photo, the late J Batty.*

Plate 11. Atherton, No.1. Seen on the approach to Atherton by 'The Hollow' is SLT No.1 TF 2072 of 1930. This, the oldest bus in the fleet, had been completely rebuilt by Bond of Wythenshawe in 1953 thus hiding its origins extremely well having lost all traces of its angular front and with a curved rear dome and radiused corners to the rubber mounted windows. Not surprisingly No.1 saw service elsewhere on the system upon closure of the St. Helens route and was in service on the last day of SLT operation in 1958. *Photo, the late J. Batty.*

Gibfield

Plate 12. Gibfield, No.46. Leaving the chimneys of Atherton in the distance, the route to St.Helens takes trolleybus No.46 along Wigan Road and over the former LNWR Leigh to Bolton line after crossing the Gibfield colliery mineral line at Worthington Fold. The road narrowed here and the overhead, rather than being hung from span wires, was supported from the bracket arms of former trampoles. Gibfield colliery, to the left of camera, dated from the late 1820s becoming the largest and most important of Lord Lilford's Lancashire collieries. The Gadbury brick works, situated to the right of camera, ensured constant supplies for the mining operations and was connected to Gibfield via the railway track across Wigan Road. No.46, the last of 16 Roe bodied Guy BT 2 axle trolleybuses delivered in December 1933, remained in largely unrebuilt condition until withdrawal in November 1956. *Photo, the late J. Batty.*

Plate 13. Gibfield, No.16. This desolate view of No.16 heading towards Hindley and on to St. Helens having just crossed the Gibfield colliery railway track typifies one type of SLT 'trolleyscape' namely railways, terraces, rough roads and puddles. Trains between Leigh and Bolton are expected in both directions as No.16 climbs the rise over the railway. Note the LNWR lower quadrant signals to the left of the picture. The scene is lifted a little by the Ford Prefect's polished chrome embellishments. Today this location is the junction of the A577 with Atherleigh Way.

Photo, the late J.Batty.

Ticket No.3748. The first tickets issued by South Lancashire Tramways, printed by the Bell Punch Company, carried 'named' destination stages indicating the precise journey and were colour coded according to value. Subsequent changes saw the introduction of tickets having numbered but unnamed stages with the fare overprinted in black. White tickets with red fare overprints were in use at the time of introduction of trolleybuses, coloured tickets being re-introduced in the mid 1930s, the 1d example shown here being green.

Ticket, courtesy Brian Hughes.

Plate 14. Gibfield. On 2nd April 2002, the terraced rows visible in the distance viewed towards Hindley along Wigan Road at Gibfield remain as a reference point for the location of the old mineral railway that crossed in the foreground connecting the Gadbury brick works to the left with Gibfield Colliery. A visible reminder of the coal and railway heritage of this area is Wigan Road's gentle rise to the level of the former trackbed of the ex LNWR Kenyon Junction to Bolton railway, progressively closed between 1963 and 1969, and which was crossed by an overbridge at this point. Today a road sign marks the beginning of the A579 Atherleigh Way opened in 1985 which follows the trackbed by-passing Leigh and Pennington to join the Lowton St. Mary's By Pass near Pennington Flash. This reaches the A580 East Lancashire Road and a connection with the M6 motorway via Winwick Lane. The sign also serves to identify the A577 road to Wigan which trolleybuses followed as far as Hindley before turning left onto the A58 along Liverpool Road towards Platt Bridge. Gone is the once industrial and sometimes desolate topography with its associated smoke and grime, replaced today with vegetation, breathable air and a cleaner if somewhat sterile environment.

Photo, D.J.Sweeney.

Plate 15. Towards Hindley, No.46. No.46 ambles along Wigan Road towards Smallbrook Lane and Hindley having crossed the Leigh to Bolton railway line. The Atherton to St. Helens route had reversing triangles at Hindley Green, Hindley Church, Ashton, *Ram's Head* at Haydock and the *Huntsman Inn* at Blackbrook. These four wheel Guy trolleybuses were the favourites for the numerous short workings, known locally as 'jiggers'. However in this case No.46 is providing a through service to St. Helens. After 1952 the journey was timed at 68 minutes requiring 8 SLT and 4 St. Helens trolleybuses. Weekend services were met by 9 and 3 respectively.

Photo, the late J.Batty.

Hindley

Plate 16. Hindley Green, No.43. Operating a Hindley local 'jigger' between Leigh Road and Church Street along the length of Atherton Road is No.43 pictured in the Leigh Road reverser. The conductor prepares to board the platform as the bus draws forward and begins the left turn into Atherton Road towards the centre of Hindley. The occupant of the pram is doubtless oblivious to the goings on as the gentleman with coat belt twisted uses one hand to direct the pram around the corner. No.43 carries the attractive first post war livery of red with two white bands and a grey roof.
Photo, Author's collection.

Plate 17. Hindley Green. With Hindley Green Post Office on the corner, the Leigh Road junction with Atherton Road remained largely unchanged on 17th August 1998, save for truncated chimneys, burglar alarms and skyward reaching modern street lighting. The most significant change is the traffic at this junction which made crossing the road to take this photograph a time consuming affair.
Photo, Author.

Plate 18. Hindley Green, No.41. No.41 has encountered trouble in Atherton Road having just left the Leigh Road reverser. One trolley boom remains on the wires. In 1956 traffic was light and the bus causes no obstacle. Little attention is paid to 41's predicament from either side of the road by the passers by. Beyond St. John the Evangelist church to the right lies Hindley Green post office. Rebuilt No.41 in the single cream band livery provides great contrast to 43 seen before in the reverser.
Photo, C.Carter.

Plate 19. Atherton Road, Hindley, No.43. No.43 having travelled the length of Atherton Road deposits its passengers before drawing forward to reverse into Church Street Hindley. Beyond the bus Eli Brindley & Co. advertise graded red shale for tennis courts. The Rex cinema featured Mon/Tue *Battle Stations* starring John Lund and William Bendix, *Devil Goddess* with Johnny Weissmuller, Wed /Thur, *Dakota Incident*, Linda Darnell and Dale Robertson of Wells Fargo fame, plus *No Man's Woman* with Marie Windsor and John Archer. Finally Tyrone Power and Maureen O'Hara star in *The Long Grey Line* on Fri/Sat. These are the cinema attractions for week commencing 5th November 1956. The trolleybuses on the St. Helens route had just days to run, No.43 being withdrawn upon closure of this route. *Photo, Author's collection.*

Plate 20. Church Street, Hindley, No.43. There is time for a cheery smile for the camera and a chat to two passers by as No. 43 awaits the allotted time to return to Leigh Road. Judging by the upturned collar to the driver's coat there is a chill to this November day in 1956. Perhaps in a few days the focus of his attention will be less on the weather and shoppers and more on a new Daimler CVG5K diesel bus which will replace his long serving trolleybus. *Photo, Author's collection.*

14

Plate 21. Church Street, Hindley. Church Street on 17th August 1998, retained the characteristic slate roofed corner property albeit vacant. Note the survival of the attractive ridge tiles and finial. Beyond, the Rex cinema has become the Monaco ballroom whilst the church grounds are now bounded by a low height wall.

Photo, Author.

Plate 22. Atherton Road/ Liverpool Road junction. A busy scene in Hindley on 17th August 1998, with traffic flowing between Atherton Road and Wigan Road. To the left is Market Street. St. Peters church dwarfs the *Bird I'th Hand* public house on the corner of Liverpool Road into which St. Helens bound trolleybuses took a left turn from Atherton Road.

Photo, Author.

Plate 23. Hindley, St. Helens No.311. Seen from immediately in front of the Church Street trolleybus reverser, Atherton bound St. Helens trolleybus No.311 turns into Atherton Road, Hindley, from Liverpool Road, by St. Peter's Church school on a wet November day in 1956, just days before closure of the Atherton-St. Helens trolleybus route. At the same time a Lancashire United, Northern Counties bodied Guy Arab III passes the *Bird I'th Hand* public house as it joins Wigan Road, having entered Hindley along Market Street from Westhoughton.

Photo, Author's collection.

15

Plate 24. Hindley South. (railway station) St. Helens No.312. Leaving Hindley via Liverpool Road, St. Helens Sunbeam No.312 pulls out from a trolleybus stop to pass a parked Morris Minor adjacent to a milk advertisement. Hindley South Station lies beyond. This trolleybus was fitted experimentally in 1955 with continental style trolley retrievers, the ropes and drums of which can be seen below the platform window. Apparently the experiment was not a success, the ropes tending to foul other high vehicles. No.312 remained the only St. Helens trolleybus so fitted.

Photo, the late J.Batty.

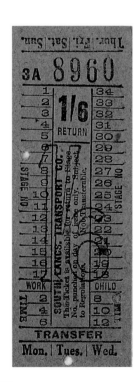

Plate 25. Hindley South (railway station) No.10. No.10, having just passed the station, descends the grade on its way to Atherton. The overhead wiring was originally equipped with positive and negative wires set at a spacing of 18 inches matching the trolley mountings on the SLT lowbridge buses. Many stretches of tramway bracket arm suspension were renewed with span wires and BICC twin line steel hangers. In this view, 18 inch hangers support the wiring to St. Helens whilst that to Atherton has later 24 inch spacing causing the booms on No.10 to splay.

Photo, the late J.Batty.

Ticket No.8960. Tickets used by the SLT on the St. Helens route were replicas of the St. Helens Corporation design. Note the overprint duplicating the printed ticket value. The general change around 1948 to TIM (Ticket Issuing Machines Ltd.) tickets did away with special tickets on this route although St. Helens Corporation used green paper in their machines.

Ticket, courtesy Brian Hughes.

Plate 26. Hindley South. Nos.11 and 14. Nos.11 and 14 in Liverpool Road by Hindley South station are operating the basic service with No.14 about to pass the station en route to Atherton. Note the wiring causing No.14's booms to splay on the 24" spacing whilst No.11's appear rather better mannered. This area, with numerous colliery workings, was criss crossed by a complicated rail network .There were three stations carrying the name Hindley. To make matters worse Hindley South was also known as Hindley & Platt Bridge and there was also Platt Bridge station! Hindley South was on the GCR Glazebrook to Wigan Central line. Hindley Green with Platt Bridge to the west, was on the LNWR Tyldesley to Wigan line whilst Hindley North was on the L&Y Manchester to Wigan Wallgate line. Renamed Hindley on 6th May 1968, this station remains open. Hindley Green closed in 1961 and Hindley South in 1964.

Photo, the late J.Batty.

Joint Operators—St. Helens Corporation Transport—South Lancashire Transport Company

Service 1 ST. HELENS (Ormskirk Street)—HAYDOCK—ASHTON—PLATT BRIDGE—HINDLEY—ATHERTON (Punch Bowl)

Service 2 ST. HELENS (Ormskirk Street)—HAYDOCK—ASHTON (Robin Hood)

MONDAY TO FRIDAY

	am	am	am	am	am	am	am	am	am	am	am	am	am	am	am
St. Helens (Ormskirk Street) dep	...	...	...	...	...	...	4·54	...	5 06	...	5 18	...	5 30	5 42	5 54	6 06
Blackbrook (Ship Inn) ,,	...	...	...	...	...	...	5 03	...	5 15	...	5 27	...	5 39	5 51	6 03	6 15
Haydock (Rams Head) ,,	...	...	...	...	...	...	5 13	C	5 25	C	5 37	C	5 49	6 01	6 13	6 25
Ashton (Robin Hood) ,,	...	...	...	...	...	...	5 21	5 21	5 33	5 33	5 45	5 45	5 57	6 09	6 21	6 33
Platt Bridge Depot ,,	4 58	5 04	5 10	5 16	5 22	5 28	...	5 36	...	5 48	...	6 00	6 12	6 24	6 36	6 48
Hindley (Bird-in-Hand) ,,	5 02	5 08	5 14	5 20	5 26	5 32	...	5 40	...	5 52	...	6 04	6 16	6 28	6 40	6 52
Atherton (Punch Bowl) arr.	...	5 25	...	5 37	...	5 49	...	5 57	...	6 09	...	6 21	6 33	6 45	6 57	7 09

	am		pm	pm	pm	pm	pm	pm	pm							
St. Helens (Ormskirk Street) dep	6 18	and	1006	1018	1030	1042	1054	1106	1118	...	...	...	...	...	...
Blackbrook (Ship Inn) ,,	6 27	every	1015	1027	1039	1051	1103	1115	1127	...	...	...	...	...	...
Haydock (Rams Head) ,,	6 37	12	1025	1037	1049	1101	1113	1125	1137	...	...	...	...	...	...
Ashton (Robin Hood) ,,	6 45	mins.	1033	1045	1057	1109	1121	1133	1145	...	...	...	...	...	...
Platt Bridge Depot ,,	7 00	until	1048	1100	1112	1124	1136	1148	1200	...	...	...	...	...	...
Hindley (Bird-in-Hand) ,,	7 04		1052	1104	...	...	...	...	...	...	...	...	...	...	...
Atherton (Punch Bowl) arr.	7 21		1109												

SATURDAY

	am	am	am	am	am	am	am	am	am	am	am	am	am	am	am
St. Helens (Ormskirk Street) dep	...	...	...	...	...	...	4 20	4 54	...	5 06	...	5 18	...	5 30	5 42	5 54
Blackbrook (Ship Inn) ,,	...	...	...	...	...	...	4 29	5 03	...	5 15	...	5 27	...	5 39	5 51	6 03
Haydock (Rams Head) ,,	...	...	...	...	...	...	4 39	5 13	C	5 25	C	5 37	C	5 49	6 01	6 13
Ashton (Robin Hood) ,,	...	...	...	...	...	...	4 47	5 21	5 21	5 33	5 33	5 45	5 45	5 57	6 09	6 21
Platt Bridge Depot ,,	4 47	4 58	5 04	5 10	5 16	5 28	...	...	5 36	...	5 48	...	6 00	6 12	6 24	6 36
Hindley (Bird-in-Hand) ,,	4 51	5 02	5 08	5 14	5 20	5 32	...	...	5 40	...	5 52	...	6 04	6 16	6 28	6 40
Atherton (Punch Bowl) arr.	5 08	...	5 25	...	5 37	5 49	...	...	5 57	...	6 09	...	6 21	6 33	6 45	6 57

	am	am		pm	pm	pm	pm	pm	pm	pm	pm			
St. Helens (Ormskirk Street) dep	6 06	6 18	and	1006	1018	1030	1042	1054	1106	1118	1175	...	...	...
Blackbrook (Ship Inn) ,,	6 15	6 27	every	1015	1027	1039	1051	1103	1115	1127	1134	...	...	...
Haydock (Rams Head) ,,	6 25	6 37	12	1025	1037	1049	1101	1113	1125	1137	1144	...	...	...
Ashton (Robin Hood) ,,	6 33	6 45	mins.	1033	1045	1057	1109	1121	1133	1145	1152	...	...	...
Platt Bridge Depot ,,	6 48	7 00	until	1048	1100	1112	1124	1136	1148	1200	...	...	...	...
Hindley (Bird-in-Hand) ,,	6 52	7 04		1052	1104	...	...	...	...	...	...	...	...	...
Atherton (Punch Bowl) arr.	7 09	7 21		1109	...	...	...	...	...	...	...	...	...	...

Platt Bridge

Plate 28. Platt Bridge Depot, No.1. With Platt Bridge depot entrance to the right, No.1 stands in Liverpool Road on a St. Helens service. A 'goal post' arrangement supports the depot entrance wiring. The only other example on the system was at Atherton depot. Platt Bridge depot was built just after the turn of the century when the South Lancashire Tramways Company was extending its Atherton to Haydock tram services. Even then the route was worked by trams from Atherton depot. During the first few months of trolleybus operation the route was again worked from Atherton with the trolleybuses returning to depot using the single overhead positive wire and earth return via tram track and trailing skate. Until 1904 Wigan Tramways, whose services ran as far as Templeton Road had a separate tram depot at Platt Bridge. Rebuilt No.1 presents a modern appearance and belies its age to the unwitting onlooker.   *Photo, the late J.Batty.*

Plate 29. Capp Street. On 17th August 1998, a Ford Escort passes the Capp Street entrance to the former Platt Bridge depot at the point where No.1 had stood some 42 years earlier. To the right of the Ford Transit can be seen the sign and entrance to Springbank estate within which the depot buildings still stand. The houses in the distance towards the site of the former Hindley South Station remain largely unaltered.

Photo, Author.

Plate 30. Platt Bridge Depot, No.40. Standing at the depot doors at Platt Bridge on 24th June 1956, the day of the Omnibus Society special tour of the system in trolleybus No.1, is Guy BT No.40 with rebuilt front. The lowbridge double deckers standing in front of No.40 are Northern Counties bodied Guy Arab II No.284, FTD 189, and Weymann bodied Arab III No.383, KTB 114. To No.40's left is No.310, FTE 331, a Massey bodied Guy Arab II and a Leyland TD7 diverted from Alexander. Probably the most eye catching vehicle is CTF 438, a 1938 Leyland TS8 originally with a Roe B32F body, rebodied by Plaxton in 1953 with an FC35F body.   *Photo, The late E.K.Stretch.*

Plate 31. Former depot buildings. On August 17th 1998 a concrete fence marks the edge of the Springbank Estate and bars the way to the former depot buildings. A centre pair of wooden doors remains. A lone former traction pole acting as a lamp post remains as a tacit reminder of the former occupants of the building.   *Photo, Author.*

Along tram tracks at Templeton Road.

Plate 32. Templeton Road, No.39. About half a mile south of Platt Bridge depot the trolley wires left Liverpool Road taking the trolleybuses sharp left onto Lomax Street then right onto Templeton Road thus avoiding the centre of Platt Bridge. This 400 yard stretch of potholed, unadopted and unmetalled former tram road brought the trolleybuses to a road junction on Warrington Road where they crossed into Lily Lane thence to Ashton in Makerfield. Notable were the tram tracks which remained in situ with paving between and 18 inches to either side of the rails. With the Warrington Road/Lily Lane junction in the distance, No.39 rattles along the dusty tracks towards Hindley.

Photo, the late E. K. Stretch.

Plate 33. Templeton Road, 1985. The stone paved tram tracks in Templeton Road remained when photographed on 20th September 1985, providing not so much a reminder of trolleybuses which it last saw in 1956, but of the trams, the last of which rumbled along 26 years earlier in 1930! This 55 year legacy of tramway operation, which succumbed to tarmacadam not long after, must have attained something of a record. *Photo, Author.*

Plate 34. Templeton Road, No.46. About to leave Templeton Road and cross Warrington Road into Lily Lane is the ubiquitous No.46 on a through service to St. Helens. To the left of the bus, Warrington Road took the A573 through Golborne and on to Warrington, some 9 miles distant. In the other direction the A58 to Wigan travelled through Platt Bridge before becoming the A 573 once more.

Photo, C. Carter.

Plate 35. *Lily Lane / Warrington Road Junction.* The same location on 17th August 1998 with traffic lights and parked cars beyond the pavement marking the old exit from the former Templeton Road tramroad onto Warrington Road. A car wash and a superstore stand in place of the old buildings. Templeton Road is no longer a thoroughfare, being a property access only road.

Photo, Author.

Bamfurlong.

Plate 36. *Bamfurlong, Bolton Road, No.41.* The A58 left Platt Bridge in the direction of Ashton in Makerfield, Lily Lane becoming Bolton Road. Seen on Bolton Road, Bamfurlong, by Riding Lane is No.41 on its way to Atherton. Reductions in colliery workings in this area meant that plans to introduce additional shuttle services were not implemented. Consequently, a reverser originally planned for this location was never constructed.

Photo, Author's collection.

Ashton in Makerfield

Plate 39. Ashton in Makerfield No.4. Save for two men chatting outside Unsworth's radio and electrical shop next to Timothy Whites, Gerrard Street is surprisingly deserted as unrebuilt trolleybus No.4 runs through Ashton on its way to St. Helens from Atherton. In the distance the *Cross Keys Inn* is visible opposite the zebra crossing with the trolleybus reverser alongside in Princess Road. No.4 was transferred to Atherton depot following the closure of the St. Helens route, surviving until the end of the system in 1958 as the last fundamentally unrebuilt lowbridge Guy. *Photo, R. Stephens.*

Plate 40. Warrington Road, Ashton in Makerfield, No.16. Approaching Ashton from St. Helens, No.16 casts a shadow in the late afternoon sun as it makes its way along the A49 in Warrington Road. With Monica Terrace to its right and a Smith's of Wigan coach close behind, the trolleybus will soon make the sharp right turn into Gerrard Street and the centre of Ashton. The continued use of tramway bracket arms along this section to Haydock Park with the overhead to one side of the road meant that trolley booms were at full stretch for St. Helens bound buses.

No.16 carries the second post war livery of red with a grey roof but was later repainted red with a single cream band. Note the gas lamp to the nearside of the bus.

Photo, Author's collection.

Joint Operators—St. Helens Corporation Transport—South Lancashire Transport Company

Service 1 ST. HELENS (Ormskirk Street)—HAYDOCK—ASHTON—PLATT BRIDGE—HINDLEY—ATHERTON (Punch Bowl)

Service 2 ST. HELENS (Ormskirk Street)—HAYDOCK—ASHTON (Robin Hood)

SUNDAY

	am	am		om	pm	pm	pm	pm	pm		pm	pm	pm
St. Helens (Ormskirk Street) dep	8 30	9 00	and	1230	1242	1254	1 06	1 18	1 30	and	1006	1018	1030
Blackbrook (Ship Inn) .... ,,	8 38	9 08	every	1238	1251	1 03	1 15	1 27	1 39	every	1015	1027	1039
Haydock (Rams Head) .... ,,	8 47	9 17	30	1247	1 01	1 13	1 25	1 37	1 49	12	1025	1037	1049
Ashton (Robin Hood) .... ,,	8 54	9 24	mins.	1254	1 09	1 21	1 33	1 45	1 57	mins.	1033	1045	1057
Platt Bridge Depot .... ,,	9 08	9 38	until	1 08	1 24	1 36	1 48	2 00	2 12	until	1048	1100	1112
Hindley (Bird-in-Hand) .... ,,	9 12	9 42		1 12	1 28	1 40	1 52	2 04	2 16		1052	1104	...
Atherton (Punch Bowl) ....arr.	9 27	9 57		1 27	1 45	1 57	2 09	2 21	2 33		1109	...	...

	pm	pm	pm	pm									
St. Helens (Ormskirk Street) dep	1042	1054	1106	1118									
Blackbrook (Ship Inn) .... ,,	1051	1103	1115	1127	...	...	...	...	...	...	...	...	
Haydock (Rams Head) .... ,,	1101	1113	1125	1137	...	...	...	...	...	...	...	...	
Ashton (Robin Hood) .... ,,	1109	1121	1133	1145	...	...	...	...	...	...	...	...	
Platt Bridge Depot .... ,,	1124	1136	1148	1200	...	...	...	...	...	...	...	...	
Hindley (Bird-in-Hand) .... ,,	...	...	...	...	...	...	...	...	...	...	...	...	
Atherton (Punch Bowl) ....arr.	...	...	...	...	...	...	...	...	...	...	...	...	

MONDAY TO FRIDAY

	am	am	am	am	am	am	am	am	am	am	am	am	am		pm
Atherton (Punch Bowl) ....dep	...	...	...	...	...	...	...	...	5 26	5 38	5 50	6 02	6 14	and	1038
Hindley (Bird-in-Hand) .... ,,	...	...	5 02	...	5 14	...	5 26	...	5 43	5 55	6 07	6 19	6 31	every	1055
Platt Bridge Depot .... ,,	4 47	4 59	5 06	C	5 18	C	5 30	C	5 47	5 59	6 11	6 23	6 35	12	1059
Ashton (Robin Hood) .... ,,	5 02	5 14	5 21	5 26	5 33	5 38	5 45	5 50	6 02	6 14	6 26	6 38	6 50	mins.	1114
Haydock (Rams Head) .... ,,	5 10	5 22	...	5 34	...	5 46	...	5 58	6 10	6 22	6 34	6 46	6 58	until	1122
Blackbrook (Ship Inn) .... ,,	5 20	5 32	...	5 44	...	5 56	...	6 08	6 20	6 32	6 44	6 56	7 08		1132
St. Helens (Ormskirk Street) arr.	5 29	5 41	...	5 53	...	6 05	...	6 18	6 29	6 41	6 53	7 05	7 17		1141

	pm	pm	pm	pm											
Atherton (Punch Bowl) ....dep	...	1050	1102	1114	...	...	...	...	...	...	...	...	...		...
Hindley (Bird-in-Hand) .... ,,	1104	1107	1119	1131	...	...	...	...	...	...	...	...	...		...
Platt Bridge Depot .... ,,	1108	1111	1123	1135	...	...	...	...	...	...	...	...	...		...
Ashton (Robin Hood) .... ,,	...	1126	...	...	...	...	...	...	...	...	...	...	...		...
Haydock (Rams Head) .... ,,	...	1134	...	...	...	...	...	...	...	...	...	...	...		...
Blackbrook (Ship Inn) .... ,,	...	1144	...	...	...	...	...	...	...	...	...	...	...		...
St. Helens (Ormskirk Street) arr.	...	1153	...	...	...	...	...	...	...	...	...	...	...		...

Haydock

Plate 41. Haydock Park, No.10. Travelling from Ashton towards St. Helens, Warrington Road became Lodge Lane with Haydock Park racecourse to the left. Before reaching the A580 East Lancashire Road the trolleybuses turned at Old Boston Corner from the A49 to take the A599 Penny Lane to Haydock travelling under the East Lancs Road. No.10 is pictured in October 1956 turning from Lodge Lane into Penny Lane. Today the M6 motorway crosses Penny Lane at the photographer's position, running parallel with Lodge Lane. *Photo, Author's collection.*

Plate 42. Haydock, Penny Lane, St. Helens No.306. About to pass beneath the East Lancashire Road on Penny Lane having travelled from Atherton, St. Helens No.306 will shortly leave the SLT overhead to rejoin the wires of its native system as it enters Haydock. The East Lancashire Road was being constructed at the time of trolleybus introduction between Ashton and Haydock in 1931. Today the view is not so rural with the Old Boston trading estate to the left and the M6 motorway dominating the background. *Photo, The late E. K. Stretch.*

Haydock, Ram's Head.

Plate 43. Haydock, Ram's Head, No.41. The *Ram's Head* at Haydock, situated at the point where Church Road becomes Clipsley Lane, marked the boundary between the SLT and St. Helens trolleybus systems. Alongside in Kenyons Lane South was a reverser, in which No.41 is seen on 2nd November 1956. The trolleybus was operating a Monday to Friday afternoon extra duty which involved its using every intermediate turning point between Atherton and Haydock. The service was :- Depot - Leigh Road - Haydock - Leigh Road - Hindley - Leigh Road - Ashton - Atherton - Depot.

Photo, The late E. K. Stretch.

Plate 44. Ram's Head. The *Ram's Head,* a substantial brick built building rebuilt to its current state in 1896, remained on 17th August 1998 as an imposing marker of the former boundary of the two trolleybus systems. St. Helens Corporation had commenced the introduction of trolleybuses in 1927, three years before the SLT. The SLT converted the Ashton to Haydock section concurrently with St. Helens' introduction of trolleybuses between St. Helens and Haydock, both sections becoming operational on 21st June 1931, thus permitting the jointly worked through service. Note the building's substantial chimney stacks and the decorative styling at roof level together with flower baskets and upper storey window boxes.

Photo, Author.

The Huntsman.

Plate 45. The Huntsman. At the St. Helens end of Clipsley Lane stands *The Huntsman* at the junction with West End Road and Vicarage Road. There was a trolleybus reverser located in Vicarage Road, from where the Austin Metro is leaving to take Clipsley Lane. This reverser in St. Helens territory was seldom used by the SLT but was shown on SLT trolleybus destination blinds as 'Huntsman'.

Photo, Author.

Blackbrook

Plate 46. Blackbrook, No.1 and St. Helens No.306. A reciprocal arrangement existed between St. Helens Corporation and the SLT whereby trolleybuses which became defective in each other's territory would be attended to by local repair crews. There was such an occurance in May 1956 when SLT No.1 travelling to St. Helens lost a trolleyhead under Corporation wires in Blackbrook Road. The St. Helens overhead linesman has the attention of two young onlookers as he effects a repair from the tower wagon parked immediately behind No.1. Meanwhile, St. Helens No.306, returning to town on a 3A shortworking to Blackbrook edges slowly past with outstreched booms, having just left the Blackbrook turning circle situated alongside the *Ship Inn*, just visible beyond the tower wagon. *Photo, Author's collection.*

Joint Operators—St. Helens Corporation Transport—South Lancashire Transport Company

Service 1 ST. HELENS (Ormskirk Street)—HAYDOCK—ASHTON—PLATT BRIDGE—HINDLEY—ATHERTON (Punch Bowl)

Service 2 ST. HELENS (Ormskirk Street)—HAYDOCK—ASHTON (Robin Hood)

SATURDAY

	am	am	am	am	am	am	am	am	am	am	am
Atherton (Punch Bowl) ......dep	...	...	...	...	...	...	...	5 09	...	5 26	5 38
Hindley (Bird-in-Hand) .... ,,	...	...	...	5 02	...	5 14	...	5 26	...	5 43	5 55
Platt Bridge Depot .... ,,	...	4 47	4 59	5 06	C	5 18	C	5 30	C	5 47	5 59
Ashton (Robin Hood) .... ,,	4 50	5 02	5 14	5 21	5 26	5 33	5 38	5 45	5 50	6 02	6 14
Haydock (Rams Head) .... ,,	4 58	5 10	5 22	...	5 34	...	5 46	...	5 58	6 10	6 22
Blackbrook (Ship Inn) .... ,,	5 08	5 20	5 32	...	5 44	...	5 56	...	6 08	6 20	6 32
St. Helens (Ormskirk Street) arr.	5 17	5 29	5 41	...	5 53	...	6 05	...	6 18	6 29	6 41

	am	am	am		pm	pm	pm	pm	pm	pm	
Atherton (Punch Bowl) ....dep	5 50	6 02	6 14	and	1038	...	1050	1102	1114	...	...
Hindley (Bird-in-Hand) .... ,,	6 07	6 19	6 31	every	1055	1104	1107	1119	1131	...	...
Platt Bridge Depot .... ,,	6 11	6 23	6 35	12	1059	1108	1111	1123	1135	...	...
Ashtyn (Robin Hood) .... ,,	6 26	6 38	6 50	mins.	1114	...	1126	...	...	1152	...
Haydock (Rams Head) .... ,,	6 34	6 46	6 58	until	1122	...	1134	...	...	1200	...
Blackbrook (Ship Inn) .... ,,	6 44	6 56	7 08		1132	...	1144	...	...	1210	...
St. Helens (Ormskirk Street) arr	6 53	7 05	7 17		1141	...	1153	...	...	1219	...

SUNDAY

	am	am	am	am	am		pm	pm	pm	pm	pm	pm	pm	pm	pm	pm
Atherton (Punch Bowl) ....dep	...	...	...	9 32	1002		1232	...	...	1 02	...	...	1 38	1 50	2 02	2 14
Hindley (Bird-in-Hand) .... ,,	...	...	...	9 47	1017	and	1247	...	1 19	...	...	1 55	2 07	2 19	2 31
Platt Bridge Depot .... ,,	8 21	8 51	9 21	9 51	1021	every	1251	1259	1 11	1 23	1 35	1 47	1 59	2 11	2 23	2 35
Ashton (Robin Hood) .... ,,	8 35	9 05	9 35	1005	1035	30	1 05	1 14	1 26	1 38	1 50	2 02	2 14	2 26	2 38	2 50
Haydock (Rams Head) .... ,,	8 42	9 12	9 42	1012	1042	mins.	1 12	1 22	1 34	1 46	1 58	2 10	2 22	2 34	2 46	2 58
Blackbrook (Ship Inn) .... ,,	8 51	9 21	9 51	1021	1051	until	1 21	1 32	1 44	1 56	2 08	2 20	2 32	2 44	2 56	3 08
St. Helens (Ormskirk Street) arr.	8 59	9 29	9 59	1029	1059		1 29	1 41	1 53	2 05	2 17	2 29	2 41	2 53	3 05	3 17

	pm		pm	pm	pm	pm	pm									
Atherton (Punch Bowl) ....dep	2 26	and	1038	...	1050	1102	1114	...	...	...	...	...	...	...	...	...
Hindley (Bird-in-Hand) .... ,,	2 43	every	1055	1104	1107	1119	1131	...	...	...	...	...	...	...	...	...
Platt Bridge Depot .... ,,	2 47	12	1059	1108	1111	1123	1135	...	...	...	...	...	...	...	...	...
Ashton (Robin Hood) .... ,,	3 02	mins.	1114	...	1126	1138	...	...	...	...	...	...	...	...	...	...
Haydock (Rams Head) .... ,,	3 10	until	1122	...	1134	1146	...	...	...	...	...	...	...	...	...	...
Blackbrook (Ship Inn) .... ,,	3 20		1132	...	1144	1156	...	...	...	...	...	...	...	...	...	...
St. Helens (Ormskirk Street) arr.	3 29		1141	...	1153	1205	...	...	...	...	...	...	...	...	...	...

Via Church Street, Parr Street, Higher Parr Street, (in via Higher Parr Street, Corporation Street, Cotham Street), Park Road, Blackbrook Road, West End Road, Clipsley Lane, Church Road (Haydock), Penny Lane, Lodge Lane, Warrington Road, Gerard Street, (Ashton), Bolton Road, Lily Lane, Warrington Road, Walthew Lane, Liverpool Road (Hindley), Atherton Road, Corner Lane, Smallbrook Lane, Wigan Road.

C—Connects with through bus at Ashton

Workmen's and Children's Fares between Atherton and Ashton—S.L.T. conditions apply.

Workmen's and Children's Fares between Ashton and St. Helens—St. Helens conditions apply

Plate 47. Corporation Street, No.9. Beyond Blackbrook, the trolleybuses followed the A58 into St. Helens until, at the junction of Parr Street and Corporation Street, the inbound wiring followed the latter to the right to commence a circuit through the town centre, eventually rejoining the inbound wires via Parr Street. No.9 runs along Corporation Street having just passed over Shaw Street station bridge. St. Helens trolleybus depot was situated in Hall Street to the right of No.9. Two gentlemen head that way from behind the bus whilst to the left steps and doorways receive the cleaner's attention.

Photo, Author's collection.

Plate 48. Victoria Square, No.8. St. Helens Leyland PD1, No.43, DJ 9919, one of three similar vehicles with lowbridge East Lancashire L53R bodywork delivered in 1947, stands alongside the bus shelter in Victoria Square prior to departure on service 47 to Rainford, as SLT Guy No.8 makes its way along Corporation Street. Note the painted radiator surround of the PD1, those of PD2s usually being unpainted but polished. The trolleybus is about to pass the Town Hall off to its right before bearing left into Cotham Street to reach the Atherton route terminus in Ormskirk Street. Meanwhile a Ribble Leyland PD2 behind the St. Helens bus waits for the car following No.8 to pass before leaving Hardshaw Street to join Corporation Street. In this October 1952 view the trolleybus is seen as rebuilt some two years previously at which time it was repainted into red with a grey roof livery. It later received a final repaint into the red with a single cream band livery. Somewhat surprisingly it was withdrawn from service in August 1956, some three months before the abandonment of the St. Helens route, the first rebuilt trolleybus to be taken out of service apart from accident damaged No.25 withdrawn in November 1955.

Photo, Author's collection.

Plate 49. St. Helens Town Hall, No.6. With St. Helens' splendid town hall of 1876 as background, No.6 prepares to bear left from Corporation Street into Cotham Street. The policeman has to control not only traffic along these two roads but also that emerging from Victoria Square facing the Town Hall. The trolleybus follows the outer set of wires, those on the nearside being used by St. Helens services 4 and 6, Moss Bank to Parr and St. Helens Junction to Dentons Green respectively. No.6 carries the two band livery and is in similar condition to No.9 in the following photograph. However, note the difference in location of destination apertures. No.6 received a front only rebuild around 1954.

Photo, C.Carter.

Plate 50. Cotham Street, No.9. The corner building behind No.9 stands at the point where Cotham Street crossed Claughton Street into which the overhead for St. Helens services 4 and 6 turned, crossing the Atherton route wires from the nearside. No.9, this time in the earlier livery, again under a single pair of wires, follows Cotham Street on a damp day towards Sefton Place terminus, the conductor having already turned the destination blind for the return to Atherton.

Photo, Author's collection.

Plate 51. Cotham Street. On 17th August 1998, the old buildings at the upper end of Cotham Street remain and, along with St. Helens Town Hall, provide a visual flashback to the days when the SLT Guy trolleybuses glided silently past. The property at the corner of Claughton Street, occupied by Age Concern, still retains its distinctive curved arch door. One of the former dwellings nearer the Town Hall is now a coffee shop.

Photo, Author.

Plate 52. Sefton Place, No.14. The Atherton route terminus in St. Helens was Ormskirk Street in Sefton Place and was shared with St. Helens short workings to Ashton, Haydock and Blackbrook. In 1952, No.14 stands beside a deserted bus stop in typical SLT weather, having turned into Sefton Place from the exit to Cotham Street behind the bus. The Ridings furniture shop, occupying part of the Imperial Buildings block, offers Indian carpets on no deposit terms and also has a line in cycles. No.14, recently rebuilt with deepened side panels and a modern look to the front, contrasts greatly with Nos.6 and 9 seen previously in Cotham Street. This trolleybus received a further repaint into the single cream band livery and was somewhat surprisingly withdrawn when the St. Helens route closed in November 1956.

Photo, Roy Marshall.

Plate 53. Sefton Place, St. Helens No.305. Between Haydock and St. Helens, in St. Helens territory, SLT and St. Helens trolleybuses, operating the joint service to Atherton, shared the wires with St. Helens Corporation trolleybuses on service 3 to Haydock, *Ram's Head* on which service St. Helens Roe bodied Sunbeam W No.305 awaits departure from Sefton Place in April 1956. This service had operated between Ackers Lane and Haydock until the Ackers Lane route closed in February 1952. There were three parallel sets of wires in Ormskirk St., those on the nearside used by Atherton route services. St. Helens services to Moss Bank, Dentons Green and Ackers Lane to St. Helens Junction had used the centre pair of wires until these routes closed in February 1952, after which the overhead emerging from Baldwin Street in the background had only been used to permit Parr service trolleybuses to gain access to Sefton Place from Claughton Street. The circular Rainhill, Prescot services used the outer set of wires.

Photo, Martin Brown.

Plate 54. Sefton Place, No.40. With a St. Helens Massey bodied Ransomes trolleybus close behind, unrebuilt No.40 will have a full load for the journey back to Atherton. This time the offer not to be missed at Ridings is a Wilton carpet, a limited quantity consignment apparently having just arrived from Belgium: Cash or terms as usual ! Most of those on the pavement seem to have a seat on the bus as their greater concern. No.40 could provide no greater contrast with No.14. Apart from half drop windows having been replaced by sliding ventilators, the trolleybus is in almost original condition down to the eight leg trolley gantry, guttering over the top deck windows and drainage pipes running down the pillars at both ends of the bus. The rear platform window remains glazed rather than panelled over and a makers badge is still affixed to the driver's door. By way of contrast the Ransomes behind No.40 has no offside drivers door, access being by way of the nearside on all St. Helens prewar trolleybuses ! No.40 later received a new front as seen in the photograph at Platt Bridge depot. *Photo, C. Carter.*

Plate 55. Sefton Place, No.10. SLT Guy No.10 looks as though it will be lightly loaded on departure from St. Helens for the return run to Atherton as it stands in a deserted Sefton Place. Whilst the photographer has the attention of at least one upper deck passenger, the timekeeper's attention appears to have been distracted by some occurence well to the rear of the trolleybus in the direction of the Cotham Street junction with Ormskirk Street. The main interest is not so much activity, or lack of it, but in the front end of No.10, seen as rebuilt around 1951. In December 1954 the trolleybus returned to Atherton Howe Bridge depot for a final repaint in this livery after which it emerged with rubber mounted upperdeck front windows, destination aperature and cab side windows to combat water ingress. At the same time the mudguards over the rear wheels were modified to incorporate an additional fairing between the rear wheels. Photographs prior to these modifications are rare hence this noteworthy inclusion.

Photo, Author's collection.

30

Plate 56. Sefton Place. Sefton Place on 17th August 1998 is pedestrian friendly ! Beyond *The Sefton* is Baldwin Street with the exit from Cotham Street to the right beyond the Royal Bank of Scotland. Buses and taxis still pass along Ormskirk Street turning right into Bridge Street. The dress styles of the 1950s, with headscarves and belted coats, contrast with today's casual, less formal, but more practical attire.   *Photo, Author.*

Plate 57. Sefton Place, No.1. The first trolleybus in the fleet, Guy BTX No.1 stands on Ormskirk Street's granite setts in 1953 just prior to its dispatch to bodybuilder S.H.Bond of Wythenshawe. It returned in the summer of that year having been rebuilt using the original frames but with a much more modern, less angular appearance.   *Photo, Author's collection.*

Plate 58. Ormskirk Street, No.17. No.17 leaves Sefton Place to return to Atherton in pursuit of two St. Helens buses as the trio pass the Mersey furniture showrooms in Ormskirk Street. The East Lancashire bodied bus heading the line is about to bear left into Church Street. No.17 will follow taking it onward to Parr Street to join the inward bound wires at Corporation Street. The bus in front of No.17 is of interest being a London Transport style RT, one of 40 such buses delivered new to St. Helens in 1950-1952 to full LT specification. The use of the destination aperture to display the route numbers was a St. Helens pecularity, though perhaps not as strange as the SLT which used no numbers at all ! The wiring to the right took Rainhill / Prescot bound trolleybuses into Bridge Street .

Photo, the late J.Batty.

Plate 59. Ormskirk Street. A glance on 17th August 1998 along Ormskirk Street towards Church Street provides easy clues to the path taken by the Atherton bound trolleybuses. The key landmark to the left is the Globe building, now home to Boots opticians. Note the sympathetic 'in character' rebuilding at roof level which, being slightly lower, gives a better view of the amazingly unaltered row of four chimney pots on the building beyond! The old buildings in Church Street have been demolished but their line is perpetuated in the new shopping centre.

Photo, Author.

A JOURNEY ALONG THE ROUTES:
2. LEIGH TO BOLTON.

Leigh Terminus - Spinning Jenny Street.

Plate 60. Leigh Terminus, Nos.57, 45 and 62. The Leigh to Bolton trolleybus service commenced on Sunday 17th December 1933. SLT trams had run south beyond Leigh to Lowton St. Mary's but this southern portion of the former tram route was replaced on the same day by a motor bus service operated jointly by Lancashire United Transport and Leigh Corporation. Leigh trolleybus terminus was located on private land off Spinning Jenny Street. Furthest away from the public conveniences waiting to depart for Bolton is No.57, one of a batch of six three axle Roe bodied Leyland TTB trolleybuses numbered 54 to 59 introduced in 1938. The nearside wiring was used by the Mosley Common service. Guy BT No.45 operating this service awaits the departure to Atherton depot of No.62, a wartime Karrier W with Weymann utility bodywork. In 1956 this bus received a modified cab front panel with headlamps mounted on the wings, emerging from Atherton depot with the incorrect registration FDT 454 as seen here. This was quickly corrected to FTD 454. Note the array of overhead fittings and the 18" and 24" wiring spacings at the terminus exit.

Photo, C. Carter

Plate 61. Leigh Terminus, No.1 Passengers on No.1's platform are about to perform the time honoured activity of disembarking on the move as the trolleybus, approaching the terminus, slows to take the sharp left hand turn from King Street into Spinning Jenny Street. The date is 16th August 1958 and rebuilt No.1 presents a modern appearance in the final days of SLT operation. The imposing three storey building on the corner of Twist Lane and King Street still stands today as the most prominent landmark associated with the former terminus location.

Photo, the late Reg Wilson.

33

Contrasting pairs at Spinning Jenny Street.

Trolleybus and motorbus

Back end views

The old and the new

Plate 62. Leigh Terminus, No.55 and Bolton PD2/4 No.446. LUT had opened a motor bus station at Spinning Jenny Street in 1927. Upon the introduction of trolleybuses all but one of the motor bus services were banished to side streets. Latterly, service 16 to Horwich, shared by LUT, Bolton Corporation and Leigh Corporation used the terminus, although only LUT and Bolton operated any vehicles on it. Roe bodied Leyland trolley No.55 waits alongside DBN 349, a Bolton Leyland PD2 No.446. Bolton's 100 Leyland bodied Leyland PD2/4s of 1948/9 were a rarer variety than the norm, being air braked as opposed to the then usual vacuum brakes. Trolleybus No.55 was the sole member of the batch to retain front panel access for the towing hook and continuous beading at 'top of wheel arch' height. *Photo, Author's collection.*

Plate 63. Leigh Terminus, Nos.63 & 68 (Middle) A view towards the terminus exit into King Street on 21st August 1958, just 10 days before final closure, Karrier W No.63 and Sunbeam MS2 No.68 wait to depart on Mosley Common and Bolton services respectively. Note the effect of the upward pressure from the trolley booms on the slack overhead. No.68 carries rear panel advertising for Hulton Service Station, a Ford franchise garage located by the Hulton Lane turning circle removed in 1956 upon replacement of Bolton local trolleybus services. Note the angular fabricated rather than pressed rear dome of wartime built No.63, a common economy feature of utility bus body construction.

Photo, P.J. Thompson (Photosales)

Plate 65. Spinning Jenny Street, No.58. With Twist Lane in the background, No. 58, destination blind already set for the return to Bolton, has turned from King Street and passes a smart black Austin A30 parked by the Spinning Jenny Street entrance to the Regal where *Perri* is showing. Note the traction pole mounted Trolleybus Stop, interesting in that the sign was at the opposite side of the road to the actual unloading point. *Photo, Author's collection.*

Plate 66, The Spinning Jenny Street Mural. One Thomas Highs was born in Leigh, c1720 and in later years experimented with machinery for the textile industry at his home, 59, King Street, Leigh. In 1767, he employed John Kay of Warrington to construct a working model of his apparatus for demonstration purposes. In 1785, a number of industrialists brought legal action against Richard Arkwright who claimed to have patented a similar, if not identical, device for spinning. During the court case, in which Highs was called upon to give evidence, it transpired that John Kay had later been employed by Arkwright, and had made machinery for him from ideas gleaned whilst in the employ of Thomas Highs. The court found against Arkwright and as a consequence he lost his monopoly over the cotton industry, much to the delight of local industrialists.

The mural, as incorporated into the building on the corner of Spinning Jenny Street and King Street, and photographed on 8th February 1984, commemorates the belief that Thomas Highs was the rightful inventor of the 'Spinning Jenny'. The buildings on Spinning Jenny Street were demolished in 1990 to make way for a new road, Spinning Jenny Way. The mural itself can now be seen in the foyer of Leigh Town Hall.

Photo, D.J.Sweeney.

Plate 64. Leigh Terminus, Nos.69 & 26.(opposite) In this 14th July 1953 view, the angular front and work stained early livery of 22 year old lowbridge Guy BTX No.26 makes it look decidedly down at heel alongside the stylish highbridge Weymann body of 5 year old Sunbeam MS2 No.69. However, No.26, with its upright stance, assumes an air of dignity as the two trolleybuses pose with their drivers. Indeed its solid Roe body was to soldier on for another two years without a repaint until withdrawal in October 1955. One could be forgiven for believing that 69, with its deep windscreen and modern lighting, might have been a driver's preferred choice when trying to follow the wires in the dense smogs that all too often descended upon SLT territory! *Photo, Author's collection.*

Plate 67. Twist Lane / King Street. Little remains on 30th July 1998 to indicate the old terminus location save for *Edison's* (formerly the *Eagle & Child*) standing at the Twist Lane junction with King Street. The photograph was taken from a low height boundary wall of a car rental premises at the point where the trolleybuses entered the terminus. The trolleybuses have gone as has the Regal cinema, closed on 30th December 1968 and subsequently demolished to make way for Spinning Jenny Way, a busy thoroughfare taking traffic to join Atherleigh Way bypassing Leigh to the west.

Photo, Author.

. **Plate 68. King Street, No.64.** No.64 passes along a traffic free King Street in April 1956. The exit from Leigh Corporation bus station is visible beyond the Regal cinema. Owned by Associated British Cinemas Ltd. and able to accommodate 1564 people, the Regal opened on Saturday 25th June 1938. The cinema made history on 8th August 1949 when the European premiere of *Command Decision* starring Clark Gable, Van Johnson and Walter Pidgeon was shown in the presence of the Mayor and Mayoress (Councillor and Mrs. T. Hourigan), members and officials of the Council and officers and men from the Burtonwood Air Base. This was the first time a film in Britain had received a premiere outside the capital.

Photo, Martin Brown.

Plate 69. King Street /Spinning Jenny Way. Seen alongside Spinning Jenny Way in February 2002, where the Regal cinema once stood, is the *Goose at the Spinning Jenny* public house. Lancashire, the home of the cotton industry with its humid climate, saw the mid 18th century bring technological advance to cotton spinning with which the names of James Hargreaves, Richard Arkwright and Samuel Crompton are synonymous. Whilst others laid similar claim, history records James Hargreaves as the inventor in 1764, of the machine eventually capable of spinning more than 100 threads simultaneously from which this pub and Leigh's former trolleybus terminus street took their names.

Photo, D.J.Sweeney.

Plate 70. King Street, No.53. The 16th August 1958 sees a smart Leyland trolleybus No. 53 with its destination blind already set for return to Atherton passing the Leigh Corporation bus station nearing the terminus. The bus, with a variety of Ford and Morris cars in attendance, appears lightly loaded with just one passenger ready to hop off when the bus takes the left turn into Spinning Jenny Street .

Photo, the late Reg Wilson.

Plate 71. King Street, No.49. Some two and a half years earlier, the driver of a solitary Austin car signals to turn right into Lord Street as trolleybus No.49, with the terminus to the left in the distance, loads at Leigh market place. The stained stonework of King Street's buildings make the cream coloured litter bin all the more prominent. There were twelve Leyland TTBs in the fleet numbered 48 - 59. No. 49, almost identical to 53 seen earlier, belonged to the first batch of 4 vehicles, delivered March 1936, owned by Bolton Corporation, but operated by SLT.

Photo, the late J. Batty.

Plate 72. The Avenue, No.13.

An interesting spectacle occurring whenever the route was obstructed was the turning back of trolleybuses by reversal into unwired side streets by means of jumper cables. One pair of bamboo poles was hooked onto the overhead enabling the bus to be powered via insulated trailing cables and a second pair of poles connected onto hooked down trolley booms . No.13, a lowbridge Guy BTX, is seen on 16th June 1957 reversing by this method into The Avenue at the North end of Leigh town centre before returning to Atherton. What was uneventful on a fine mid summer's day could cause hairs to stand on end during inclement weather giving cause to ponder whether certain sensations were caused by something other than poor circulation! Such a practice would be unlikely to be given approval today!

Photo, The late E. K. Stretch.

LEIGH—ATHERTON—FOUR LANE ENDS—BOLTON
Trolley Vehicle Service

MONDAY TO FRIDAY

		am	am	am	am	am	am	am	am	am	am	am	am	am	am	am
Leigh, Spinning Jenny Street	dep.	...	...	...	...	...	...	...	...	5 26	5 35	5 44	5 52	6 1	6 9	6 18
Atherton, Depot	,,	4 34	4 43	4 43	4 52	5 0	5 9	5 17	5 26	5 34	5 43	5 52	6 0	6 9	6 17	6 26
Atherton, Punch Bowl	,,	4 38	4 47	4 47	4 56	5 4	5 13	5 21	5 30	5 38	5 47	5 56	6 4	6 13	6 21	6 30
Four Lane Ends	,,	4 50	4 59	4 59	5 8	5 16	5 25	5 33	5 42	5 50	5 59	6 8	6 16	6 25	6 33	6 42
Bolton, Howell Croft	arr.	5 6	5 15	...	5 24	5 32	5 41	5 49	5 58	6 6	6 15	6 24	6 32	6 41	6 49	6 58

		am	am	am	am		pm	pm	pm	pm	pm	pm	pm	pm
Leigh, Spinning Jenny Street	dep.	6 26	6 35	6 44	6 52	and	1018	1026	1035	1044	1052	1055	11 3	1111
Atherton, Depot	,,	6 34	6 43	6 52	7 0	every	1026	1034	1043	1052	11 0	11 3	1111	1119
Atherton, Punch Bowl	,,	6 38	6 47	6 56	7 4	8½ minutes	1030	1038	1047	1056	11 4	11 7	1115	...
Four Lane Ends	,,	6 50	6 59	7 8	7 16	until	1042	1050	1059	11 8	1116	...	...	...
Bolton, Howell Croft	arr.	7 6	7 15	7 24	7 32		1058	...	...	...	...	...	...	...

		am	am	am	am	am	am	am	am	am	am	am		pm	pm
Bolton, Howell Croft	dep.	...	...	...	5 6	5 15	5 24	5 32	5 41	5 49	5 58	and	1032	
Four Lane Ends	,,	5 0	...	...	5 20	5 29	5 38	5 46	5 55	6 3	6 12	every	1046	1051
Atherton, Punch Bowl	,,	5 11	...	...	5 31	5 40	5 49	5 57	6 6	6 14	6 23	8½ minutes	1057	11 2
Atherton, Depot	,,	5 15	5 25	5 34	5 35	5 44	5 53	6 1	6 10	6 18	6 27	until	11 1	11 6
Leigh, Spinning Jenny Street	arr.	5 23	5 33	5 42	5 43	5 52	6 1	6 9	6 18	6 26	6 35		11 9	...

		pm	pm	pm	pm	pm	pm	pm	pm
Bolton, Howell Croft	dep.	1041	...	...	1049	...	...	1058	...
Four Lane Ends	,,	1055	...	11 0	11 3	...	11 9	1112	1117
Atherton, Punch Bowl	,,	11 6	11 9	1111	1114	1117	1120	1123	1128
Atherton, Depot	,,	1110	1113	1115	1118	1121	1124	1127	1132
Leigh, Spinning Jenny Street	arr.	...	...	...	...	...	...	...	

Railway Stations on or near the route Howe Bridge Station. Atherton Central Station. Bolton Howell Croft, for Bolton (Gt. Moor St. and Trinity St.) Stations

Plate 73. The Hippodrome, Leigh Road. Leigh Road and the Hippodrome cinema seen about 1949. In the distance a newly delivered Sunbeam MS2 trolleybus leaves Leigh heading towards Atherton. The Hippodrome had a chequered career opening as a theatre as evidenced by the Civic Theatre lettering above the third storey windows. However, pictures had been shown as early as 1910 and by November 1924 it was being advertised as the Hippodrome Super Cinema. The last silent movie shown on 14th February 1931 was *The Divine Lady* starring Corrin Griffiths. Complete modernisation took place during summer 1939. After a brief spell of live entertainment in 1955 the Hippodrome returned to films under the Rank ownership becoming the Odeon in 1956 before a further name change to The Classic in 1967 and The Cannon under Cannon group ownership in 1985 with closure in October 1989. The building reopened for a short period as Laser Quest. *Photo, Wigan Heritage Services.*

Plate 74. Former Hippodrome. On 30th July 1998, the former Hippodrome was in a sorry state with all references to its theatrical or motion picture past having been obliterated. Even the bus stop appears to stoop in sympathy! The property was for sale and some minor repair work was underway but in today's multiscreen, video, CD ROM world, its heyday is over.

Photo, Author.

Atherleigh

Road realignment at Atherleigh

From Leigh the road took the trolleybus route through Atherleigh and on to Howe Bridge, Atherton. During August 1958 road realignment to ease the bend through Atherleigh was underway, the opportunity being taken to lift redundant tram tracks! The impending closure of the trolleybus system meant there was never any intention to rewire the realigned bend and only minimal adjustment to the overhead using adjustable leg hangers sufficient to enable trolleys to pass was undertaken. As a result trolleybuses had to negotiate the roadworks and the revised alignment at dead slow speed with their booms at full stretch. Those passing towards Atherton could hug the bollards whilst Leigh bound trolleybuses were forced to the middle of the road through the new alignment and had to face oncoming traffic as well as keep their booms on the wires!

Plate 75. Atherleigh. On 25th August 1958, No.60, a utility bodied Karrier W, swings its booms to full stretch as its driver eases slowly through the roadworks keeping as close as possible to the bollards. Some minor assistance was provided by way of adjustable leg hangers on the nearest span wires repositioning the Atherton bound wires as far as possible towards the Leigh bound wires. The pavements on the outside of the bend became much wider extending up to the bollards nearest the camera and concrete lighting columns were installed. The column by the telegraph pole gained a new lantern glass before being replaced. It has a few more days to serve as a traction pole.
Photo, the late E.K .Stretch.

Plate 76. Atherleigh. On the same August day, No.16, a Guy BTX with rebuilt front approaches Atherleigh bend from Atherton, the driver choosing his line away from the nearside kerb. Note the temporary wiring arrangement with the Leigh bound positive wire suspended from adjustable leg hangers and the negative moved across to the line ears formerly supporting the positive wire. A couple of new concrete lighting columns are already in place.
Photo, the late E.K.Stretch.

Howe Bridge

Atherton Howe Bridge Depot

Howe bridge depot was built in 1901 by the South Lancashire Tramways Company to coincide with the commencement of tram services to Lowton St. Mary's to the south and Four Lane Ends at the boundary with Bolton to the north. The depot originally sat on a 4,142 acre site, later extended to 5,067 acres in 1936 and was initially designed to house 50 tramcars. The South Lancashire Tramways Company decided on the Howe Bridge depot location with its associated power station in Atherton Urban District, halfway between Leigh and Atherton, depriving Leigh of a valuable rating asset as a result of a disagreement with Leigh officialdom. The company established its headquarters there, ultimately the headquarters of the South Lancashire Transport Company and its successor Lancashire United Transport. Motor buses were housed across the road in a purpose built depot, the former tram depot eventually becoming the bus overhaul works. Interestingly there was a rail connection to the Kenyon Junction to Bolton line of the LNWR .including colliery sidings to service the power station. 'South Lancashire Tramway Company' siding still appeared in the Railway Clearing House *Handbook of Stations* in 1956 !

Plate 77. Atherton Howe Bridge depot. Leyland sent their photographer to Atherton in 1936 following delivery of the first four Roe bodied Leyland TTB trolleybuses Nos.48 to 51, registered ATE 792 to 795. In this staged photograph numbers 48 and 49 'ply the main route' whilst No.51 emerges from the depot. At this time the depot entrance wiring was unconnected to the route wiring, frogs being added during the war. Note the gas lamp, tram tracks, shaded fleet numerals, stencil indicators and front panel access to the towing bracket on No.49. This latter feature was only retained by one Leyland, No.55, from a later batch. These four trolleybuses were the property of Bolton Corporation, each costing £2000 when new. On disposal to Birds at Stratford upon Avon upon closure of the Bolton local services in 1956, the quartet realised a total of £360 !

Photo, Wigan Heritage Services.

Plate 78. Howe Bridge Depot. Seen from the Leigh direction on 14th March 1958, the power station cooling tower dominates the view with the SLT/LUT main offices to the right. The power station building stands behind the cooling tower whilst the depot buildings remain hidden behind the offices. The Lancashire United Transport bus depot was directly opposite on the other side of the road. Sadly the entire site was demolished during the latter part of 1998.

Photo, W. Ryan.

Plate 79. Howe Bridge, No.67. With a rural backdrop No.67 stands close by the depot entrance awaiting a new crew whilst on service to Bolton. Not surprisingly, the depot was a 'crew change' spot for SLT and LUT crews. No.67 was withdrawn prematurely in April 1958 following a collision which damaged the cab nearside, this after having received a repair to the rear some months earlier from another mishap.

Photo, Author's collection.

Plate 80. Atherton Howe Bridge depot, No.53. After a change of crew, the conductress at the end of her duty makes her way back to the depot as a new driver draws trolleybus No.53 away from the bus stop to pass underneath the depot entrance wiring. Prominent at the end of the boundary wall and marking the entrance to the depot is the white banded post bearing the notice which reads " No Entry Except For Trolleybuses". Illumination at the entrance is provided by the lantern on the traction pole. *Photo, Photobus.*

Plate 81. Howe Bridge, No. 64. Opposite the trolleybus depot, a couple of LUT's utility bodied Guy Arabs peep out from the bus depot as No.64 heads towards Leigh, with a coal lorry in close pursuit. No.64, showing 'Depot', may well be on test with a mechanic with rolled back sleeves and grubby hands accompanying the driver. This was the least altered of the utility trolleybuses retaining drop down windows apart from the offside upper deck. The headlights remain in the front panel rather than being exiled to the front wings.   *Photo, Roy Marshall.*

Plate 82. Howe bridge, Nos. 62 and 66. With the depot entrance and company offices in the background, Karrier W No.62, and Sunbeam MS2 No.66 pass as they operate the Leigh to Bolton service. Again, one of the area's ubiquitous coal lorries follows No.66. Originally built with a utility style fabricated angular rear dome, No.62 has received a rather neater, contoured replacement.
Photo, Author's collection.

Plate 83. Howe Bridge, Nos. 54 and 27. Leyland TTB No. 54 on service to Bolton is closely followed by Guy BTX No.27 destined for Mosley Common. Above the Austin A30 can be seen the depot wiring which, on exit towards Atherton, ran parallel for 50 yards or so before joining the route wiring. Meanwhile, on the bus garage forecourt, an LUT Roe bodied single decker, with LUT promotional advertising, awaits its next turn of duty.

Photo, P.J.Thompson, (Photosales)

Plate 84. Main offices, No.7. Rebuilt Guy BTX No.7 leaves the depot to take up service to Swinton, augmenting Swinton depot's allocation on the Atherton to Farnworth route. This destination was usually displayed until Worsley was reached after which the blind would be changed to show Farnworth, although No.7's duty could have been a short working. Taking to the road at the same time, as if doubtful about No.7's reliability, is BTF 576, former bus No.23, a Roe bodied Leyland TS7 which, converted to a towing vehicle, remained in that role until withdrawn in 1964. Note the collapsible staging on the roof of BTF 576 enabling fitters to attend to the trolleyheads of vehicles in service.

Photo, Photobus.

Plate 85. Atherton depot, No. 58. Travelling from Atherton on 24th August 1958, No.58 is about to pass the depot buildings and offices on Leigh Road. The bus carries that wonderful advertising paradox referring to Woodbines as the 'great little cigarette'!

Photo, the late Reg Wilson.

44

Around the depot yard.

Plate 86. Atherton depot.
Pictured in the depot yard around 1936 are Guy trolleybuses Nos.47, 26, 40, 21, 30 and 10. No.47 was a highbridge, Guy bodied, former Guy demonstrator which came into SLT ownership in 1935. Registered JW 5370, No.47 left SLT for a few months in 1939 on loan to Southend Corporation. The original sloping cab panel seen here was later replaced around 1938 with an assembly similar to the other trolleybuses alongside. The bus, always the 'odd man out' was withdrawn in 1951, the first trolleybus to be taken out of use.

Photo, R. M. Hannay.

Plate 87. Atherton depot, No. 47.
No.47 is seen in Atherton depot yard having acquired its later style front panel. Note the remnants of wartime livery along the base of the cab panel.

Photo, Author's collection.

Plate 88. Atherton depot. A sad event during the summer of 1998 was the demolition of both the former SLT depot buildings and the former LUT bus depot opposite. Pictured here on 30th July 1998, in a view directly comparable with that previously of No. 47, the removal of the old power station roof is underway. By November the whole site was in the final stages of demolition.

Photo, Author.

Plate 89.   Atherton depot, Nos. 33 & 20. In happier times on 2nd November 1957, Nos.33 and 20 await their next duties. The view permits an interesting comparison of Guy BT No.33 in 'as built' 1933 condition and rebuilt Guy BTX No.20 of 1931 which originally had an appearance similar to that of 33.   As with contemporary railway property, the era of engineering minimalism had yet to dawn and the substantial nature of the buildings gave rise to the belief that they would be there for ever!

Photo, P.J.Thompson.
(Photosales)

Inside Howe Bridge Depot.

Plate 90. Atherton depot, No. 40. An interesting feature within the depot to the rear of the building was the traverser and turntable built in 1933 by S. H. Heywood & Co. Ltd. Reddish, on which Guy No.40 is seen. Operated by two tramcar type controllers, one to traverse and the other to turn, the equipment collected power through two trolley poles running under wiring visible in the top right of the picture. Maximum safe load was 9 tons. Whilst the 3-axle Leylands at around 8 ton 15cwt. were just within this, could it be that the weight of the post-war Sunbeams, at 9 ton 16cwt 2qrs., was conveniently overlooked?

Photo, A. Ingram.

Plate 91. Atherton depot, No. 32. No.32 is seen over the pit receiving attention to its rear axle, its nearside half shaft lying by the rear wheel. Repairs were successfully completed and No.32 ran until final closure as one of just a few Guy BTs remaining in service. With a front only rebuild, the trolleybus retains much originality behind the front bulkhead including shallow bottom panels and beading below the waist rail. An earlier Woodbines advert is carried. The angular front of the unrebuilt bus alongside belongs to Guy BTX No.15.

Photo, Author's collection.

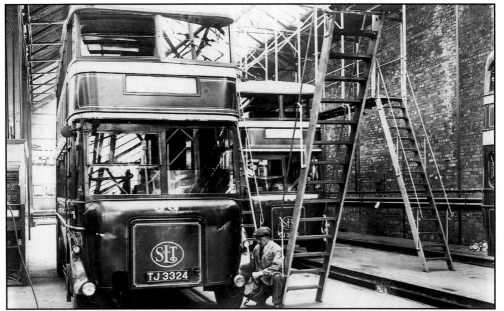

Plate 92. Atherton depot, Nos. 35 & 33. On casting his eye around the front cab panel, the fitter checking tyre pressures on almost new Guy BT No.35 is probably relieved that he is not employed as the resident bodybuilder! Nevertheless the odd dents received by 35 cannot detract from the ornate paintwork and panel lining that was the style in the 1930s. Far more satisfying to be taken to work in a vehicle exuding craftsmanship rather that the corporate image, raspberry ripple, mobile billboards of today.

Photo, A. Ingram.

The former London & North Western Railway at Howe Bridge.

Northwards from Howe Bridge depot, the wires soon ran underneath the bridge carrying the former LNWR Tyldesley to Wigan line via Hindley Green. Howe Bridge station was known as Chowbent until April 1901, a name which persisted with locals for many years afterwards. The line connected west of the bridge with that running from Kenyon Junction to Bolton Great Moor Street. The station which closed on 20th July 1959, had, up to the early fifties, been particularly busy handling up to 500 people on Saturday morning holiday specials. Following closure of the line in 1969 the bridge was dismantled but the bridge abutments remained in place and saw subsequent use in the 1980s supporting a Bailey bridge providing road transport for extracted minerals from open cast workings. That task complete, all traces of there ever having been a bridge at this location have now disappeared.

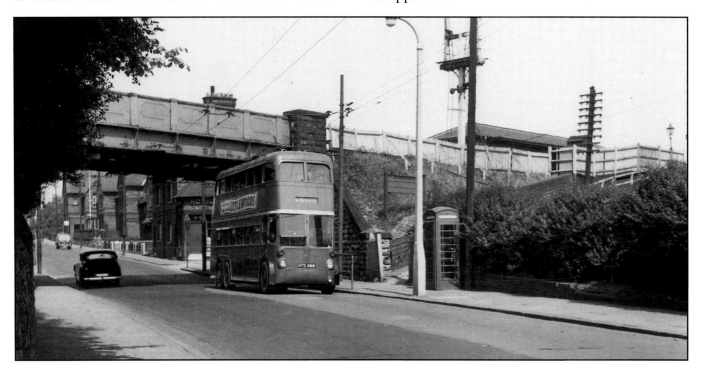

Plate 93. Howe Bridge, No. 71. Seen on 22nd June 1956, Weymann bodied Sunbeam MS2 No.71, the last trolleybus delivered to the SLT in 1948, slowly emerges to avoid dewiring, from the minimal clearance of Howe Bridge railway bridge bound for Leigh. Bridges tended to be problematical for trolleybuses and not just because of clearance. The relatively rigid support afforded to the overhead under bridges was far less forgiving than span wire suspension and spirited attempts at passing under bridges could result in trolley poles parting company with the wires. Visible beyond are houses built by Fletcher Burrows for colliery workers and their families as part of the Howe Bridge Model Village.

Photo, the late E.K.Stretch.

Plate 94. Howe Bridge, rebuilding the railway overbridge. This interesting view of activities on the 14th July 1957 shows the severed overhead and replacement rolled steel beams awaiting unloading from a bogie bolster. Note the former private owner wooden bodied railway wagons.

Photo, Wigan Heritage Services.

The rebuilding of Howe Bridge railway bridge.

A major event during the summer of 1957 was the rebuilding of Howe Bridge which involved complete replacement of the overbridge and major work on the abutments. Disruption to trolleybus services was inevitable and a one day cessation of operation occurred on Sunday 14th July when replacement motor bus services were operated. The Leigh to Bolton service ran as service 82 via Wigan Road and Lovers Lane and the Atherton to Leigh portion of the Mosley Common service as 84. The date was significant in heralding in these new service numbers which were to become the replacement motor bus services after SLT closure in 1958.

Plate 95. Howe Bridge, No.69. A few days later a Bedford coal lorry follows Sunbeam No.69 under the skeleton of the replacement bridge. Note the realigned Leigh bound wiring suspended from an adjustable leg hanger. From this point it was a straight run beyond the bridge up Leigh Road to Atherton

Photo, C. W. Routh.

Plate 96. Howe Bridge, No.71. The pathway to the Fletcher Burrows built colliery workers' houses provides an ideal vantage point from which to appreciate the tight fit for trolleybuses under the bridge, the power cables on the roof of Sunbeam No.71 almost touching the running wires!. This view towards Leigh also identifies the contractor who without doubt would not have found having to contend with trolleybuses conducive to a speedy conclusion of his contract!

Photo, Author's collection.

49

Plate 97. Howe Bridge, Nos.42 & 70. The final result of the bridge rebuild was quite pleasing as seen here on 31st August 1958 with Howe Bridge railway station remaining open and services advertised. A grey roofed trolleybus, Guy No.42, bound for Mosley Common passes Sunbeam No.70 on the Bolton to Leigh service and there is little to suggest that this is the last day of trolleybus operation. No.42 was the only trolleybus to survive until closure with the earlier grey roof livery and one of only 3 Guy BTs remaining in service, the others being Nos.32 and 44. all with rebuilt fronts.

Photo, J. C. Gillham.

Plate 98. Howe Bridge, No.58. The parked Vauxhall together with Leigh bound trolleybus No.58 passing cautiously under the new railway bridge cause little obstruction to traffic on 31st July 1958. Overhead wire splicing ears visible between No.58's trolleyheads and the first twin line hangers mark the point at which the overhead was severed during construction of the new bridge. Visible beyond the bridge on the rising gradient are Howe Bridge model village houses whilst in the distance another trolleybus climbs Leigh Road's gentle rise towards Atherton. *Photo, P.J.Thompson, (Photosales)*

Plate 99. Howe Bridge. Seen almost ten years after the last day of trolleybus operation, the bridge, albeit without the trolley wires, remains, though it too was removed after closure of the railway line in 1969. Emerging from the bridge on the Manchester to Liverpool route 39 is front entrance Northern Counties bodied Guy Arab V No.237, a type which became synonymous with Lancashire United Transport. These Guys were for many years the standard equipment operating the 82 Leigh to Bolton former trolleybus service.

Photo, Jim Saunders.

Plate 100. Howe Bridge. In the early 1980s, a temporary Bailey Bridge was erected at Howe Bridge, seen here on 7th April 1985, as an access road for opencast coal extraction from Millers Lane which went out by road transport. The former trackbed of the railway at Howe Bridge, including the east curve, was utilised and also a section of the Bolton & Leigh trackbed between Howe Bridge Jct. and Gibfield, to exit on Wigan Road, Atherton. Wigan Metro opposed the plan and the government inspector rejected the Opencast Executive's application in 1978. However, the inspector's decision was overruled by the then Secretary of State for Energy, Tony Benn. After a lengthy court case on appeal, Tony Benn got his way and opencasting at Millers Lane went ahead. The rebuilt bridge, as seen in **plates 97, 98 & 99** was only demolished about two years before the opencast plans emerged. As a finale to all of this, in the year 2000, a gas pipeline was laid under the road at Howe Bridge and great difficulty was encountered by the contractors in overcoming an impenetrable barrier to their pipeline, namely the bridge foundations. *Photo, D.J.Sweeney.*

Plate 101. Howe Bridge. Today one could be forgiven for passing this location without realising that a railway line crossed by bridge at this point. The Fletcher Burrows houses remain as does the narrow road immediately beyond this point, the road rising gently towards Atherton. Also surviving is a public telephone box at this point though by 30th July 1998, the traditional GPO K6 has been replaced by a modern British Telecom example.

Photo, Author.

Plate 102. Leigh Road, Atherton, Nos.60 & 44. Karrier No.60, waits at roadworks on the approach to Howe Bridge railway bridge whilst Guy No.44 runs up Leigh Road, towards Atherton from the depot to take up service to Swinton on 2nd November 1957. Following the Guy, a Humber 16 is about to pass an old style school sign for Howe Bridge primary school. No.44 was the only trolleybus to receive an all over red livery. No.60 has acquired new front cab panels at which time all lamps have been replaced by wing mounted units.

Photo, P.J.Thompson.
(Photosales)

Plate 103, Atherton Cenotaph, No.54. With Atherton's memorial to those who fell during wartime in the background, No.54 coasts down the gentle grade from Atherton to Howe Bridge on 8th March 1958. It is interesting to ponder the former use of the traction pole with its bracket arm. No doubt it originally suspended tramway wiring. However the arm most probably held a mercury vapour street lantern until made redundant by the new concrete column alongside.

Photo, P.J.Thompson,
(Photosales)

Plate 104, Atherton Cenotaph, No.70. With Atherton Cenotaph on the left and the houses along Hamilton Street in the background, Sunbeam No.70, with a gentle hum from its powerful 115 h.p. 'Metrovick' motor glides effortlessly up the rise to Atherton with the service to Bolton on 8th March 1958. Hamilton Street was home to a local coal merchant, one of three brothers, known as 'Baggy Lee' to his customers.

Photo, P.J.Thompson,
(Photosales)

Plate 105. Leigh Road, No. 64. With Atherton *Punch Bowl* pub in his sights marking the end of Leigh Road's straight run up from Howe Bridge, the driver of No.64 keeps the power on for just a little longer as the trolleybus passes Bee Fold Lane, Atherton Central Park and the cobbles of Stanley Street to his right on 31st July 1958. This stretch from Atherton down to Howe Bridge has changed little over the years though the trolleybus and this Bedford articulated lorry have been replaced by vehicles making much more noise.

Photo, P.J.Thompson ,
(Photosales)

Atherton: the hub of the system

Apart from the numerous short workings all basic services either terminated in, or passed through Atherton. Ahead of the introduction of a one way traffic scheme in 1967, trolleybus wiring ran clockwise, around the four sides of a rectangle, following the long main street Market Street, Wigan Road, the long back street Mealhouse Lane and Church Street. A glance at the map will show that this circuit was not a complete loop as there was no connection from Mealhouse Lane into Church Street, However turn back provision was available by way of Bag Lane, wired to permit trolleybuses to regain the Market Street wires from Mealhouse Lane.

Farnworth route services entered Atherton's Market Street via Tyldesley Road and terminated in Wigan Road whilst St. Helens services had their own reverser and terminus in Lambeth Street. Meanwhile Leigh to Bolton and Leigh to Mosley Common through services also loaded in Wigan Road.

During the last few years of operation, childhood shopping trips to Atherton, far from being boring were eagerly awaited, since wherever one was, there was always trolleybus activity; perhaps a chance to see the lowbridge Guys, a few still in grey roof livery, or some of the original 1 - 10 batch of 1930. Finally, until the St. Helens route closure in November 1956, there was entertainment in Wigan Road, during the wait for the Bolton bus home, provided by St. Helens route trolleybuses using the Lambeth Street reverser, occasionally with an extra splash of colour from a red and cream St. Helens Corporation trolleybus operating the joint service.

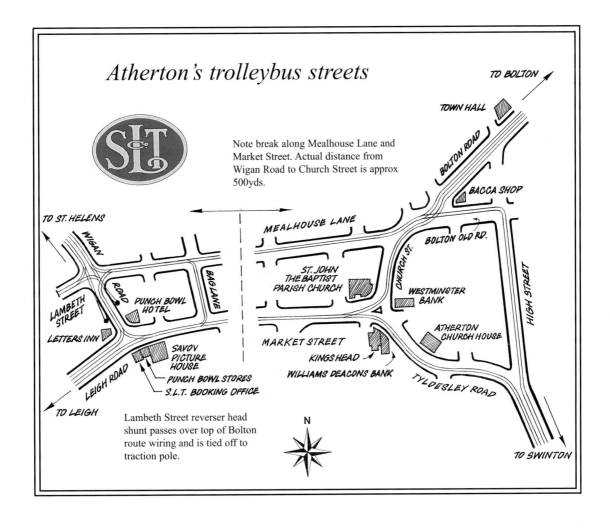

Atherton's trolleybus streets

Note break along Mealhouse Lane and Market Street. Actual distance from Wigan Road to Church Street is approx 500yds.

Lambeth Street reverser head shunt passes over top of Bolton route wiring and is tied off to traction pole.

Plate 106. The Punch Bowl, Nos.12, 55 & 56. Leigh Road entered Atherton town centre at the junction of Market Street and Wigan Road. With Atherton Savoy cinema behind, Guy No. 12 operating the Farnworth service via Swinton is about to turn from Market Street into Wigan Road. The wires to the right of camera will be taken by Leyland No. 55 bound for Leigh. The third trolleybus is Leyland No.56. Next to the Punchbowl Stores was the SLT booking and enquiries office. Two way traffic apart from trolleybuses is clearly evident. The date is around 1956 judging by an early version of a Jacob's Cream Crackers advertisement carried by No.12.
Photo, Dennis Gill.

Plate 107. Atherton Savoy. In the summer of 1998 the traffic signs and road markings tell all. The former Savoy Picture House has gone the way of many similar establishments looking all the more forlorn having lost its canopy. Commissioned by The Eagle Picturedrome Co. Ltd. of Wigan on 17th January 1927 and with a resident orchestra, the first film shown was *The Sea Beast* starring John Barrymore. Closure came in August 1967. Amongst the last films was *The Great St. Trinian's Train Robbery* with Frankie Howerd and Dora Bryan. Following closure the building became a Bingo Hall and when photographed on 4th August 1998 was 'The Atherton Snooker and Social Club'.   *Photo, Author.*

Plate 108. Punch Bowl, No.37. On the 2nd November 1957, Guy BT No.37, in service on the Farnworth route, turns into Wigan Road from Market Street. The *Punch Bowl* hotel's sign hangs prominently from the building's corner whilst behind the trolleybus, the stores of the same name stand alongside the Savoy Picture House. By this time No.37 was one of only two trolleybuses to remain in service in the early post war livery of red with a grey roof and two white bands, the other being Guy BT No.45.
Photo, P.J.Thompson (Photosales)

54

Plate 109. Punch Bowl. A comparable view in the summer of 1998. The Punch Bowl Stores, now The Chocolate Box is 'To Let' and Stone Products UK Ltd. Fireplace Centre, later a DIY centre, occupies the former SLT Booking office. The *Punch Bowl* pub remains, with a later pub sign now in Market Street rather than on the corner as seen in the view of No.37.

Photo, Author.

Plate 110. Wigan Road, Nos.61 & 65. In a 'duo directional traffic' Wigan Road in 1958, Karrier W No.61 pulls away from the Bolton bus stop, whilst behind it, similar bus No.65 slows down for the Mosley Common bus stop. Visible behind No.65 is the wiring at the A 579 Leigh Road junction. Detail differences between the two utility trolleybuses are No.65's retained front panel mounted headlights and the louvres over the upper deck windows lost by 61 upon body overhaul.

Photo, Author's collection.

Plate 111.Wigan Road, No.1. Operating a Saturday lunch time shuttle between Leigh and Tyldesley on 21st December 1957 is No.1 waiting in Wigan Road. On departure the bus will turn sharp right into Mealhouse Lane. Beyond the bus the St. Helens route wiring in Wigan Road and Lambeth Street has gone, having been removed one month previously.

Photo, P.J.Thompson, (Photosales)

Plate 112. Wigan Road, No.10.
In 1958, Guy BTX No.10, one of the original batch of ten trolleybuses bought for the St. Helens route in 1930, turns empty from Wigan Road into Mealhouse Lane before taking the wiring in Bag Lane to regain Market Street and return to Leigh. By this time, the only remaining wiring in Wigan Road was that leading into Mealhouse Lane, the St. Helens route having closed in 1956. No.10, with its new front and deepened side panels,(the front end rubber mounted windows were a later modification), survived the St. Helens route closure and displays the last version of the Jacob's Cream Crackers advertisement to be carried by SLT trolleybuses.

Photo, Author's collection

Plate 113. Mealhouse Lane, No.63.
This 14th July 1953 view sees Karrier No.63 about to restart having just deposited a bus crew in Mealhouse Lane. The trolleybus looks 'spick and span' having not long received its final repaint replacing its 'red with a grey roof' livery. The front lamps are for the time being retained in the cab panels, though No.63 received repairs quite late in its career to the cab area including a rubber mounted nearside cab front window, new panels and wing mounted lamps. Uniquely it retained a louvre over the upper deck front windows only.

Photo, Authors collection

Plate 114. Church Street, No. 64.
The remaining side of the Atherton trolleybus rectangle was Church Street which ran down from Mealhouse Lane to join Market Street at the junction with Tyldesley Road. On 21st August 1958 No.64 on a Bolton to Leigh service runs past Atherton's Saint John the Baptist Parish Church. For me, this caption could never be complete without mention that my marriage banns were read here in August 1975, though I was married to my wife Susan in Stourbridge Worcestershire far away from SLT territory and my native Lancashire.
Photo,P.J.Thompson.
(Photosales)

Plate 115. Church Street, No.28. On 23rd June 1956, owing to obstruction of the normal Market Street, Wigan Road, Mealhouse Lane routeing, Guy No.28 is manoeuvred by bamboo poles and jumper cables from the Tyldesley Road wires into Church Street before being rewired and run 'wrong way' up Church Street. The day is dry so there should not be too many feelings of pins and needles! Close by the Westminster Bank the police, untroubled by traffic matters, watch events with interest.

Photo, The late E.K. Stretch.

Plate 116. Tyldesley Road, No.22. Guy BTX No.22 emerges from Tyldesley Road into Market Place to join Market Street and the wiring from Bolton on 27th February 1956. Farnworth route trolleybuses would pause at this point in order to let a Bolton to Leigh bus precede it along Market Street's single set of wires thus avoiding delay to the Leigh bound vehicle at the *Punch Bowl.* Although fitted with a new front No.22 never received the final livery of red with a single cream band and whilst never operating the St. Helens route, was withdrawn in November 1956 when that route closed, the SLT taking out of service the equivalent number of trolleybuses made redundant from the route closure even if not the same vehicles. To the left of the bus is the *Kings Head* and Williams Deacons bank later to become Williams and Glynn's. To the rear of No.22 stands Atherton Church House with its small spire. Flourishing in the late 19th century, 'Church Houses' provided recreational and social activities for youths from Anglican churches or Sunday schools. In time they lost popularity and after incurring financial loss this property in Tyldesley Road was demolished in 1971.

Photo, the late J.Batty.

Plate 117. Church St. and the Kings Head. Church Street on 4th August 1998 looking towards the *Kings Head* and former Williams Deacons bank. An annual feature of the island alongside the obelisk at the year end was a Christmas tree bedecked in white lights as is custom in Scandinavian countries. It is also pleasing to see that the church has received attention to its stained stonework permitting a full appreciation of its architectural attributes. The area between the obelisk and the church was pedestrianised in 2002, traffic from Church Street now passing the obelisk on the opposite side to reach Market Street.

Photo, Author.

Plate 118. Market Street, No.58. This delightful early post war view of Market Street Atherton dominated by the Parish church of St John the Baptist encapsulates so much about northern workaday British streets of the late 1940s; headscarved ladies with wicker shopping baskets, prolific cigarette advertising, no double yellow lines, and granite setts where cyclists' worst fears might be tram tracks, though in this case the electric transport is South Lancashire Transport's Leyland trolleybus No. 58 bound for Leigh.

Photo, Wigan Heritage Services.

58

Plate 119. Market Street. Fifty years on so much of this view of Market Street remains recognisable. Things are not so bad, roofs have been repaired and buildings, including the church, cleaned up. Street lighting has been improved and everyone must agree that, apart from the garish zig-zag lines associated with the pelican crossing, the current road surface is an improvement

Photo, Author.

Plate 120. Market Street, No.35. Guy BT No.35 moves cautiously along a busy Market Street towards the junction with the overhead from Bag Lane. The BT in the final livery remains little altered, carrying an eight leg trolley gantry and, albeit dented, its original bulging front cab panel, replaced on many unrebuilt Guys with a flat panel.

Photo, Author's collection.

Plate 121. Market Street / Bag Lane, Nos.55 & 59. Trolleybus No.59 emerges from Bag Lane having used this wiring to reach Market Street from Mealhouse Lane and return to Leigh. No.59 will be followed to the Punch Bowl by another Leyland No.55 and a Karrier W. With popular appreciation of its reliable simplicity, the Morris Minor remains a common sight on British streets and would not be out of place if seen at this spot today.

Photo, Author's collection.

Plate 122. Market Street, No.18. Seldom photographed was the view from the Savoy cinema towards the *Letters Inn* pub on the corner of Leigh Road and Wigan Road. In a shower of sleet (SLT photographers had to be waterproof and weather resistant !) Guy No.18 has deposited its Atherton bound passengers in Market Street and will shortly draw forward to take the right hand wiring into Wigan Road to the Farnworth route loading point. Consumption of the breakfast advertised on No.18's rear panel was probably advice well taken if the weather was to live up to its promise. *Photo, P.J.Thompson, (Photosales)*

Plate 123. Punch Bowl, No.68. Completing a trolleybus tour around Atherton brings us back to the *Punch Bowl* where an inspector exchanges a brief word with the driver of smart Sunbeam No.68 before its departure to Leigh on the Bolton to Leigh service. The date is 27th February 1956 and the trolleybus carries an early Jacob's advertisement. The junction of the Bag Lane wiring with that in a deserted Market Street can be seen in the distance.
Photo, the late J.Batty.

.......and on to Bolton.

Plate 124. The Bacca Shop, No.62. Trolleybus No.62 en route to Bolton has emerged from Mealhouse Lane, the exit of which is visible between the two buildings behind the bus, and will shortly leave Church Street to take Bolton Road to its left. The photograph was taken from the rear upper deck of a Farnworth route trolleybus at its loading point in Bolton Old Road. The irregular shaped white building behind 62 was a well known Atherton fishmongers owned by the Norris family for about three generations. Before the last war they would turn out at 4 a.m. and drive to Fleetwood where they would buy their stock direct from the trawlers as they landed their catch. Note the trolleybus overhead feeder cable conduit running up the traction pole to the right of the picture. This location was always known to locals by the landmark of the 'Bacca Shop' situated out of view to the right of the traction pole. *Photo, the late J.Batty.*

Plate 125. The Bacca Shop. This classic 1947 'trolleyscape' view shows the 'Bacca Shop' with the Bolton route wiring disappearing to the left along Bolton Road and to its right, Bolton Old Road into which runs the single pair of wires belonging to the Farnworth route. The clock tower of Atherton Town Hall stands prominently to the left along Bolton Road. This was a busy spot for trolleybuses since in addition to buses to and from Bolton, all buses to Farnworth and Mosley Common traversed this junction. Note the overhead feeder conduit on the traction pole outside the 'Bacca Shop', visible in the previous photograph of No.62. The heavyweight nature of SLT overhead fittings is noticeable as is the mixture of 18" and 24" spacer bars, themselves of a variety of designs. Close inspection will reveal that the frog and the Bolton bound wiring are suspended directly above the cats eyes following a change to the road alignment and kerb position after which the SLT decided to leave the overhead unaltered. Bolton bound trolleybuses negotiated this junction with care.

Photo, Wigan Heritage Services.

61

Plate 126. The Bacca Shop. On 30th July 1998 the Bacca Shop stands prominently under a threatening sky. Property to the left of Mealhouse Lane and in Church Street has been demolished permitting improvements to the road layout greatly easing the traffic flow past this point and on to Bolton.

Photo, Author.

Plate 127. The Bacca Shop, No.68. Pictured in 1956 Leigh bound No.68 pauses to unload before passing the Bacca Shop and into Church Street. The advertisements for Bolton's Hippodrome and Grand Theatre in Churchgate go unnoticed and business at Woodwards AA and RAC accredited garage behind the trolleybus cannot be that brisk, the one visible mechanic having time to spare. In addition to car repairs, Woodwards also did light haulage and operated a small fleet of coaches for private hire. Summer Sundays could be busy with coaches hired from other operators to meet demand, such was the travel boom in the 1950s.

Photo, Author's collection.

Plate 128. Bolton Old Road, No.55. Bolton Old Road rejoined Bolton Road about a quarter of a mile beyond Atherton Town Hall in the direction of Atherton Central Station. With the Atherton roads blocked on 23rd June 1956, trolleybus No.55 powered via jumper cables, uses Bolton Old Road as an emergency turning point before returning to Bolton.

Photo, The late E.K.Stretch.

Plate 129. L&Y overbridge, Atherton Central, No.54. Below overhead wiring supported by a mixture of ancient span wire fittings and former tram pole bracket arms, trolleybus No.54 and a Morris Cowley, travelling towards Atherton, pursue a cyclist across the bridge taking Bolton Road over the former Lancashire and Yorkshire Railway Manchester to Liverpool line. Atherton Central Station to the left of the photograph remains open today as 'Atherton', one of the few stations in the area south of Bolton towards Pennington to survive the 1960s onslaught on railways in this region.
Photo, the late J.Batty.

LEIGH—ATHERTON—FOUR LANE ENDS—BOLTON
Trolley Vehicle Service

SATURDAY

		am	am	am	am	am	am	am	am	am	am	am	am	am	am	am	am
Leigh, Spinning Jenny Street	dep.	...	...	...	...	...	5 26	...	...	5 52	...	6 9	...	6 26	...	6 44	
Atherton, Depot	"	4 34	4 43	4 52	5 9	5 26	5 34	5 43	5 52	6 0	6 9	6 17	6 26	6 34	6 43	6 52	
Atherton, Punch Bowl	"	4 38	4 47	4 56	5 13	5 30	5 38	5 47	5 56	6 4	6 13	6 21	6 30	6 38	6 47	6 56	
Four Lane Ends	"	4 50	4 59	5 8	5 25	5 42	5 50	5 59	6 8	6 16	6 25	6 33	6 42	6 50	6 59	7 8	
Bolton, Howell Croft	arr.	5 6	...	5 24	5 41	5 58	6 6	6 15	6 24	6 32	6 41	6 49	6 58	7 6	7 15	7 24	

		am				am	am	am	am	am	am	am	am	am		
							pm	pm	pm	pm	pm	pm	pm	pm	pm	
Leigh, Spinning Jenny Street	dep.	6 52				1018	1026	1035	1044	1052	1055	11 3	1111	1120	
Atherton, Depot	"	7 0		and		1026	1034	1043	1052	11 0	11 3	1111	1119	1128	
Atherton, Punch Bowl	"	7 4		every		1030	1038	1047	1056	11 4	11 7	1115	1123	1132	
Four Lane Ends	"	7 16		8¼ minutes		1042	1050	1059	11 8	1116	1119	...	...	...	
Bolton, Howell Croft	arr.	7 32		until		1058	11 6	1115	...	...	...	...	...	...	

		am	am	am	am	am		pm	pm	pm	pm	pm	pm	pm	
Bolton, Howell Croft	dep.	...	5 6	5 24	5 41	5 58	and	1032	1041	1049	...	...	1058	pm	
Four Lane Ends	"	5 0	5 20	5 38	5 55	6 12	every	1046	1055	11 3	...	11 9	1112	...	
Atherton, Punch Bowl	"	5 11	5 31	5 49	6 6	6 23	8¼ minutes	1057	11 6	1114	1117	1120	1123	1125	
Atherton, Depot	"	5 15	5 35	5 53	6 10	6 27	until	11 1	1110	1118	1121	1124	1127	1129	
Leigh, Spinning Jenny Street	arr.	5 23	5 43	6 1	6 18	6 35		11 9	1118	...	...	...	...	...	

		pm	pm	pm	pm	pm
Bolton, Howell Croft	dep.	...	11 6	...	...	1115
Four Lane Ends	"	1117	1120	1120	1134	1140
Atherton, Punch Bowl	"	1128	1131	1121	1134	1140
Atherton, Depot	"	1132	1135	1135	1138	1144
Leigh, Spinning Jenny Street	arr.					

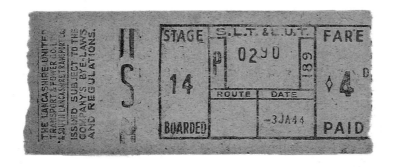

Whilst it was 1948 before TIM tickets were in general use on the SLT, they made occasional appearances before then, this early example printed in red ink and dating from 1944.

Ticket, courtesy Brian Hughes.

63

Over Hulton

Plate 130. *New Brook Road, No. 62.* Northwards from Atherton Central Station a narrow Bolton Road soon met New Brook Road at the former boundary of Atherton and Over Hulton in Westhoughton Urban District. No. 62 has just crossed the boundary and faces the long climb up New Brook Road, steady at first but steeper up Firs Brow beyond the distant house by Breeze Hill Road. The road levelled out beyond Hulton Park gates before another gentle climb to reach Four Lane Ends. The date is 31st August 1958, the last day of SLT trolleybus operation.

Photo, Walter E. Amos.

Plate 131. *New Brook Road, No.63.* Leigh bound No.63 descends Firs Brow during 1956. Leaving Atherton, the surroundings changed upon reaching Over Hulton. Rows of terraces were replaced by suburban housing punctuated by open spaces, green fields and woodlands. Beyond the stone wall behind No.63 lie the fields and woods of Hulton Park which belonged to the late Sir Geoffrey Hulton, land which had been leased to the Co-operative Society.

Photo, the late J.Batty.

Plate 132. *New Brook Road.* What used to be an SLT trolleybus is, on 30th July 1998, First Bus service 582 to Leigh. Single decker, R639 CVR, a Volvo B10 BLE bodied by Wright of Northern Ireland descends a largely unchanged Firs Brow. The photograph was taken a little further up New Brook Road than the previous picture in order to capture the Speed Camera sign and cycle lanes. That pavement does not seem to have improved much!

Photo, Author.

Plate 133. Firs Brow, No. 57.
Just visible at the top of Firs Brow is the 'Park Gates' bus stop, the New Brook Road entrance to the private Hulton Park normally being closed. Unspoilt woodland was all that was to be seen beyond the gates' iron railings making any opportunity to visit the woods, especially in Spring when carpeted by bluebells, one not to miss. The 90 h.p. 'Metrovick' motor of Leyland No.57 ensures a sprightly climb up New Brook Road which apart from a red trolleybus and a lone pedestrian is deserted.
Photo, P.J.Thompson, (Photosales)

Plate 134. Firs Brow. The winter of 1955 sees a sudden heavy snowfall in full control of Firs Brow. The worst fears of the driver of the Guy Arab III single decker in the distance would have been confirmed as he struggled with his coach to the bottom of the Brow only to see cars, lorries and buses strewn across the road blocking it in both directions. Awaiting rescue, Lancashire United Leyland TS7 No.108 appears to have done the best, with a Phillipson's Albion lorry having secured second place ahead of an LUT Guy Arab IV on service 50 from Warrington. The nearest trolleybus is No.65, whilst another Karrier No.61 and a Sunbeam stand with their trolley booms on the Leigh bound wires in a fruitless attempt to pass. *Photo, Bolton Evening News.*

Plate 135. New Brook Road, No.70. Passing what is now Thirlmere Road to its left, Sunbeam No.70 has the road to itself in 1956, apart from parked Austin and Rover cars, as it ambles from Four Lane Ends towards Firs Brow and on towards Atherton. Living as a youth on this stretch of New Brook Road on the outside of the bend gave me a commanding view of approaching trolleybuses all the way from the 'Park Gates' to Crescent Avenue near Four Lane Ends.

Photo, the late J.Batty.

Plate 136. Crescent Avenue, No.63. In 1956 Karrier No.63 still has all light units mounted in the cab front panelling as it passes Crescent Avenue on the gradual descent down New Brook Road from Four Lane Ends. The other end of Crescent Avenue emerges at Four Lane Ends next to shops and the Leigh bound bus stop.

Photo, the late J.Batty.

Workmen's and Day Return tickets were introduced in 1933. Whilst the Workmen's tickets, overprinted 'W' were lettered 'S.L.T.Co.-L.U.T. & P.Co., Ltd.' the Day Returns were simply lettered 'South Lancashire Transport Co.' and were usually overprinted 'R'. Normal practice was to punch the tickets to indicate the date of the month as well as the stage and to cancel them on the return journey to indicate the hour, the figures 1 to 12 at both ends of both tickets being provided for this purpose.

Tickets, courtesy Brian Hughes.

66

Four Lane Ends

Four Lane Ends: The Bolton Boundary.

Having ascended Firs Brow, New Brook Road's gentle climb through Over Hulton brought Bolton bound trolleybuses to Four Lane Ends where the A579 crossed the A6 from Westhoughton Urban District into Bolton Borough to become St. Helens Road. The A6 approached Four Lane Ends from Westhoughton as Manchester Road crossing the A 579 to head eastwards towards Little Hulton as Salford Road.

Four Lane Ends was the southernmost point reached by Bolton local trolleybus services, the trolleybuses reversing into a back street alongside the *Hulton Arms* hotel just south of the A6. On 25th March 1956 trolleybuses operating Bolton local services were replaced by Bolton Corporation motor buses, the Four Lane Ends service continuing to use the same location to reverse. Meanwhile operation of the through trolleybus service from Leigh to Bolton continued.

Until replacement of the remaining trolleybus services in August 1958, no through tickets were issued in either direction beyond Four Lane Ends. Separate fare collection on behalf of Bolton Corporation and the SLT necessitated the conductor's ritual of swapping ticket machines before working through the bus afresh issuing a new ticket to each passenger following departure from Four Lane Ends. SLT ticket machines were used throughout but tickets issued on the Bolton side whilst lettered SLT & LUT were distinguished by green striped edges and permitted free onward travel by motor bus to Trinity Street railway station.

During the autumn of 1955, SLT and Manchester trolleybuses came within sight of each other at Four Lane Ends as deliveries of new BUT 9612T's from body builders H.V. Burlingham Ltd. of

Plate 137. Four Lane Ends, No.61. A clear March day in 1956 sees Karrier W No.61 having arrived at Four Lane Ends from Bolton, 'laying over' before proceeding down New Brook Road through Over Hulton towards Atherton on the through service to Leigh. At this time, until 25th March, the local Bolton to Four Lane Ends service was still worked by trolleybuses, the reverser wiring used by this service visible in the foreground. The *Red Lion* public house stands behind No.61 beyond the traffic lights at which a Vauxhall and a Morris Minor wait to leave New Brook Road. Out of view to their left and diagonally opposite the *Red Lion* lies the *Hulton Arms*. Shops alongside the trolleybus, with its early Jacob's advert, comprised the Leyro Newsagency, run for many years by the Boon family, bread and fruit and vegetable shops and a butchers. The playground of St. Andrews junior school lay immediately behind the row of shops. Retrieval of mis-kicked footballs from the rear of the Newsagents premises had to be conducted with diplomacy if future supplies of sweets were to be ensured! 'Hot Bovril for Cold Knights' would, without doubt, have been most welcome during the previous winter months.

Photo, the late J.Batty.

Blackpool were towed in groups of three or four along the A6 passing beneath the SLT wires on their way to Manchester.

The unblemished red paintwork of these brand new trolleybuses provided stark contrast to the antique appearance of most of the SLT fleet. Ironically, whilst the Manchester trolleybus system outlived that of the SLT by eight years, abandonment, yet to start with the SLT in March 1956, had already commenced in Manchester, the last trolleybuses running on service 212 along Rochdale Road to Moston in April 1955, some six months before the main delivery of the BUTs had begun. One trolleybus No.1302, delivered some months ahead of the rest, arrived just in time to work briefly on service 211 to Moston via Oldham Road before its closure on 7th August 1955.

Lancashire United's motor bus services 38 (Wigan to Manchester), 50 (Bolton to Warrington) and 59 (Bolton to Wigan) all passed through Four Lane Ends. Childhood trips on the 38 to Manchester and the dentist had the added bonus of running under the SLT Farnworth route wires between Little Hulton and Swinton; an upper deck front seat on the Guy Arab operating the 38 providing a grandstand view of the trolleybuses. Peak hour 'duplicates' returning from Manchester on service 38 often ran only as far as Four Lane Ends turning left down New Brook Road to return to Atherton depot. A request to a friendly conductor resulted in a free ride home down New Brook Road. Response to "Wer d'ya want droppin' luv?", would have the LUT off service 38 Guy pull up at the trolleybus stop half way to the Park Gates!

Plate 138. Four Lane Ends. On 30th July 1998 the scene is little altered at Four Lane Ends. Puddles from a recent shower remain at the entrance to the former trolleybus reverser, whilst a steady stream of cars provides a constant reminder of the shift away from public transport to the traffic congested roads of today. To the rear of the Ford Fiesta is Crescent Avenue marked by a 30 m.p.h. sign. Today, children attending St. Andrews school have a longer walk from Four Lane Ends, a new school building being located at the opposite end of Crescent Avenue, the old school having been demolished to make way for houses.

Photo, Author.

Plate 140. Four Lane Ends, Nos.64 and 67 (opposite). Following the failure of No.67, seen in the preceding picture, relief eventually arrived with the next service bus No.64 which, having loaded, pulls out to pass the defective trolleybus. A Bolton Corporation Leyland PD2 on the trolleybus replacement service 17 to Four Lane Ends stands a little distance behind, its driver contemplating the manoeuvre into Back Manchester Road alongside the Hulton Arms, made awkward by trolleybus 67 partly occupying the position from where he would reverse. After replacement of trolleybuses by motor buses on the Four Lane Ends local service to Bolton, the reverser remained in use by occasional short workings from Atherton, vehicles under test and driver training trips from Atherton depot.

Photo, the late J.Batty.

Plate 139. Four Lane Ends, Nos.67 & 68. Turning the clock back once again to Spring 1956 sees varied trolleybus activity at Four Lane Ends. A lady waits patiently to board as passengers alight from Bolton bound Sunbeam MS2 No.68. Meanwhile the booms of trolleybus 67 are being lowered, the bus having become defective immediately upon pulling away down New Brook Road towards Leigh. Strangely, the destination blind shows Bolton and has probably been turned from Leigh to dissuade prospective passengers. Visible beyond the shadows cast by the trees in the spring time sun and by now only used occasionally, is the reverser wiring in Back Manchester Road alongside the *Hulton Arms.* Note the SLT reverser light standing to the right of the road junction sign and the Shell / BP filling station hidden to the left.

Photo, the late J.Batty.

Plate 141. Four Lane Ends, No.63. Passengers are about to alight from Karrier W No.63 as it draws to a halt alongside the bus stop for Bolton at Four Lane Ends. This photograph taken in March 1956 looks down New Brook Road from the entrance to the filling station which stands next to the *Hulton Arms*. No.63 was later to receive wing mounted front lights and quite late in its career a rubber mounted nearside cab front window. The substantial brick wall catching the afternoon sun was a recent replacement for a rather rickety wooden fence.

Photo, the late J.Batty.

Plate 142. Four Lane Ends, No.61. On a dull winter's day in early 1958 Karrier W No.61 stands at the bus stop for Bolton with New Brook Road curving away into the distance towards Atherton. No.61 carries the third and last version of the Jacob's advertisement

Photo, Dennis Gill.

Reversing at Four Lane Ends.

Plate 143. Four Lane Ends, No.57. Viewed in the same direction as the previous photograph but some two years earlier when the Bolton local service was still operated by trolleybuses, Leyland No.57 is about to reverse into Back Manchester Road before returning to Bolton. This photograph taken from outside the Leyro Newsagents affords a good view of 'period' petrol pumps and the traction pole mounted bus stop sign with Crescent Avenue to its left. Advertisements borne by the trolleybus promote a choice of alcoholic drinks; either beer in the form of Tetley's, or Dewar's whisky for those seeking something more medicinal! *Photo, the late J.Batty.*

Plate 144. Four Lane Ends Reverser, No.56. Alongside the *Hulton Arms* in Back Manchester Road, its blind still showing Four Lane Ends, trolleybus 56 waits to return to Bolton in early March 1956. Bearing witness here to SLT economy in construction of the overhead is the reuse of former tramway cap and cone hangers together with absence of cast runner bars at the point of intersection of the wires at the frog. Runner bars provided stiffening to prevent flexing of the wires from upward pressure of the trolleys which could cause wires to fracture. Note the lamp, suspended and powered from the overhead, towards the rear of the reverser wiring and the frog pull off wire running up and across the bracket arm suspension. Frogs were spring loaded and arranged on the SLT such that all manoeuvres using the Atherton side of a reverser required a frog change using a pull handle on a nearby traction pole. So for example the frog at Four Lane Ends reverser was set such that exit towards Bolton did not require a frog pull.

Photo, the late J.Batty.

Plate 145. Four Lane Ends Reverser, Nos. 57 & 59. Just days before replacement by motor buses, Leyland trolleybuses 57 and 59 operate the Bolton to Four Lane Ends service. No.59, seen parked in the Back Manchester Road reverser, awaits its driver, whilst No.57, its blind already turned for return to Bolton, is ready to draw forward before reversing. In the distance beyond the A6 traffic lights, stands the road sign marking the Bolton Borough boundary. The trolleybus reverser lamp seen alongside the *Hulton Arms* would have provided only minimal illumination.

Photo, the late Jack Batty.

Plate 146. Four Lane Ends reverser. On 30th July 1998 a Land Rover Discovery passes the location of the trolleybus reverser in what was Back Manchester Road, now renamed Fletcher Street. The *Hulton Arms* and *Red Lion's* dominance of Four Lane Ends is accompanied by the Shell garage forecourt sign, a somewhat more prominent feature than the small signs associated with the garage in trolleybus days. Meanwhile a delivery van, partly obscured by the cyclist, occupies the Four Lane Ends bus stop lay by.

Photo, Author.

Bus stop alterations at Four Lane Ends.

Plate 147. Four Lane Ends, No.55. During the Spring of 1956 work commenced to relieve the obstruction caused by Leigh bound trolleybuses waiting at Four Lane Ends by provision of a bus stop lay by directly in front of the row of shops. The scope and progress of this work is clearly evident from this rear upperdeck window of a trolleybus waiting at the temporary bus stop towards which two ladies cautiously make their way. Two other trolleybuses operating the Leigh to Bolton service are visible including No.55 waiting for traffic lights in St. Helens Road with Bolton Corporation's JBN 158, a 1956 Metro Cammell Orion bodied Leyland PD2/13 returning to Bolton on trolleybus replacement service 17. This local Four Lane Ends service was usually operated by Bolton's Leyland PD2s or Crossley DD42/3s. A replacement traction pole is in position to which a new span wire with an adjustable leg hanger is attached by the usual SLT expediency of double wrapping the wire around the pole rather than using a pole strap. The bracket arm and sodium vapour lamp were transferred to this pole at a later date. All Bolton traction poles and those of Westhoughton carrying street lamps were for many years painted green with the top three feet silver. This new pole never received its silver top, apparently overlooked upon completion of the lay by.

Photo, the late J.Batty.

Plate 148. Four Lane Ends, Nos.69 & 57. With lay by work completed Sunbeam trolleybus No.69 has ample space on its offside so as not to impede traffic. The bus stop now has the added luxury of a shelter and the Leigh bound wiring has been realigned to permit the trolleys to pull in. Leyland No.57, followed by a sedate trio of cars crosses the A6 into St. Helens Road, the approach to the traffic lights having acquired white lining.

Photo, the late J.Batty.

Plate 149. Four Lane Ends, No.70. If a typical 1950s view of 'The SLT' at 'Lane Ends', as it was known for short, was etched in the subconscious mind then this would probably be it: a work stained red three axle trolleybus, in the wet! A lonesome figure loiters on the corner behind Sunbeam No.70 whilst there will be brief respite from the dampness with the prospect of crusty loaves for some in the shop alongside. The thought of winning the pools was also a warming one. What would 'Lane Ends' and public transport be like in 15 or so years time ?

Photo, Author's collection.

Plate 150. Four Lane Ends, Guy Arab V No.234. And so to March 1973! The bread shop is still open, indeed the sun is out for a change. Strange in Lancashire that shop blinds come down not to stop the rain but to keep the sun out! A Ford Escort Police Panda car and a Hillman Imp are a sign of the times The bus to Leigh is still a red one, but what a bus! If the SLT trolleybuses had their following then the Guy Arabs of Lancashire United certainly did. LUT remained faithful to the reliable Guys with their Gardner 6LW engines, purchasing 30 footers between 1956 and 1968 until they were no longer manufactured.

Standing in exactly the same position as trolleybus 70 in the previous photograph is Northern Counties bodied front entrance Guy Arab V No.234 of 1966, freshly repainted. The bus is operating the former Bolton to Leigh trolleybus service.

Photo, Jim Saunders.

73

But back to the SLT.....

Plate 151. Four Lane Ends, No.61. With the traffic lights out of action, trolleybus No.61, still with headlights mounted in the front panel, crosses the A6 from St. Helens Road in 1956 under the watchful eye of the point duty policeman, a Ribble lowbridge Leyland PD2 simultaneously turning into St. Helens Road from Manchester Road on service 313 Chorley to Bolton. The overhead wiring from Four Lane Ends to Bolton was owned and maintained by Bolton Corporation, section breakers marking the boundary of ownership being visible just behind No.61's trolley heads. Normal practice was for both positive and negative wires to have section insulators at half mile intervals as was the case with Bolton's wiring. However the SLT adopted an earth return system obviating the need for negative wire section insulators south of Four Lane Ends.

Another peculiarity manifested itself at this point but only after dusk! Most SLT trolleybuses had interior lighting powered in series from traction voltage. Only Guy No.47 plus Karriers Nos.60 to 63 and Sunbeams Nos.66 to 71 had battery lighting. Non battery fitted Leigh bound trolleybuses approached Four Lane Ends with increasingly dim interior illumination which, often accompanied by an audible flash, suddenly regained normal brilliance as the trolley heads crossed the section breakers; this owing to the distance of Four Lane Ends from the nearest feeder on the Bolton side! Being reasonably flat terrain, the progress of trolleybuses suffered little from the effects of reduced voltage. *Photo, Author's collection.*

St. Helens Road.

Plate 152. St. Helens Road, No.59. St. Helens Road is well salted on the 19th February 1956 as an empty No.59 waits to depart Four Lane Ends for Bolton. Beyond the post office stands the crown green boundary wall. The access between the bowls club and the post office was briefly used as a reversing point by Bolton Corporation buses during the construction of the bus stop lay by on the other side of the traffic lights at Four Lane Ends. Today where was once the crown green stands the Over Hulton Conservative Club and whilst the stone built *Red Lion* public house remains, all the other property has been demolished to make way for the overbridge across the M61 which runs parallel with the A6 at this point. *Photo, the late J.Batty.*

Plate 153. St. Helens Road, No.56. A little later that day, at the same bus stop with St. Helens Road disappearing into the distance towards Bolton, Leyland trolleybus No.56 stands at the point which today is the M61 overbridge. Number 56's rear platform panel has seen better days and was later replaced. Note the trolley retriever, clearly visible against the shadow below the rear panel. A collie dog keeps a watchful eye on the gentleman walking with the aid of a stick towards the junction of Plodder Lane with St. Helens Road, visible just in front of the trolleybus. The option of a Mackeson on this cold February day in 1956 might be well worth considering.   *Photo, the late J. Batty.*

Plate 154. St Helens Road, No. 64. On a warmer day in March 1956, Karrier W No.64 hurries along St. Helens Road towards Four Lane Ends past the junction with Plodder Lane into which a car now turns. Plodder Lane will take the driver approximately 2 ½ miles due east past the Great Lever and Farnworth golf course into Farnworth almost to the terminus of SLT's Atherton to Farnworth route. Trolleybus No.64 carries a Dulux/Dulite advert, the only trolleybus to do so. The well maintained quality of the Bolton Corporation overhead combined with this long straight stretch of St. Helens Road down towards Four Lane Ends often made for some inspired running when the silence of the trolleybuses at speed, apart from the swish of the trolley heads on the wires, could really be appreciated.

Photo, the late J.Batty.

On the Bolton side of Four Lane Ends, tickets from green striped rolls were issued and were valid for free onward travel to Trinity Street Station, this example dating from 1957.

Ticket, courtesy Brian Hughes.

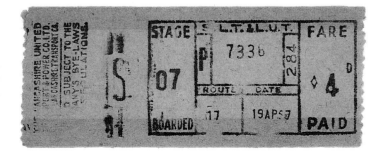

Plate 155. St. Helens Road, No.56. The bus stop sign takes on a certain irony in this early 1958 view of trolleybus No.56 snowbound on St. Helens Road. Even if enthusiastically wielded a couple of shovels would not see 56 freed quickly to continue its journey to Bolton such was the drifting along St. Helens Road. Indeed No.56 was destined to spend the night in winter blizzard conditions before being freed the following day. *Photo, Bolton Evening News.*

Horridge Fold.

Plate 156. Horridge Fold, No.54. On a clear March day in 1956, trolleybus No.54, operating on the through service to Leigh, follows the gentle curve of St. Helens Road through Horridge Fold alongside the stone retaining wall beyond which lies 'Whitegate Farm' before the straight run down past the fields to Four Lane Ends. The bus has not long passed the Hulton Lane turning circle, still in operation on the 11th of March. This permitted trolleybuses operating the local service to Hulton Lane to turn back to Bolton. Between Hulton Lane and Horridge Fold a clear vista across the fields of Gannet Fold farm to Deane and beyond permitted a tantalising glimpse of a tramcar stored alongside Booths Steelworks which was rail connected to the Bolton Great Moor Street to Kenyon Junction line. The tram, ex Hull Corporation car 132 rescued by Jack Batty, appeared there in 1955 for temporary storage before removal to Crich Tramway Museum and eventual restoration at the Hull Transport Museum. *Photo, the late J.Batty.*

Hulton Lane

Plate 157. Hulton Lane turning circle, Nos. 54, 56 & 68. In addition to the service to Four Lane Ends, SLT trolleybuses also operated a Bolton local service to Hulton Lane. A detached reversing triangle installed at the junction of Hulton Lane and St. Helens Road in December 1933 when the SLT began trolleybus operation from Leigh to Bolton, was replaced in 1936 by a turning loop upon commencement of Bolton local trolleybus services. This permitted the Hulton Lane service trolleybuses to turn back towards Bolton. Following replacement by motor buses on 25th March 1956, this loop had no further use and was quickly dismantled, the only wiring to be removed on this route before the final SLT closure in August 1958. Seen just days before the replacement of the Hulton Lane trolleybus service., Leylands Nos.54 and 56, partly visible, wait in the loop on the Hulton Lane service whilst Sunbeam No.68 passes along St. Helens Road to Bolton on the through service from Leigh.

Photo, the late J.Batty.

Plate 158. Hulton Lane, No.59. Terraced houses at the top of Hulton Lane provide the backdrop to trolleybus No.59 and its crew photographed in the Hulton Lane loop before returning to Bolton in March 1956 just before this trolleybus service finished. Leyland trolleybuses Nos.48 to 51 were purchased by Bolton Corporation ostensibly for the Bolton local services, although operated by the SLT. Whilst not always these four trolleybuses, it was indeed rare for anything other than the Leylands 48 to 59 to operate the services. Upon closure of the Bolton local services the SLT returned 48 to 51 to Bolton Corporation for disposal, 52 to 59 remaining in service until final SLT closure in 1958.

Photo, the late J.Batty.

Plate 159. Hulton Lane, No.55. Hulton Lane disappears into the distance with the bridge over the Bolton Great Moor Street to Kenyon Junction railway line just at the limit of vision. At a similar distance beyond the bridge Hulton Lane joined Wigan Road in Deane. Had the politics of the day been different, trolley wires might well have enabled No.55 to follow Hulton Lane down to Deane and complete a circular service back into Bolton via Wigan Road. However expenditure constraints ensured that this was not to be and on 11th March 1956, No.55 can only complete the tight turn back onto St. Helens Road to reach Bolton. No.55 was the least altered of the Leyland trolleybuses retaining the double rear platform window and beading under the waist rail.

Photo, the late J.Batty.

Plate 160. Hulton Lane, Nos.56 and 58. (below). Probably the last photograph of the Hulton Lane turning circle in operation. Trolleybus No.56 has departed for Bolton whilst No.58 waits in the loop. Dominant in the background is the Ford garage later changing franchise to Volkswagen. Spare ground to the left of the trolleybuses used at the time as a lorry park later became a football pitch. The author remembers assembling scratch teams from Bolton School to play the locals on this pitch, the shop on the opposite corner providing welcome refreshments after 90 minutes! The cliche 'Not a level playing field!' emanated from these games!

Photo, the late J.Batty.

Plate 161. Hulton Lane. A Renault dealership occupies the old Ford garage site and adjacent land on 30th July 1998, some 16 months before the installation of traffic lights at this junction. The old garage building which was a former Bolton Corporation tram depot and terraces along St. Helens Road provide for instant identification of the Hulton Lane trolleybus terminus. The bus stop in the foreground for the present day Leigh to Bolton bus service 582 is a few yards forward from the old trolleybus stop which was located to permit passengers on the Hulton Lane service to alight before the trolleybus turned into the loop.

Photo, Author.

Daubhill

Plate 162. St. Helens Road, No.59. Leigh bound trolleybus No.59 is pursued by a learner driver in an Austin Somerset as they pass between parked Ford Popular and Hillman cars on the climb away from Daubhill railway station. A steady westerly breeze whisks the smoke away from the chimney stack of Tootal's Sunnyside Mills. Such stacks which dominated the urban skyline in the first half of the twentieth century have all but disappeared today, taking with them not only their darkening pollution but also the associated cotton, coal, steel and other heavy industries, for generations the heartbeat of industrial conurbations such as the 'North West'. The Bolton and Leigh Railway, later to become part of the LNWR system, tunnelled under St. Helens Road on its way from Bolton's Great Moor Street station at a point marked by the billboards seen beyond the cars. This alignment, opened on 2nd February 1885, was a diversion on what was Lancashire's first public railway, the first section from the Bolton Derby Street terminus to Wm. Hulton's Collieries at Pendlebury Fold near Chequerbent having opened for the carriage of goods on 1st August 1828. This followed Royal Assent received on 31st March 1825. Part of the original alignment crossing St. Helens Road at Daubhill Bar in the far distance was retained to provide access to Sunnyside Mills and often provided the spectacle of an ex LMSR Stanier 8F 2-8-0 locomotive slowly shunting mineral wagons across the road until the line's closure in 1967.

Photo, the late J.Batty.

Plate 163. Daubhill Station, No.49. With Morris Green Lane to the left of camera and access to Daubhill railway station behind the shops, newly delivered trolleybus No.49 loads for Bolton in 1936 as a bemused passer-by in St. Helens Road wonders why anybody would want to photograph a new fangled trolleybus! Why not wait for one of Bolton Corporation's trams? However, with the introduction of Bolton owned Leyland trolleybuses Nos.48 to 51 on March 28th that year, the tram tracks in St. Helens Rd. had become disused, though trams remained in service elsewhere in Bolton until 29th March 1947 when the last route to Tonge Moor was closed. Meanwhile Daubhill station, known since its relocation in 1885 as Daubhill and Rumworth, remained open until 3rd. March 1952. A detached triangle, used only emergencies, was located in Perth Street just beyond Morris Green Lane. This was removed around 1945. Enriching this 'period' view of the trolleybus in original condition with its stencil destination indicator are the setts, gas lamps and flat caps.

Photo, Author's collection.

Derby Street.

Plate 164. Derby Street, No.61.
St. Helens Road continued towards Bolton becoming Derby Street near Sunninghill School beyond which lay the long descent into Bolton. The hill climbing abilities and rapid acceleration of the trolleybuses made them masters of the climb up Derby Street with its numerous stops and pedestrian crossings. Pictured in March 1956 having passed the *Ram's Head* almost at the crest of the climb is Karrier No.61 carrying the first version of the Jacob's Cream Crackers advertisment. Note the whitened edges to the doorsteps of the slated roof dwellings on the opposite side of the road to the parked Hillman Minx.

Photo, the late J. Batty.

Plate 165. Derby Street, No.70. The driver of the LUT Northern Counties bodied Guy Arab III will be pleased at the opportunity of an unimpeded climb up Derby Street as he passes Sunbeam MS2 No.70. In 1999 a good number of Derby Street's slated roof buildings remain including those to the left of the trolleybus up as far as the National Westminster Bank on the corner of Cricket Street. What was the florists has become the Al Noor Indian takeaway. However the *Crown Hotel* next to the bank and the properties opposite including a newsagents and pub have been demolished. The Bolton Corporation owned and maintained overhead was arguably the best on the system. The Bolton tower wagon carried complete span wire and twin line hanger assemblies to enable speedy replacement without splicing should the need arise, made possible by the equi-distant positioning of opposite traction poles. Note also the use of pole straps for span wire to traction pole attachment unlike the SLT which relied upon double wrapping the wire around the poles. Curiously however the negative wire was rather loosely suspended on the climb out of Bolton giving rise on occasions to wayward trolley booms. *Photo, the late J.Batty.*

Plate 166. Derby Street, No.53. A lady with head scarf and shopping basket directs a calming hand to an excitable dog as Leyland No.53 begins Derby Street's climb from Bolton. In this early 1950s view, the trolleybus, in sparkling condition, still carries the first post war livery of red with a grey roof and two white bands plus large fleet numerals. During the coronation of Queen Elizabeth, this trolleybus was one of several in the fleet decorated with union flags along both trolley poles. It became a distinctive sight in its early livery with these adornments together with the bright yellow Tizer advertisement and was one of the last 'highbridge' trolleybuses to be repainted red with a single cream band during 1954.

Photo, Roy Marshall.

LEIGH—ATHERTON—FOUR LANE ENDS—BOLTON
Trolley Vehicle Service

SUNDAY

		am	am	am	am	am	am	am	am	pm	pm	pm	pm	pm	pm	pm	pm
Leigh, Spinning Jenny Street	dep.	...	...	9 48	1018	1048	1118	...	1148	...	1218	...	1248	1 3	1 18	1 26	...
Atherton, Depot	"	8 56	9 26	9 56	1026	1056	1126	1141	1156	1211	1226	1241	1256	1 11	1 26	1 34	1 43
Atherton, Punch Bowl ...	"	9 0	9 30	10 0	1030	11 0	1130	1145	12 0	1215	1230	1245	1 0	1 15	1 30	1 38	1 47
Four Lane Ends ...	"	9 12	9 42	1012	1042	1112	1142	1157	1212	1227	1242	1257	1 12	1 27	1 42	1 50	1 59
Bolton, Howell Croft ...	arr.	9 28	9 58	1028	1058	1128	1158	1213	1228	1243	1258	1 13	1 28	1 43	1 58	2 6	2 15

		pm	pm			pm	pm	pm	pm	pm	pm	pm	pm
Leigh, Spinning Jenny Street	dep.	1 44	1 52	and		1018	1026	1035	1044	1052	1055	11 3	1111
Atherton, Depot	"	1 52	2 0	every		1026	1034	1043	1052	11 0	11 3	1111	1119
Atherton, Punch Bowl ...	"	1 56	2 4	8¼ minutes		1030	1038	1047	1056	11 4	11 7	1115	...
Four Lane Ends ...	"	2 8	2 16	until		1042	1050	1059	11 8	1116	...	...	...
Bolton, Howell Croft ...	arr.	2 24	2 32			1058	...	...	...	...	...	...	...

		am	am	am	am	am	am	am	pm	pm	pm	pm	pm	pm	pm	pm	pm
Bolton, Howell Croft ...	dep.	...	9 28	9 58	1028	1058	1128	1158	1213	1228	1243	1258	1 13	...	1 28	...	1 43
Four Lane Ends ...	"	...	9 42	1012	1042	1112	1142	1212	1227	1240	1255	1 10	1 25	1 27	...	1 42	1 57
Atherton, Punch Bowl ...	"	...	9 55	1025	1055	1125	1155	1225	1240	1255	1 10	1 25	1 38	...	1 53	...	2 8
Atherton, Depot ...	"	9 35	9 59	1029	1059	1129	1159	1229	1244	1259	1 14	1 29	1 42	1 49	1 57	2 5	2 12
Leigh, Spinning Jenny Street...	arr.	9 43	10 7	1037	11 7	1137	12 7	1237	1252	1 7	1 22	1 37	1 50	1 57	2 5	2 13	2 20

		pm	pm	pm		pm	pm	pm	pm	pm	pm	pm	pm	pm	pm
Bolton, Howell Croft ...	dep.	...	1 58	2 6	and	1032	...	1041	...	...	1049	...	...	1058	...
Four Lane Ends ...	"	...	2 12	2 20	every	1046	1051	1055	...	11 0	11 3	...	11 9	1112	1117
Atherton, Punch Bowl ...	"	...	2 23	2 31	8¼ minutes	1057	11 2	11 6	11 9	1111	1114	1117	1120	1123	1128
Atherton, Depot ...	"	2 22	2 27	2 35	until	11 1	11 6	1110	1113	1115	1118	1121	1124	1127	1132
Leigh, Spinning Jenny Street...	arr.	2 30	2 35	2 43		11 9	...	...	...	...	...	...	...	...	...

Bolton

Plate 167. Deane Road Junction, No.58. At the bottom of Derby Street inward bound trolleybuses bore left towards the junction of Deane Road and Moor Lane following the latter to reach the right turn into Ashburner Street and thence to Howell Croft terminus. Outward bound trolleybuses departing Howell Croft regained the inward route in Derby Street via Great Moor Street. With Deane Road disappearing into the distance No. 58 turns into Moor Lane at what could have been a trolleybus junction had Bolton's post war plans to introduce trolleybus operation along Deane Road and Wigan Road up Hulton Lane to reach the wiring

in St. Helens Road come to fruition. After the Hulton Lane turning circle was removed in 1956 there were no frogs on the Bolton owned overhead. Cynically, the general lack of activity in this photograph causes one to wonder whether a trolleybus service along Deane Road would have been a paying proposition !
Photo, the late J.Batty.

Plate 168. Moor Lane, No.58. In the days when the standard colour for a car was black, trolleybus No.58 follows Moor Lane's one-way loop from the Deane Road junction past the depot of fruit and vegetable wholesalers E. Johnson & Son and a trio of cars including two Austins before slowing to take the right turn into Ashburner Street to reach the Bolton unloading point just beyond the Odeon cinema. It is interesting to compare the simplicity in 1956 of the trader's telephone number, Bolton 237, with the mind boggling numbers of today!

Photo, the late J.Batty.

Plate 169. Ashburner Street, No.27. Trolleybus No.27 sets down all Bolton bound passengers alongside the junior library in Ashburner Street prior to moving into the Howell Croft terminus. This early post war view shows the Guy BTX prior to its front only rebuild still very much in original condition save for the replacement of the drop windows with sliding ventilators. The trolleybus retains its eight leg trolley gantry and has an inset rather than flush replacement panel for its staircase lower deck window. Lowbridge trolleybuses more or less disappeared from the Bolton route basic service after the introduction of the Sunbeam MS2s in 1948, though they still appeared occasionally on unadvertised Saturday extras from Atherton.

Photo, Roy Marshall.

Plate 170. Howell Croft, No.55. Having deposited its passengers in Ashburner Street, No.55 threads its way past the bonded warehouse of brewers Magee Marshall & Co. Ltd into Howell Croft terminus in 1956. This bus station, opened in July 1948, replaced the original terminus, originally in Howell Croft South, and had two parallel bus stop lanes. Had plans come to fruition for trolleybus operation by Bolton Corporation along Deane Road, two lines of overhead wiring would have been provided through the bus station, the Deane Road service being to the left of the picture. *Photo, Dennis Gill.*

Plate 171. Howell Croft. On 30th July 1998 there is nothing to suggest that trolleybuses previously plied their way through here. The characteristic architecture of the library building and what is now the Lever Chambers Centre for Health to the left of the telephone booths provide instant identification of the location of the former terminus entrance. A market now truncates Ashburner Street whilst to the extreme right of the photograph, behind the site of the former Magee Marshall warehouse, stands Bolton's Octagon theatre within which the author recalls two memorable performances of D.H.Lawrence's '*A Collier's Friday Night*' and J.B.Priestley's '*An Inspector Calls*'. Some things do not change one of which is former SLT weather: predictably unsettled ! *Photo, Author.*

Plate 172. *Howell Croft*. Against a backdrop dominated by Bolton's Town Hall clock, one of the Corporation owned Leyland trolleybus operating a local service to Hulton Lane awaits departure time in this 1948 view of Howell Croft terminus. Prolific advertising on SLT trolleybuses in the early post war years is evidenced by those either side of the destination indicator box. The trolleybus would run as far as the junction of Hulton Lane with St. Helens Road. Waiting to depart on the service 38 to the Deane end of Hulton Lane is BBN 181, a Bolton Corporation Massey bodied Leyland TD5c, No.223 which entered service in 1941. At this time span wires, visible above the TD5c, had been suspended over the second lane in Howell Croft terminus in anticipation of the introduction of trolleybuses along Deane Road. This was not to be. The span wires were quickly removed and Bolton placed in service a fleet of 100 Leyland PD2/4s during 1948/9 which not only sealed the fate of any future introduction of trolleybuses but also allowed the withdrawal of elderly pre-war stock. Behind the TD5c stands a new Craven bodied Crossley DD42/3, itself one of a large batch of buses delivered in 1946/7, which had replaced Bolton's last trams.   *Photo, Bolton Evening News.*

Plate 173. *Howell Croft, No.70.* In this view of Howell Croft taken around 1952 trolleybus No.70 waits to depart for Hulton Lane whilst Bolton Crossley No.247, second in the batch, is waiting to operate a duty on service 3 to Townleys hospital. The trolleybus has yet to receive its final overhaul and still carries the red with a grey roof livery. Of far greater significance is the employment of this Sunbeam on the Hulton Lane service, normally the preserve of the Leylands. This is the only photograph which has come to light of one of these fine vehicles operating the Hulton Lane local service.

Photo, Roy Marshall.

Plate 174. Howell Croft, No.51. Again around 1952 trolleybus No.51 on service to Leigh still carries the first post war livery with two white bands. Leigh bound trolleybuses initially loaded at the first shelter, behind the Leyland PD2, giving Leigh passengers priority before drawing forward to the Hulton Lane boarding point to pick up those who would otherwise use the Bolton local service The PD2 No.404 is on Daubhill service 17, a source of confusion when diesel buses took over services to Hulton Lane and Four Lane Ends as these were also allocated the service number 17 ! The situation was rectified when the SLT trolleybuses were finally replaced, the Leigh to Bolton service becoming number 82 and those to Daubhill, Hulton Lane and Four Lane Ends becoming Nos. 79, 80 and 81 respectively. (The number 17 had first been allocated in June 1940 when, under threat of German invasion, the display of destinations on trams and buses was prohibited giving way to temporary route numbers displayed by the trolley buses.) *Photo, Roy Marshall.*

Lowbridge trolleybuses at Bolton.

Plate 175. Howell Croft, Nos.13 & 63. Although the through service was by the mid fifties provided by highbridge trolleys alone, lowbridge Guys continued to make appearances on unscheduled Saturday services running between Atherton and Bolton. By 1956, wartime Guy motor buses started to be seen increasingly frequently on these Saturday extras after which time visits to Bolton by lowbridge trolleybuses became rare though not unknown. Seen in 1956 at Howell Croft, behind No.63 on service to Leigh, is lowbridge Guy No.13 working a Saturday Bolton to Atherton service. The splayed booms of No.13 arising from the close mounting on the trolley gantry are apparent when compared to those of 63.

Photo, the late J.Batty.

Plate 176. Howell Croft, No. 5. Photographs of Guy trolleybus No.5 are not so common especially since it was an early withdrawal being taken out of service when the St. Helens route closed in November 1956. The trolleybus, one of the original TF 2072 to TF 2081 registered batch of ten introduced in 1930 for the St. Helens service, received a new front and deepened side panels around 1951 but never received the final livery and was outlived by several unmodified trolleybuses including No.4 which remained in service until final closure. A rare appearance of lowbridge trolley No.5 at Bolton on an Atherton short working on July 10th 1956 is therefore noteworthy.

Photo, J.C. Gillham.

Times and technology change.

Plate 177. Howell Croft, No.69. Whilst trolleybus No.69 is in the centre of the photograph, the focus of attention at Howell Croft in 1957 is Bolton's new Daimler CVG6 No.103 on service 57 to Morris Green. The driver eyes up his new steed with its preselector gearbox and probably wonders how he managed for so many years with manual gearbox buses. Apart from one or two operators such as Salford and Manchester, the North West was not home to big Daimler fleets and the introduction by Bolton of these preselector Daimlers must have been as much a revelation to the drivers as it was to the passengers who probably never had such a smooth ride, apart, of course, from the trolleybuses! Meanwhile the SLT driver of Sunbeam No.69, if given to ponder the nature of his soon to arrive trolleybus replacement, would be interested to know that Guy Arab 1Vs and Leyland PD3s with manual gearboxes were about to arrive on the scene! Meanwhile the Leyland PD2 is on service 17, this time to Hulton Lane!

Photo, the late J.Batty.

Howell Croft at night.

Plate 178. Howell Croft, No.64. It's twenty minutes past eight and there is no impending rush to board Karrier W No.64 which seems ready to depart lightly loaded for Leigh. One of Bolton's Leyland PD2/4s waits in the background alongside the Magee Marshall bonded warehouse.

Photo, the late J.Batty.

Plate 179. Howell Croft, No.69. Sunbeam No.69 on an evening short working to Atherton stands at the through service stop before pulling forward to the Hulton Lane stop in front of which two individuals pause for a chat. At the end of the bus station a right hand turn took the trolley buses into Great Moor Street and on towards the climb out of Bolton up Derby Street.

Photo, the late J.Batty.

Going

Plate 180. Howell Croft departures. Leyland No.59 prepares to turn right into Great Moor Street leaving a deserted terminus behind . The date is 23rd June 1954. No.59 carries the Belle Vue 'Showground of the World' advertisement, in those days one of the North West's star attractions. 1954 was a good year for enthusiasts of the SLT. Announcement of trolleybus abandonment was just over a year away and no end was in sight. Apart from Guy demonstrator No.47, the entire fleet was still in service. Trolleybus repaints were still underway, Leyland No.48 had just emerged with its rebuilt front and one or two others including Guy No.24 were yet to be rebuilt! Trolleybus travel, possible between Farnworth and Prescot in conjunction with the St. Helens system was taken for granted. Just over four years later it was all gone .

Photo, Author's collection.

Going !

Plate 181. Howell Croft. No trolley wires in this 1960s view of Howell Croft. A Lancashire United Metro Cammell bodied Leyland PD3 operates the former trolleybus service to Leigh, one of 14 such vehicles delivered in 1958. Whilst LUT's Northern Counties bodied Guys were shapely buses, the PD3s were undoubtedly handsome, exposed radiators making their first appearance in the LUT fleet since 1951. Meanwhile one of Bolton's East Lancashire bodied Daimler CVG6s is visible at the Deane Road bus stop. The bonded warehouse, a dark and dominant feature of Howell Croft is hidden behind the PD3 creating a much airier impression and permitting an unobstructed view of Bolton's Town Hall buildings and quarter striking clock. All remnants of the trolleybuses have gone save for a span wire pole strap visible just above the control boxes on the lighting column.

Photo, Author's collection.

Gone !

Plate 182. On 30th July 1998 the entrance to the Octagon multi storey car park marks the exit from the former Howell Croft bus terminus, the distant library building being the sole remaining feature in view upon which to take a bearing. To the left of the picture stands Elizabeth House.

Photo, Author.

88

A JOURNEY ALONG THE ROUTES:
3. ATHERTON TO FARNWORTH VIA SWINTON.

Bacca Shop, Atherton.

Plate 183. Atherton, Bacca Shop, No.11. Having made its way along Mealhouse Lane into Church Street from the Wigan Road loading point, No.11 turns right, taking the single pair of wires into Bolton Old Road to begin the journey along the Farnworth route but only as far as Mosley Common. To the left of the bus the Bolton route wiring can be seen passing the Capstan advert in Bolton Road. Having stopped briefly to allow the conductor to alight in order to operate the junction frog, No.11 pauses once again to allow him to reboard before drawing forward to the Bolton Old Road stop adjacent to the Bacca Shop. The traction pole to the left of the bus supports the overhead wiring electrical feeder conduit in front of which hangs the Bacca Shop sign supported from the corner of that building. The frontage to Norris the fishmongers faces the camera behind the parked cars . *Photo, the late J.Batty.*

Plate 184. Atherton High Street, No.7. Having loaded in Bolton Old Road trolleybuses drew forward and took an immediate right turn into High Street at the end of which they rejoined the inward bound route in Tyldesley Road. The driver of Farnworth bound No.7, in casting a watchful eye to his right for oncoming traffic in Tyldesley Road as the trolleybus leaves High Street, will have noticed the flat back lorry owned by Canty's, a local fruit and vegetable wholesaler. Atherton Town Hall, in Bolton Road, is visible at the end of High Street. On 26th August 1958, Atherton Sailors and Soldiers Club was receiving the attention of the painters, the flag pole having been lowered for the purpose. No.7 was one of two trolleybuses of the original 1930 batch of Guy BTX vehicles, the other being No.1, which received an overall rebuild in 1953 with rubber mounted windows considerably modernising its appearance.

Photo, The late E.K.Stretch.

Plate 185. Tyldesley Road, No.16. A Fordson van keeps a watchful eye on trolleybus No.16 as it passes in the direction of Atherton along Tyldesley Road, known colloquially as Dan Lane, on a Mosley Common to Leigh service, on 21st August 1958. The shops belong to Johnny Bowker's gents outfitters whilst out of sight behind the trolleybus is the fruit and vegetable business of Joe Fullelove. Following No.16 is a Lancashire United Northern Counties utility bodied lowbridge Guy Arab II. Lee Spinning Company's Dan Lane mills dominate the background. Part of this building still remains but, alas, no longer associated with cotton.

Photo, P.J.Thompson,
(Photosales)

Plate 186. Hindsford, Nos. 57&62. Virtually unrecognisable today is this location in Hindsford with only the dwellings to the extreme right of camera remaining. The property between the trolleybuses has been demolished and the road realigned, easing the sharp bend. On August 26th 1958, Leigh bound Leyland No.57 is about to pass utility Karrier No.62, most probably also working the Mosley Common service. Note the continued use of former tramway bracket arms from which the overhead wiring is suspended. A dying breed today is the line of corner shops owned and run by real people from the community. The dehumanised out of town shopping complexes of today offer convenience and easy access to material goods but something that warms the spirit is lost in the process.

Photo, the late E.K.Stretch.

90

Tyldesley

Plate 188. Castle Street, No.11. Trolleybus No.11, followed by an LUT utility Guy Arab, passes a parked Vauxhall Victor as they run down Castle Street on their way out of Tyldesley towards Atherton in the middle of the afternoon of 15th May 1958. Much of this section of the trolleybus system saw the continued use of former tramway bracket arms, probably the most visible example of SLT economy when converting from tramway to trolleybus operation..

Photo,P.J.Thompson, (Photosales)

Plate 189. Shuttle Street, No.20. Trolleybuses travelling through Tyldesley in the direction of Worsley followed wiring which took them from Castle Street into Shuttle Street, a rather quiet backwater in comparison to the main thoroughfare, Elliott Street, which was also duo directional. On a damp day in June 1954, No.20 ambles along an almost deserted Shuttle Street past the Methodist Chapel built in 1858 and enlarged in 1875, nowadays in use as the headquarters of the Atherton and Tyldesley Scouts. Although the scene is relatively quiet, this spot could become busy as the nearby bus stop was the closest to two of Tyldesley's three cinemas, the Theatre Royal in John Street, first right behind No.20, and the New Carlton, in Johnson Street, today a bingo hall. The third cinema, the Majestic, is visible at the far end of Shuttle Street. This is now the town's public baths having replaced the 1860s built facility at the bottom of Union Street, this having been one of the first amenities of its kind in Lancashire. Visible to the rear of the trolleybus is the so called 'humidity tower' of Caleb Wright's Barnfield cotton mill. Such features were taken for granted, rather like the trolleybus, until they were no longer with us.

Photo, Author's collection.

Plate 187. (opposite) Hindsford, No.65. The towering chimney of Caleb Wright's Barnfield cotton mill in Tyldesley dominates the background as Leigh bound No.65, on the Mosley Common service, passes Ward and Goldstones, manufacturers of electrical fittings, in Tyldesley Road. Road widening is in progress in 1956. Remarkably, new BICC twin line hangers support the Tyldesley direction wiring with new span wires from at least one new traction pole. The cotton mill, like most similar concerns, was taken over by Courtaulds but has now inevitably gone. In its place in 2002 stands a Somerfield store. The properties immediately to the left of camera have gone taking with them the cigarette advertising, symbolic of the nation's preoccupation with smoking in the 1950s. The terraces in the distance remain and the bus shelter alongside, near Shakerley Road, marks the boundary where Tyldesley Road, Hindsford, becomes Castle Street, Tyldesley.

Photo, the late J.Batty.

Plate 190. Milk Street, No.65. In a similar manner to Atherton, trolleybuses followed a one way system around Tyldesley. Entering the town from Castle Street, the wires ran eastwards along Shuttle Street before a sharp right turn into Milk Street and within the space of 100 yards an equally sharp turn to the left into Elliott Street before leaving Tyldesley, heading towards Boothstown via Manchester Road. On 21st June 1956, No.65 is seen keeping to the centre of Milk Street in order to ease the left turn into Elliott Street. Prominent is the 'Halt at Major Road Ahead' sign unusually side mounted on its black and white striped column. Immediately ahead of the trolleybus, the junction wiring permitted a right turn to join the Atherton bound wiring in Elliott Street. The pull-off for this junction frog was mounted on the traction pole to the right of No.65 since the span wire on the nearside was tied back to the wall of the *Mort Arms* pub. The distant traction pole complete with bracket arm remained in situ until 1972, acting as a lighting column, 14 years after the last trolleybuses had run. *Photo, the late E.K.Stretch.*

Plate 191. Tyldesley Town Hall. Photographed from alongside the Co-operative Society shops in Elliott Street, Tyldesley Town Hall stands prominently on the corner of Elliott Street and Well Street in this view along Elliott Street towards Atherton. This photograph captures the often uninspiring flavour of industrial Lancashire towns. There was, however, a reward on a bright sunny day for taking a few steps forward into Well Street which fell away to the left, by way of an uninterrupted view across the expanse of the Cheshire Plain. The junction wiring at the exit of Milk Street is clearly visible together with bracket arm support for the overhead along the whole length of Elliott Street.

Photo, Wigan Heritage Services.

Plate 192. Elliott Street. By 17th August 1998 Tyldesley Town Hall had become home to the local housing officer and social services within Wigan Metropolitan Borough. A ramp protected by railings provides wheelchair access. One way traffic means that there is no longer a left turn from Milk Street into Elliott Street. However, the original line of this bend followed by the trolleybuses is perpetuated in the modifications to the pavement. The *Black Horse* and *Mort Arms* public houses stand either side of the exit from Milk Street whilst the original Well Street sign appears to have benefited from recent attention by the cleaners. *Photo, Author.*

Plate 193. Elliott Street, No.29. King George VI Coronation flags flutter in the breeze in this 1937 view of Elliott Street Tyldesley. Atherton bound Guy BTX No. 29 in original condition proceeds uninterrupted through the town and is about to pass youthful cyclists who need to be careful to avoid the traction pole. This pole carries a white band which, before the war, denoted it as a bus stop prior to the more familiar 'Trolleybus' stop signs appearing. An eagle eye might spot the wiring from Milk Street entering Elliott Street at a position just beyond the third bracket arm. At this date the arrangement appears to be detached wiring rather than a 'wired in' trailing frog. Most of the properties in Elliott Street remained in 1999.

Photo, A.Ingram.

Plate 194. Elliott Street, No.20. A birds eye view of trolleybus No.20 taken on 10th June 1958 in Elliott Street, Tyldesley, at colloquially known 'Bongs Square' allows a detailed study of the roof and trolley booms. Wooden decking is provided full length under the trolleys and to either side of the trolley base whilst the springs providing upward loading to the trolley booms under the running wires are clearly visible. Seldom noticed are the roof ventilators and the power cables. To the left of the bus the bracket arm doubles as a support for a street lamp whilst in Elliott St. at ground level a Civil Defence operations vehicle, a caravan mobile tea room and GPO telephone booth stand alongside.

Photo, The late R. Boardman.

Plate 195. Sale Lane, No.45. Heading eastwards from Tyldesley, Manchester Road became Sale Lane at the junction with Hough Lane. From his front seat upperdeck position the photographer was rewarded with the opportunity to capture an Atherton bound Guy BT still carrying the first post war livery of red with a grey roof and two white bands. The trolleybus is No.45 and in the latter days of the system was eagerly sought out as being the last in the fleet to retain this livery with large shaded numerals. Furthermore, apart from the provision of sliding ventilators, No.45 was largely in 'as built' condition with original cab front panel. The bus lasted in this condition almost until the end of the system being withdrawn a month or so before final closure. A Hillman estate car follows No.45 in a view that is largely unchanged in 1999.
Photo, Ribble Enthusiasts Club.

Plate 196. Parr Brow, No.29. Guy BTX No.29 was still in original condition when photographed crossing the bridge over the former LNWR Wigan to Eccles Junction railway line at Parr Brow in 1937. Note the extractor ventilators as fitted above the nearside windows of the 11 to 30 batch and the horn protruding at the base of the driver's windscreen. The Swinton destination will be changed to Farnworth upon reaching Worsley assuming the duty

is not a short working. The railway line, with nearby stations at Tyldesley and Ellenbrook, closed in 1969 and the upper structure of the bridge removed in later years to allow road widening. In 1985, the railway cutting on the left, as facing Chester Road, was filled in during a reclamation scheme.The proposed guided busway will, if constructed, use the former railway trackbed from Leigh to Ellenbrook and by use of Newearth Road, join with the A580 and all the inherant congestion. *Photo, A. Ingram.*

Plate 197. Parr Brow, No.52. On 21st August 1958, Leyland No.52 Leigh bound, from Mosley Common, climbs Mosley Common Road towards Parr Brow and is about to cross the bridge over the railway beyond which point the road continues towards Tyldesley as Sale Lane. By this time Nos.52 and 53 were the only remaining Leylands with the early style front end. Today an industrial estate occupies the open land to the left of the picture. *Photo, P.J.Thompson, (Photosales)*

Mosley Common

Plate 198. Mosley Common, Bridgewater Road, No.53. Leigh to Mosley Common service trolleybuses terminated at Mosley Common by reversing into Bridgewater Road. The driver of No.53, who has paused whilst reversing to allow clear passage of the Ford van, will need to edge back just a few inches further to allow the trolleyheads to clear the frog. No.53, one of the last repaints, always appeared well groomed and has recently received the attention of the cleaners. The trolleybus displays an early Jacob's Cream Crackers advert. Beyond the bus the winding gear of Mosley Common pit, a children's slide amongst weeds and puddles together with an early 'Slow Major Road Ahead' sign all contribute to this 1956 SLT 'Trolleyscape' view. Mosley Common colliery had, at one time, employed over 5000 miners and was the largest single colliery in the country. Its closure in February 1968 brought to an end exactly 100 years of deep mining at the site.

Photo, Author's collection.

Plate 199. Mosley Common Road, No.57. Having left the reverser, the wiring of which is visible in the background, but with its destination blind yet to be changed, No.57 gently accelerates over the setts in Mosley Common Road on the return trip to Leigh in the afternoon of 15th May 1958. Road repairs are underway in front of the Bridgewater Road reverser, the entrance to which was subsequently resurfaced with tarmac ahead of the rest of this stretch of road. A 'Jif' advert adorns the upper storey of the corner shop whilst the property next door is for sale. The bicycle next to the traction pole stands by virtue of the time honoured expedient of resting the left hand pedal on the raised kerb .

Photo, P.J.Thompson
(Photosales).

Plate 200. Boothstown, Mosley Common Road. No.2. Unrebuilt trolleybus No.2 climbs up Mosley Common Road, Boothstown and will soon cross the A580 East Lancashire Road, (road crossing sign to left of bus) en route to Atherton from Farnworth on 6th September 1955. The trolleybus, which retains its original bulbous front panel, is in sparkling condition and was a fairly late repaint into the final livery of red with a single cream band. The facing road sign warns of the junction ahead where the A577 joins the A572 in Chaddock Lane.

Photo, Author's collection.

Plate 201. Boothstown, No.2. No.2 ambles along Chaddock Lane towards Leigh Road and the junction with Simpson Road in the direction of Worsley. The trolleybus is most probably working the Farnworth service, the destination blind showing Swinton as was customary until Worsley was reached. On the corner of the bend behind the trolleybus lies Boothstown Methodist Church built in 1872, the A572 running to its left along Chaddock Lane, whilst the trolleybuses followed the A 577 to the right into Mosley Common Road towards the crossing with the East Lancashire Road. *Photo, C. Carter.*

Plate 202. Boothstown, LUT No.279. Some 15 years after the previous photograph of No.2 was taken, Jim Saunders returned to the same location and captured Lancashire United Guy Arab V No.279 in the same position on service 26 Leigh to Manchester. The church and houses in the background remain, as does the corner shop, but a snow covering marks the position of the now demolished terraces. Also once familiar but gradually disappearing underground are the erstwhile GPO overhead telephone lines, absent in this later photograph. The most interesting survivor from the trolleybus system is the traction pole with its extended bracket arm, originally supporting tramway overhead, then trolleybus wires and continuing as a street light support. Even the original lantern arrangement remains with glass reflectors and an exposed sodium vapour lamp whilst a selection of more modern street lighting can be seen towards the church.

Photo, Jim Saunders.

Plate 203. (below) Boothstown, No.42. The same former tramway traction pole with its bracket arm and street lantern is again visible as trolleybus No.42, Atherton bound in 1957, climbs Chaddock Lane towards Boothstown Methodist Church behind the camera. This view serves to remind us of a past era when polluting brick chimney stacks dominated the darkened skyline, each standing tall and gaunt over some labour intensive industrial endeavour, in this case William Yates and Sons textile factory. The sun catches the gable end of No.25 Chaddock Lane and advertisements offering a break from the daily grind either at Squires Gate holiday camp at Blackpool or, slightly nearer home, at Belle Vue, Manchester. A Foden eight wheel lorry and a Ford 'E' van follow No.42 whilst trolleybus No.4, heading toward Worsley, is about to pass a Salford Daimler CVG6 on service 26 to Leigh. Thoughts of the day are exchanged by the two men pausing to chat outside the cafe.

Photo, Roy Brook.

Plate 204. Cooper Street reverser, No.41. A trolleybus reverser was provided in Cooper Street situated off Leigh Road. Around 1940, this section of Leigh Road had been bypassed by Simpson Road for the use of ordinary traffic although trolleybuses continued to use the old road in both directions. Cooper Street reverser was interesting since it was one of only two triangles to retain detached wiring until final closure; the other being at Sandhole near Walkden. Trolleybuses turning back to Atherton were usually able to reverse into Cooper Street by gravity thus reducing work with the bamboo pole. The wires emerging from the reverser were arranged to pass above the main route wires from which they drew their current. No.41, seen here in Cooper Street on 11th June 1957, will draw forward into Leigh Road and pause whilst the conductor transfers the trolley poles onto the main route wiring. *Photo, Roy Brook.*

Plate 205. Boothstown, Leigh Road, No.35. Concrete lampposts and television aerials add to this suburban scene as trolleybus No.35 approaches Boothstown from Worsley along Leigh Road near the junction with Ellenbrook Road in 1957. The continued use of former tramway bracket arms with the overhead suspended to one side of the road results in No.35's booms stretching to reach the offset wires. In the distance, rising above Worsley Woods, is the spire of Worsley's gothic revival style church of St. Mark's, consecrated in 1846 and boasting a fine peal of ten bells, unusual for a parish church, six or eight being the norm. The open space beyond the houses was a good location from which to take in the expanse of the Cheshire plain to the south; an impressive vista to behold on a sunny day. There is a saying in the North West that if you could see such a distance it was going to rain; if you could not it was raining! Some distance beyond the trolleybus was No.276, Leigh Road, Worsley, home of the General Manager of both Lancashire United and South Lancashire Transport. *Photo, Roy Brook.*

Plate 206. Worsley, Leigh Road. No.12. January 23rd 1958 was witness to a snowfall's picturesque transformation of Worsley Wood's traditional sylvan setting for travellers along Leigh Road. The cold air feel to this day with snow laden trees, stone walls and bracket arms is well captured by Peter Thompson who would have needed to have been 'fleet of foot' in moving back out of range of the spray from the oncoming Guy lorry. Trolleybus No.12 of similar manufacture brings up the rear of a line of vehicles cautiously making their way towards Boothstown.   *Photo, P.J.Thompson. (Photosales)*

Plate 207. (below) Worsley, On 7th May 1955, the driver of trolleybus No.15, already showing Farnworth on the blind, has company in his cab as he edges past Salford City Transport Metro Cammell bodied Daimler CVG6 No.435 at its Worsley terminus on a rush hour short working service 23 to Manchester. The green Salford Daimler still retains its attractive silver roof which, whilst doubtlessly difficult to keep clean, provided a touch of character to the Salford fleet. A trolleybus turning circle, partly visible, was provided at Worsley. Behind the camera stands Worsley Court House with the waterways of the Bridgewater Canal close by. Whilst this view is now almost unrecognisable with the M60 motorway passing directly behind the bus, a wealth of local history associated with Worsley village, the Earl of Ellesmere, coaching days and canal heritage can be explored nearby .

Photo, E.Gray.

Plate 208. Worsley. Only the stone wall gives a clue as to the location of the former bus stop and turning circle. Construction of the M62 motorway, since renumbered M60, necessitated the demolition of the Gatehouse to Worsley New Hall. However, the sandstone coat of arms of the Earl of Ellesmere which had decorated the front of the Gatehouse was preserved and incorporated into the motorway bridge. This photograph dated 17th August 1998 is indeed remarkable since it captures a temporary lull in the traffic traversing the island and, at the same time, a pause in the almost ceaseless roar of lorries passing overhead. It is however no place for the pedestrian, trolleybus days being safer and somewhat quieter! *Photo, Author.*

Plate 209. Worsley, No.25. Bearing an archetypal SLT advertisement for a product which is still today the first breakfast choice in many households is No.25, on service to Atherton in Worsley Road and about to pass under the wires of the turning circle on 7th May 1955. This is the only known photograph of this trolleybus in rebuilt condition, its rarity being by virtue of an untimely withdrawal from service following a collision in dense fog with a traction pole near the junction of Manchester Road with Sale Lane on 16th November that year. *Photo, E. Gray.*

Plate 212. (opposite) Worsley Court House, No.24. With Worsley Court House away to the left of the Standard car, the driver of trolleybus No.24 has the half timbered Worsley Mill Brow in his sights beyond the Bridgewater Canal bridge on 12th February 1957. No.24 was the last trolleybus to be rebuilt re entering service some two years earlier. Whilst the original shallow side panels were retained, a single rear platform window has replaced the original full width double window. Passengers on No.24 will soon have an excellent view of The Delph, a quarried sandstone ridge visible to the left as the trolleybus makes its way over the canal bridge. The Delph had provided stone for construction of the Bridgewater Canal and was also the entrance to an underground canal network running for a total of 46 miles and extending as far as Farnworth. The canals had transported coal, up to 350 tons in an eight hour shift, from the face to the surface canal until superseded by colliery railways and had also served to drain the pits until 1968 when the last pit in the area draining into the underground canals closed. *Photo, E.Gray.*

Worsley Court House.

Plate 210. Worsley Court House, No.20. Photographed on 5th September 1957, alongside a half timbered gable end of Worsley Court House, No.20, carrying a rebuilt front and deepened side panels, moves cautiously forward under the turning circle wiring to cross the junction of Worsley Road and Barton Road. The bridge railings in the distance, behind the Atherton bound trolleybus, mark the point at which the A 572 to Swinton crosses the Bridgewater Canal. Worsley Court House, by which name this trolleybus stop and turning circle were known, was built in 1849 on the site of the village stocks for the 1st Earl of Ellesmere to house the manorial court of Worsley. Known as The Court-Leet, administrative matters relating to the manor were conducted within, a function it last performed in 1888. It continued in use thereafter as a magistrates court and later a village hall.
Photo, P.J.Thompson. (Photosales)

Plate 211. Worsley Court House. In 1966, Worsley Court House became the property of Worsley Urban District Council. It was extended in 1967 and passed to the City of Salford in 1974. Today, as a Grade 2 listed building, Worsley Court House is available for both business and private functions. Worsley village library, opened in 1972, stands alongside on the site of the village smithy. To the extreme right of the photograph, Barton Road leaves Worsley Road to run parallel with the Bridgewater Canal. Those having time to explore this area are rewarded with a remarkable insight into the transport revolution of the 18th century. Standing alongside the Bridgewater Canal is The Packet House, another Grade 2 listed mock Tudor building dating from 1760 from where, by 1781, a ticket for the Packet boat providing a daily passenger service between Manchester and Worsley could be purchased. Inevitably, competition arrived by way of the railways and the horse drawn omnibus.
Photo, Author.

Bridgewater Canal.

Plate 213. Bridgewater Canal, No.32. On 28th December 1957, trolleybus No.32 was photographed from The Delph crossing the bridge which takes the A 572 to Swinton over this northernmost stub of the Bridgewater Canal. From this point, coal which had been brought by barge along the underground canal system, would pass under the bridge to join the main stretch of the surface canal. The Bridgewater Canal, opened as far as Barton in 1761, ran at a uniform height of 83 feet above sea level throughout its 23 mile length. Whilst the name of James Brindley will be forever associated with this waterway, the engineering inspiration of John Gilbert and capital from the Duke of Bridgewater combined to ensure the success of this venture. Commencing in Leigh, the canal runs generally eastwards before turning south through Worsley to cross the Manchester Ship Canal at the famous Barton aqueduct. At Trafford Park, one of several branches linked the canal with the Rochdale Canal in Manchester whilst the main route turned westwards to meet the Manchester Ship Canal via the Hulme locks at Runcorn.

Photo, J.A.Peden.

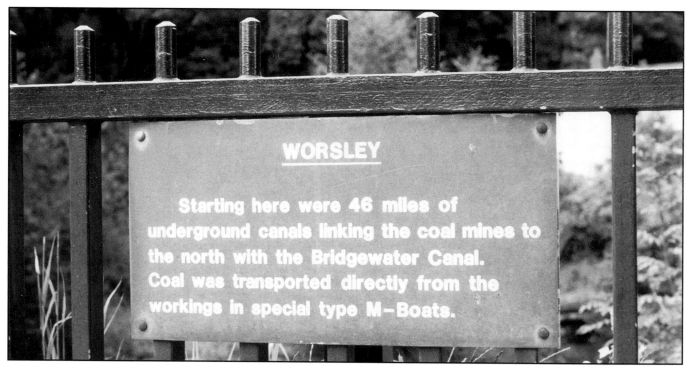

Plate 214. Bridgewater Canal. This notice is today affixed to the bridge railings facing The Delph. The so called M-Boats which were used to transport the coal from the pit workings to the surface canal, until the end of the 19th century, soon gained the nickname of 'Starvation Boats' owing to their basic skeletal construction. Each boat could transport 12 tons of coal and was propelled along the underground canal by 'leggers' who pushed against the walls and roof of the tunnels. Upon emerging at Worsley the boats were steered to the site of the present village green where the coal was weighed. Following the advent of the mineral railway network the canals continued to provide an effective pit drainage system. Today they leave their mark by way of a rust coloured discharge arising from oxidised iron salts, a feature typical of old mine workings where coal deposits are often to be found close to iron bearing rocks. The canal waters around Worsley are however not poisonous and sustain rich stocks of fish and aquatic plants.

Photo, Author.

Worsley Mill Brow.

Plate 215. Mill Brow. At Worsley Mill Brow, a half timbered property was constructed in 1903 on the site of a building complex associated with a corn mill. Mill Brow took its name by virtue of its proximity to the mill, a corn mill having stood next to The Delph since 1420. The mill's grinding stones had been driven by the waters of Worsley Brook through a 24ft. water wheel. Having at one time housed a post office, the building serves as the Mill Brow Cafe, perhaps with a potential customer, as Swinton bound trolleybus No.11 passes on 28th December 1957.

Photo, J.A.Peden.

ATHERTON—SWINTON : SWINTON—WALKDEN : WALKDEN—LITTLE HULTON AND FARNWORTH Sections (Trackless Trolley 'Buses)

MONDAY TO FRIDAY

		am	am	am	am	am	am	am	am	am		pm	pm	pm	pm	pm
Atherton, Punch Bowl	dep.	...	...	...	...	...	5 0	5 15	5 30	5 45		10 0	1015	1030	1045	11 0
Tyldesley, Co-op. Stores ...	,,	...	...	...	...	...	5 10	5 25	5 40	5 55		1010	1025	1040	1055	1110
Mosley Common	,,	...	...	...	...	...	5 20	5 35	5 50	6 5	and	1020	1035	1050	11 5	1120
Boothstown, Greyhound ...	,,	...	...	...	...	5 19	5 23	5 38	5 53	6 8	every	1023	1038	1053	11 8	1123
Worsley, Court House ...	,,	...	...	...	...	5 30	5 30	5 45	6 0	6 15	15 mins.	1030	1045	11 0	1115	1130
Swinton, Church	arr.	...	...	...	...		5 41	5 56	6 11	6 26	until	1041	1056	1111	1126	1141
Swinton, Church	dep.	4 30	4 45	5 0	5 15	5 30	5 45	6 0	6 15	6 30		1045	11 0	...	...	...
Walkden, Memorial	,,	4 42	4 57	5 12	5 27	5 42	5 57	6 12	6 27	6 42		1057	1112	...	...	...
Cleggs Lane	,,	4 47	5 2	5 17	5 32	5 47	6 2	6 17	6 32	6 47		11 2	...	...	...	...
Farnworth, Brackley Street ...	arr.	4 57	5 12	5 27	5 42	5 57	6 12	6 27	6 42	6 57		1112	...	...	...	...

		am	am	am	am	am	am		pm	pm	pm	pm	pm
Farnworth, Brackley Street ...	dep.	...	...	5 0	5 15	5 30	5 45		1030	1045	...	11 0	1115
Cleggs Lane	,,	...	...	5 9	5 24	5 39	5 54		1039	1054	...	11 9	1124
Walkden, Memorial	,,	...	...	5 14	5 29	5 44	5 59	and	1044	1059	1112	1114	1129
Swinton, Church	arr.	...	...	5 26	5 41	5 56	6 11	every	1056	1111	1124	1126	1141
Swinton, Church	dep.	4 59	5 14	5 29	5 44	5 59	6 14	15 mins.	1059	...	...	...	...
Worsley, Court House ...	,,	5 10	5 25	5 40	5 55	6 10	6 25	until	1110	...	...	...	...
Boothstown, Greyhound ...	,,	5 17	5 32	5 47	6 2	6 17	6 32		1117	...	...	...	...
Mosley Common	,,	5 20	5 35	5 50	6 5	6 20	6 35		1120	...	...	...	...
Tyldesley, Market	,,	5 30	5 45	6 0	6 15	6 30	6 45		1130	...	...	...	...
Atherton, Punch Bowl	arr.	5 40	5 55	6 10	6 25	6 40	6 55		1140	...	...	...	...

The above service will be augmented between Swinton and Farnworth as follows :—

Swinton to Farnworth.　　Mon. to Fri.—4-38 a.m., 5-8 a.m. and every 15 mins. until 8-23 a.m. then 3-8 p.m. and every 15 mins. until 6-53 p.m.

Farnworth to Swinton.　　Mon. to Fri.—5-8 a.m., 5-38 a.m. and every 15 mins. until 8-53 a.m. then 3-38 p.m. and every 15 mins. until 7-23 p.m.

Railway Stations on or near the route

Tyldesley, Stanley Street for Tyldesley Station

Moorside and Wardley Station.

Worsley Station.

Plate 216. Mill Brow. On 17th August 1998, no fewer than six businesses varying from a solicitors and an estate agent to a Chinese restaurant and a health clinic occupied the Mill Brow property. It is heartening to note the well preserved condition of this eye catching, half timbered, double gable building of 1903. Note that the ornate wrought iron support for the original cafe sign still remains albeit in retirement!

Photo, Author.

Plate 217. Worsley Green, No.42. A heavy sky threatens further snow falls to add to the already heavily laden branches of the trees alongside Worsley Green as trolleybus No.42 passes cautiously along Worsley Road on 23rd January 1958. Beyond the railings lies 'The Green' which was, until around 1903, the site of Worsley yard. Here flourished the businesses of wheelwrights and nailmakers together with timber merchants and boat builders who had nurtured their trade in conjunction with the canal development. The yard was home to a most unusual clock which was adjusted to strike 13 at 1 o'clock, allegedly on the instruction of the Duke of Bridgewater, to ensure that claimed inability to hear the clock in the noisy yard was no reason for a late return to work ! Fortunately the clock was preserved and can still be heard striking 13 in St. Marks Church!

The rectangular tower to the right of the snow covered roofs is the red brick base of the original works yard chimney, now preserved as a memorial to Francis, 3rd. Duke of Bridgewater, "The Canal Duke." The base, which was for a while a fountain, carries a Latin inscription, the translation of which provides an ample vision of this one time industrious place .

Photo, P.J.Thompson.
(Photosales)

Worsley Green.

It translates as follows:-

A lofty column breathing smoke and fire
Did I the builder's glory once inspire
Whose founder was the Duke who far and wide
Bridged water through Bridgewater's countryside

Stranger, this spot where once did never cease
Great Vulcan's year, who sleep in silent peace
But beneath my very stories does mount
That water's source, his honours spring and fount

Alas that I who gazed o'er field and town
Should to these base proportions dwindle down,
But all's not over, still enough remains
To testify past glories, duty's place.

Plate 218. Worsley Green, No.32. Fine late summer weather and an open windscreen provide the driver of No.32 with a cooling breeze on this the last day of trolleybus operation. Pedestrians enjoy a Sunday stroll in the sun. The trolleybus on its way to Atherton, is about to pass 'The Green' as it makes one of its final trips along the route through the pleasant sylvan suburbia of Worsley. Whilst two other Guy BTs, Nos.42 and 44, remained in service until the last day, No.32 was the only one to retain shallow side and rear panels albeit with a rebuilt front. *Photo, E.Gray.*

Plate 219. Worsley Road Colliery Railway Bridge No.33 (below). Some 100 years after Brindley, the deep mining industry in the South Lancashire coalfield was to take a giant leap forward with the advent of the steam powered standard gauge railway. A private colliery network developed which weaved its way through the coalfield to the interchange sidings with the national railway network. Such a line was that from Worsley canal wharf which passed over the A572 to link with the ex LNWR Tyldesley to Eccles line at Sanderson's Sidings, then north past Bridgewater Colliery, later renamed Sandhole Colliery. On 21st June 1956, a Morris Minor overtakes trolleybus No.33 which heeds the warning and keeps to the centre of the road as it passes slowly under the 15ft.6ins. high bridge at which point the overhead wires ran so closely together that there was less than twelve inches between positive and negative wires. The route to Farnworth will eventually take No.33 along the A6 on Manchester Road, past Sandhole Colliery and a detached reversing triangle which remained available for use until the end of trolleybus operation in 1958. *Photo, The late E.K.Stretch.*

Worsley Road, Colliery Railway Bridge.

Plate 220. Hazelhurst Road, No.59.(right) Beyond the industrial but paradoxically picturesque legacy of waterways, railways and half timbered buildings which are Worsley's mining and transport heritage, the wires of the trolleybus route threaded their way along the A572 through more leafy roads and genteel suburbia in Hazelhurst. On 15th May 1958, a learner driver has an unimpeded run along Worsley Road past Hazelhurst Road in trolleybus No.59. The trolleybus shows 'Depot' on its destination blind since this was the only 'non destination' display available. The appearance of highbridge trolleybuses, including the Sunbeams, beyond Worsley on the Farnworth route became quite frequent in the latter days of the system. The learner driver, assuming he is soon to pass his test, will have just over 3 months trolleybus driving ahead of him, on the SLT at least!

Photo, P.J.Thompson, (Photosales)

Hazelhurst.

Plate 221. Hazelhurst Road, No.24. On the same day as the previous photograph, No.24 passes Hazelhurst Road, off to its left, on service to Farnworth. Wall's Ice Cream is on offer at the shop opposite, but on 15th May, it does not appear that supplies will become exhausted. Judging by the lack of shadows and unbroken cloud it's probably none too warm!

Photo, P.J.Thompson, (Photosales)

ATHERTON—SWINTON : SWINTON—WALKDEN : WALKDEN—LITTLE HULTON AND FARNWORTH Sections (Trackless Trolley 'Buses)

SATURDAYS

		am	am	am	am	am	am	am	am		pm	pm	pm	pm	pm
Atherton, Punch Bowl	dep.	4 45	...	...	...	...	5 0	5 30	5 45		10 0	1015	1030	1045	11 0
Tyldesley, Co-op. Stores ...	,,	4 55	...	...	...	...	5 10	5 40	5 55		1010	1025	1040	1055	1110
Mosley Common	,,	5 5	...	...	...	...	5 20	5 50	6 5		1020	1035	1050	11 5	1120
Boothstown, Greyhound	,,	...	...	...	...	...	5 23	...	6 8	and	1023	1038	1053	11 8	1123
Worsley, Court House	,,	...	...	5 19	...	...	5 30	...	6 15	every	1030	1045	11 0	1115	1130
Swinton, Church	arr.	...	...	5 30	...	...	...	...	6 26	15 mins.	1041	1056	1111	1126	1141
Swinton, Church	dep.	...	5 0	5 30	6 0	6 15	...	...	6 30	until	1045	11 0	...	...	...
Walkden, Memorial	,,	...	5 12	5 42	6 12	6 27	...	...	6 42		1057	1112	...	...	...
Cleggs Lane	,,	...	5 17	5 47	6 17	6 32	...	...	6 47		11 2	...	...	...	...
Farnworth, Brackley Street ...	arr.	...	5 27	5 57	6 27	6 42	...	...	6 57		1112	...	...	...	...

		am	am	am	am	am	am	am	am	am		pm	pm	pm	pm	pm
Farnworth, Brackley Street ...	dep.	...	...	...	5 5	5 30	...	6 0	...	6 30		1030	1045	...	11 0	1115
Cleggs Lane	,,	...	...	...	5 14	5 39	...	6 9	...	6 39		1039	1054	...	11 9	1124
Walkden, Memorial	,,	...	...	...	5 19	5 44	...	6 14	...	6 44	and	1044	1059	1112	1114	1129
Swinton, Church	arr.	...	...	...	5 29	5 56	...	6 26	...	6 56	every	1056	1111	1124	1126	1141
Swinton, Church	dep.	...	...	...	5 44	5 59	6 14	6 29	6 44	6 59	15 mins.	1059	...	...	...	...
Worsley, Court House	,,	...	5 30	...	5 55	6 10	6 25	6 40	6 55	7 10	until	1110	...	...	...	...
Boothstown, Greyhound	,,	...	5 37	...	6 2	6 17	6 32	6 47	7 2	7 17		1117	...	...	...	...
Mosley Common	,,	5 5	5 40	5 50	6 5	6 20	6 35	6 50	7 5	7 20		1120	...	...	...	...
Tyldesley, Market	,,	5 15	5 50	6 0	6 15	6 30	6 45	7 0	7 15	7 30		1130	...	...	...	...
Atherton, Punch Bowl	arr.	5 25	6 0	6 10	6 25	6 40	6 55	7 10	7 25	7 40		1140	...	...	...	...

The service between Swinton and Farnworth will be augmented as follows :—

SATURDAY. From SWINTON to FARNWORTH 9-38 a.m. and every 15 minutes until 10-23 p.m. From FARNWORTH to SWINTON 10-8 a.m. and every 15 minutes until 10-53 p.m.

Swinton

Plate 222. East Lancs. Road, No.16. Opened in 1934, the same year as Liverpool's Mersey Tunnel, the East Lancashire Road, built at a cost of £6 million, provided a highway link between Liverpool and Salford and included features which were to become characteristic of the current day motorway system, construction of which commenced a quarter of a century later. With its gentle curves and gradients, this 25 mile, fenced boundary, 120 ft. wide highway provided a half hour journey time between Liverpool and the Salford boundary at Irlams O' Th' Height. When trolleybus No.16 was photographed crossing 'The East Lancs' Atherton bound, on 15th May 1958, one year before the opening of the Preston By Pass and the beginning of the motorway era, the A 580 was considered a fast and dangerous place. Crossing at the same time as No.16 are a Salford Daimler CVG6 and a heavily loaded Morris pickup. Meanwhile, a Seddon lorry waits patiently alongside a Lancashire United Guy Arab IV on service 31 to Mount Skip.

Photo, P.J.Thompson (Photosales)

Partington Lane.

Plate 223. Partington Lane, No.32. Just beyond the East Lancashire Road crossing, the trolleybus wires left Worsley Road to follow Partington Road up to the junction with the A6 at Swinton. Trolleybus No.32 turns from Partington Lane into Worsley Road which is deserted save for a lone pedestrian. Partington Lane was home to Swinton depot which housed most of the trolleybuses working on the Farnworth route.

Photo, C.Carter.

A new variety of tickets was introduced in the 1930s including both a standard size with 24 stages and a longer 32 stage version. Colours varied dependent upon value; this 24 stage, 3d example, which is pink, having the letter 'S' in the top left hand corner indicating its having been issued on a vehicle operating from Swinton depot

Ticket, courtesy Brian Hughes.

107

Plate 224. Partington Lane, No.29. In 1956, Atherton bound No.29 takes the right turn into Worsley Road from Partington Lane. This trolleybus was among the first to receive a rebuilt front around 1950, re entering service with a grey roof. It was therefore a late repaint into the final livery, certain others similarly rebuilt retaining the grey roof livery. Later rebuilds were subject to greater economy receiving rubber mounted windows rather than chromed windscreen surrounds and, unlike 29, retaining shallow side panels. The Swinton side of The East Lancashire Road with rows of chimney pots is in stark contrast with Worsley. Even the prospect of Heinz soup seems unable to warm the spirit of the distant pedestrian. Perhaps he was unable to get through on the telephone!

Photo, J.Fozard.

Swinton Depot.

Plate 225. Swinton Depot, No.4. At the bus stop alongside the entrance to Swinton depot in Partington Lane, trolleybus No.4 is about to pull away having 'dropped off' an off duty crew. The depot wiring frog pull-off is visible on the traction pole. No.4 was the only Guy BTX trolleybus with an unrebuilt front to remain in service until the closure of the system. For some reason it was provided with only minimal ventilation. The partly o b s c u r e d advertisement on the gable end of the terraced row promotes Quality Street chocolates which, along with the product advertised on No.4, remain ever popular today. No.4 carried a range of Kellogg's advertisements in latter years.

Photo, C.Carter.

Plate 226. Swinton Depot, No.26. Guy BTX No. 26 in largely original condition in the first post war livery makes a superb sight as it stands outside Swinton depot in exactly the same position as No.4 in the previous photograph. Note the lower saloon seating arrangement. On a fully loaded bus the rearward facing front bulkhead seats were not for the self conscious! Apart from alterations to ventilation arrangements, the only significant changes to its typical 1930s architecture have been the acquisition of a simplified trolley gantry and a change to the front profile through replacement of the front destination panel and cab panel.

Photo, the late Reg Wilson.

Plate 227. Swinton Depot, No.28. The last day of trolleybus operation was Sunday 31st August 1958. The day was sunny giving rise to the shadows on the forecourt of Swinton depot. Trolleybus No.28 stands outside the depot whilst No.6 stands behind, sandwiched between 28 and an LUT Guy Arab. Just visible is another LUT Guy of 1951 with a Weymann body, the majority of the fleet being bodied by Northern Counties. These Guys were the first outside Birmingham to have that city's style of new look front which first appeared in 1950 on Crossley, Daimler and Guy chassis purchased by Birmingham City Transport for its post war modernisation and tramway replacement programme. Today a housing estate occupies the former depot site.

Photo, Walter E. Amos.

Plate 228. Swinton Depot, No.36. This 1950 photograph of Guy BT No.36 on the setts of Swinton depot forecourt provides an interesting comparison with the view of BTX No.26 taken at the same time in Partington Lane. The two trolleybuses are in generally similar condition though No.36 retains the eight leg trolley gantry and its original bulbous cab panel. The shadow cast on the front upperdeck window by the roof dome serves to illustrate the 'V' front arrangement applied to the 2-axle Guy BTs, a feature absent on the earlier 3-axle BTXs.

Photo, the late Reg Wilson.

Plate 229. Swinton Depot, Nos.27 & 28. Amongst the last trolleybuses to be rebuilt in 1954/5 were Nos.27 and 28 pictured on Swinton depot forecourt in 1958. The economies applied to the later rebuilds are clearly evident, the retained shallow side panels imparting an incongruously 1930s look when compared with the modern front end which could not disguise the vintage. No.27 did boast the luxury of chromium plated windscreen surrounds. At some stage No.28 underwent lower deck repanelling, losing the electrical resistance box cooling louvres in the process. Nevertheless, these trolleybuses, along with Nos.6 and 24, the other later rebuilds with rubber mounted windows, were of generally similar appearance, Nos.27 and 28 even carrying the same Woodbines advertisement.

Photo, Author's collection.

Plate 231. Partington Lane, No.45. By the early months of 1958, the antiquity of the SLT trolleybus system, with careworn trolleybuses and overhead held together with splicing ears was apparent to all. However, considerations of dilapidation were displaced by incredulity when one trolleybus in particular made an appearance. This was Guy BT No.45 which, apart from sliding ventilators, remained in virtually original condition complete with bulging front cab panel. Late in the day its early two white band livery even received a touch up during which time the cab front panel was repainted, smartening its appearance considerably. The whole anachronism was enhanced by retention of large shaded fleet numerals, nearside extractor type ventilators over the lower deck windows and an eight leg trolley gantry on its grey roof. Meanwhile the lack of change to No.45 over 25 years is eclipsed by 'Kit Kat', the wrapper of which, by the end of the millenium, had not changed in over 40 years !

Photo, Author's collection.

Swinton Church.

Plate 232. Vicarage Road reverser, No.6. Prior to Partington Lane's junction with the A6, provision was made for trolleybus reversal at Swinton by means of a triangle situated in Vicarage Road alongside St. Peter's church. On 21st December 1957, trolleybus No.6 operating a Swinton to Farnworth 'jigger', is reversed at Swinton against the background of the church tower. The conductor pulls the reverser frog handle as the driver completes the manoeuvre back into Vicarage Road, monitoring his progress from his open cab door.

Photo, P.J.Thompson, (Photosales)

Plate 233. Vicarage Road reverser, No.24 (right). Some eight months earlier, on 25th April 1957, a bright sunny day with spring leaves on the trees, No.24 was completing the same manoeuvre into the Vicarage Road reverser, this time looking down Partington Lane in the direction of Swinton depot. Close inspection through the lower saloon windows once again reveals the open cab door and comparison with the previous photograph will make obvious why the conductor is absent from the platform. *Photo, P.J.Thompson, (Photosales)*

Plate 234. Partington Lane, No.36. Having left the Vicarage Road reverser and with St.Peter's church to its left, trolleybus No.36, Farnworth bound, heads along the dual carriageway portion of a deserted Partington Lane on 17th February 1956. The trolleybus which remained largely original apart from replacement of the rear platform window, was an early withdrawal, being taken out of service in April that year, some 7 months before the large scale withdrawals associated with the closure of the St. Helens route. An eagle eye will spot the retention of the drainage pipe running down the rear offside pillar from roof level. More obvious is the effect of an altercation suffered by the rear corner panel, a malady to which SLT vehicles seemed unduly prone. *Photo, W.Ryan.*

Plate 235. Swinton Church, No.22. (below) An Austin A40 Devon draws up slowly behind grey roof liveried trolleybus No.22 as it stands at the traffic lights waiting to make the left turn from Partington Lane onto Manchester Road and the A6. The arched gateway to St Peter's church remains today although it has been moved bodily nearer to the church. From this point the trolleybuses would follow the A6 as far as Little Hulton before turning right in the direction of Farnworth.

Photo, C. Carter.

Plate 236. Swinton Church, No.10. A cup of Ty-Phoo tea on a damp and blustery day in 1957 might well be on the minds of those aboard Atherton bound No.10. The trolleybus awaits additional passengers in Partington Lane opposite Swinton church alongside one of the area's less architecturally memorable structures, namely the SLT bus shelter! Upon return to the depot, the fitters will be disappointed to find that attention is required to a leaking oil seal on No.10's leading driving axle.

Photo, Dennis Gill.

Plate 237. Swinton Church, No.55. Fine weather in 1958 finds highbridge trolley No.55 on the Farnworth service in Partington Lane Swinton against a background of youthful trees. In the same way that a cup of tea might have been appropriate in the photograph of No.10, 'Sunfresh' could well be welcome on this day. A final word is exchanged between the crew as the driver prepares to climb into the cab. Both seem oblivious to the destination blind showing Farnworth whilst working a duty in the Atherton direction. Previously the preserve of lowbridge trolleybuses, it was quite common in later days to see all types of highbridge buses, including the post war Sunbeams, operating this service after it was realised that sufficient clearance existed under bridges along the route.

Photo, Author's collection.

Plate 238. Swinton Church, LUT Guy Arab No.382. Situated a short distance behind the Atherton bound trolleybus stop opposite Swinton Church in Partington Lane was the motor bus stop shelter, which, whilst spartan, at least boasted the luxury of windows! In spring sunshine, passengers climb aboard lowbridge Weymann bodied Lancashire United Guy Arab III No.382 on service 20 to Hollins Green from Farnworth. Whilst the wires of the trolleybus route turned left from Partington Lane into Chorley Road running to Farnworth via Little Hulton, the Guy will have taken the direct route from Farnworth via Kearsley reaching Swinton via Station Road, visible beyond the bus. From Swinton the motor bus will follow the trolley wires to the other side of the A580 East Lancashire Road before turning from Worsley Road into Folly Lane towards Monton. Visible through the branches of the tree is one of the recently erected concrete lighting columns which, with a consciously designed profile and pendant lanterns, were not unattractive. *Photo, Roy Marshall.*

Plate 239. Partington Lane. On 4th August 1998, with forty years of growth behind them, the trees have transformed Partington Lane. Photographed from the location of the former trolleybus reverser, off to the left in Vicarage Road, a Timeline Mercedes minibus operating service 484 from Prestwich to Eccles can be seen making the right turn from Station Road into Chorley Road. Visible through the trees is the repositioned stone gateway to St. Peter's church. *Photo, Author.*

The Bull's Head, Swinton.

Plate 240. The Bull's Head, No.30. Looking along a largely deserted Chorley Road, at least by today's standards, No.30 slows to take the right turn into Partington Lane around 1956. At this time, *The Bull's Head* still sported a half timbered appearance to its upper storey. The suspension of the SLT overhead was such that those waiting to board in Partington Lane witnessed the gross undulations and heaving of the wiring heralding the arrival of the trolleybuses as they turned the corner. Without wishing to resort to overly picturesque imagination, the wiring's movements in rising and sinking with the passage of the trolley heads was akin to the motion bestowed upon flotsam by the passage of waves!

Photo, C.Carter.

Plate 241. The Bull's Head, No.16. In 1958 *The Bull's Head*, having been repainted during April 1957, had a much lighter look about it as trolleybus No.16 begins the turn into Partington Lane after having given way to the Morris Oxford. Plenty of pedestrian activity here. Despite its rebuilt front, the two letter registration of No.16 gives its age away. Even in 1958 it seems that fathers pushed prams!; but how often do we see wicker shopping baskets in this age of the plastic carrier bag?

Photo, Author's collection.

115

Plate 242, The Bull's Head. On 4th August 1998 the view was pretty much the same. Chimney stacks have either disappeared or have been reduced in height. *The Bull's Head* has stood the passage of time; not so the railings on the corner which have most probably had an argument with a lengthy trailer during the sharp left turn into Station Road. Damage caused in this way to the railings at this location was frequent. As predicted the ubiquitous plastic carrier bag is in evidence.

Photo, Author.

Plate 243. Chorley Road, No.27. Having rounded the corner from Partington Lane, No.27 stands at the Farnworth bound time point in Chorley Road on 21st September 1957. Beyond this point towards Manchester, relief from the somewhat claustrophobic roads and pavements associated with rows of terraced property came in the form of the spacious grass expanse in front of Swinton Town Hall.

Photo, P.J.Thompson,
(Photosales)

Chorley Road, Swinton.

Plate 244. Chorley Road, No.16. Just visible behind trolleybus No. 16 standing at the time point in Chorley Road is Swinton Town Hall seen beyond Partington Lane. No.16 presents a smart appearance on 10th July 1956. This trolleybus received an early rebuild around 1950 including deepened side panels after which it re entered service in the red with a grey roof livery. This rebuild was early enough for it to receive one more repaint into the final livery before repaints ceased in mid 1955. In 1956 the first of the concrete lighting columns have already arrived. *Photo, J.C.Gillham.*

Swinton Town Hall.

Plate 245. Swinton Town Hall.
Swinton Town Hall was formally opened on 17th September 1938. Swinton and Pendlebury had become a Municipal Borough in 1934 and architects Sir Percy Thomas and Ernest Prestwich were awarded the contract to design the new town hall. The main contractors were J. Gerrard and Sons Ltd., the building being constructed on the spacious site formerly occupied by the Swinton Industrial School, demolished in 1933 after closure some eight years earlier. Whilst plain and functional in appearance rather than bearing outright architectural pedigree, the two storey building set back from the main A6 in spacious lawns nevertheless presents an imposing appearance. The building was always something of a eye catcher for those having travelled from Little Hulton along Chorley Road's terraced rows. As if taking their cue, the SLT trolley wires disappeared to the right of the Town Hall down Partington Lane whilst Chorley Road continued beyond the traffic lights into Pendlebury and on to Salford. The sign in the foreground directs the way to local government departments and Crompton House. The extension to the rear of the original town hall building was added in 1974.

Photo, Author.

Moorside.

Plate 246. Moorside, Nos.45, 28 & 18. Having meandered their way through the industrial backstreets of Tyldesley, through Boothstown and the tree lined roads of Worsley, the trolleybuses found themselves amongst somewhat more purposeful traffic beyond Swinton as they travelled towards Little Hulton along the A6. Even so, everything ground to a halt when religious processions or similar activities associated with local wakes took to the roads. Trolleybus services were cut short or temporarily discontinued. Waiting for such a procession to pass along Manchester Road, Moorside towards Swinton in May 1957, are three trolleybuses; No.45, with its trolley booms lowered, ahead of Nos.28 and 18.

Photo, R. C. Jackson.

Plate 247. Moorside, No.24. With trolleybus No.24 parked in a side street, out of the path of the procession, away from the overhead wires, a policeman keeps an eye open for potential obstructions as the choir boys and clergy followed by the banner carriers proceed steadily along Manchester Road from Swinton. Meanwhile the event has attracted a few onlookers observing the activity from the pavement in front of the houses. Soon No.24 will receive power from the overhead by means of trailing cables attached to its lowered trolley booms allowing it to regain the overhead wires in Manchester Road.

Photo, R.C.Jackson.

Plate 248, Moorside, No.24. Following the passage of the procession in May 1957, trolleybus No.24 on service from Farnworth is manoeuvred, under power from trailing cables, out of the side street and back onto Manchester Road to rejoin the wires towards Swinton. In front of the trolleybus is the Swinton Co-operative whilst to the immediate left of No.24 two ladies visit the somewhat more diminutive Moorside Co-operative corner shop. Meanwhile this unorthodox trolleybus manoeuvre attracts the attention of a small group of onlookers. *Photo, R.C.Jackson.*

Plate 249, Sandhole, Nos.24 & 7. Just one week before final closure in August 1958, trolleybus No.24, closely followed along Manchester Road by a Rover, passes Farnworth bound No.7 which is approaching the detached reversing triangle serving Sandhole colliery. By this time motor buses were operating many of the duties on the Farnworth route owing to a decreasing number of available trolleybuses. This stretch of road between Sandhole and Moorside was formerly known as Wardley Lane. Today the view is not so rural, the M60 motorway and its connections dominating the background. The overhead at this point is supported by twin line hangers acquired second hand from the St. Helens system whilst the span wire has been transferred to a new traction pole standing alongside that carrying the street lamp, the latter having become weakened through internal corrosion necessitating the fitting of bracing plates half way up the pole.   *Photo, The late E.K.Stretch.*

Plate 250. Sandhole detached triangle. Bridgewater Colliery, later known as Sandhole, lay to the south of Manchester Road and the ex L&Y Manchester to Wigan railway Line. The colliery, connected to the ex LNWR Tyldesley to Eccles line via Sanderson's Sidings, closed in 1962, though a washery remained operative until 1966. An occasional trolleybus service for colliery workers operated from Swinton to Sandhole, a reverser in Sandhole Lane remaining in use up to the end of trolleybus operation in 1958. It seemed strange travelling along Manchester Road to come upon a Guy BT in the reverser, peeping out from the gap in the hedge. The overhead arrangement was interesting, having no frogs and being completely detached from the main route wiring. Movements in and out of the reverser required three transfers of the trolley booms; the first, upon arrival from Swinton, onto a tied off spur, visible with its spacer bar and insulators, in front of the nearest traction pole followed, after reversal into Sandhole Lane, by a second transfer to a parallel set of wires. When setting off for Swinton, trolleybuses would use these exit wires, tied off on the Sandhole Lane side, drawing as far across Manchester Road as their fully extended trolley booms would permit. Finally the conductor would swing the booms over to the other side of the road onto the Swinton bound wires. What was an incredible manoeuvre in trolleybus days would be simply suicidal against today's mad traffic dash along the A6. Visible, on 23rd August 1958, with Sandhole Lane to the right, are the electricity feeder cables crossing the span wire to the detached spur.   *Photo, The late E.K. Stretch.*

Walkden

Plate 251, Walkden, No. 27. Despite showing Swinton on its destination blind, No.27 approaches Walkden on service to Farnworth on 2nd April 1958. To the rear of the trolleybus a Ford Popular waits for a Morris Minor to clear its path before joining the A6 from Hodge Road, whilst an LUT Guy Arab IV on service 38 to Manchester disappears in the distance towards Swinton. The two ladies, one carrying a young child, will have just a short walk to the junction of the A6 with the A575, Farnworth to Worsley Road, at Walkden Memorial island. *Photo, P.J.Thompson (Photosales)*

Plate 252. Walkden Memorial. In trolleybus days Walkden Memorial was a key journey landmark standing on an elongated island where the A575 Bolton Road from Farnworth crosses the A6 into Memorial Road leading to Worsley. Bridgewater Road also converged at this point as the B5232 from Boothstown. A trolleybus turning circle was provided and is seen in the latter days of the system viewed towards Manchester Road from what was Manchester Road West until renamed High Street in 1965. Beyond the monument stands St.Pauls church whilst visible between the traction pole and the monument is the Manchester Road bus shelter located outside the *Stocks Hotel* out of view behind the shops to the left. Oh for the days when there was time to sit and ponder! A wealth of interesting 'street furniture' is on view including belisha beacons, ancient and modern street lighting, traction poles and trolley wires. Note the span wire supporting the turning circle frog. *Photo, Walkden Heritage Unit,*

Plate 253. Stocks Hotel, No.58. Standing alongside the Manchester Road bus stop shelter outside the *Stocks Hotel* in 1958 is highbridge Leyland trolleybus No.58, a relative newcomer to the Farnworth route formerly the preserve of the lowbridge Guys until the last few months of operation. Judging by the apparel there is a chill to the day. It is however interesting to witness the change in fashion over the years especially the predominance in the 1950s of headscarves.

Photo, J.Fozard.

Plate 254. Stocks Hotel. On the 4th August 1998, some forty years later, the 1898 built *Stocks Hotel* had reached its century whilst retaining much of its external character. Traffic lights at the road junction have replaced the island whilst the monument has been relocated beyond the *Stocks Hotel* on Manchester Road. Standing in the same position as the trolleybus in the previous photograph is a First Manchester Leyland Atlantean on service 39, Leigh to Manchester. The destination display comprising route number and intermediate destinations in two route boxes above the ultimate destination was introduced by Manchester Corporation Transport. The same layout was applied to the new Lancashire United buses purchased to replace the trolleybuses from 1956, an influence brought to SLT / LUT by Mr. C.C.Oakham, formerly Chief Engineer in Manchester who replaced Mr. E.H.Edwardes as General Manager in 1955.

Photo, Author.

Plate 255. Walkden, Manchester Road West, No.37. The warmth of a late summer day ensures that benches on both sides of Manchester Road West Walkden are put to good use on 6th September 1955. The driver of trolleybus No.37 appears similarly relaxed as he waits to depart for Farnworth. Note the spare wheel mounted on the nearside of the Ford estate car making its way around the island from the monument just visible on the extreme right. For some reason Barclays Bank on the corner of Manchester Road West and Bolton Road seems to be a popular meeting place. This building, visible in the previous photograph taken in 1998, allows comparison and identification of location. *Photo, Author's collection.*

Plate 256. Walkden, Manchester Road West, No.36. Three buses pausing on their duties in June 1954 emphasise the width of Manchester Road West Walkden on approach to the Memorial from Little Hulton. Decorations around the monument are associated with the diamond jubilee of Worsley Urban District Council. Trolleybus No.36 stands in the same place as No.37 in the previous photograph whilst another Guy BT, partially visible, has stopped alongside Barclays Bank. Standing in front of No.36 is LUT No.447, a Foden PVD6G with Northern Counties bodywork. Foden buses were uncommon but found popularity with several fleets in the North West including Warrington, Chester and Lancashire United Transport in whose fleet they were a variation on the Guy Arab 6LW/Northern Counties theme. They were popular with the depot fitters who would have been at home working on their Gardner engines. The Foden carries the red livery with a grey roof in which it was delivered. Trolleybus No.36 retains the earlier 'two white band' livery, whilst the partially visible Guy BT has been repainted into the final livery of red with a single cream band.

Photo, Author's collection.

Plate 257. Walkden, Manchester Road West, No.2. Displaying its original rear platform double window and beading below the waistrail, trolleybus No.2 pauses alongside Walkden Co-operative in Manchester Road West before proceeding towards Little Hulton to join Manchester Road East. An overhead feeder cable from Walkden sub station is visible to the right of the bus, suspended from the traction pole which also serves as a lighting column outside the Palace cinema. Supporting the bicycle is an SLT timekeepers hut with its telephone attached to the back wall. Note the feeder cable suspended above the hut.

Photo, Author's collection.

Plate 258. Walkden, Manchester Road West, No.38. Trolleybus No.38 draws the attention of an inspector on 20th June 1954 at the 'alighting only' bus stop alongside the Palace cinema in Manchester Road West, Walkden. After the war most Guy BTs had the extractor type ventilators above the nearside windows removed when sliding ventilators were fitted. Three of the class however retained these ventilators including No.38, the others being Nos.35 and 45, both of which remained in service until 1958, No.38 being withdrawn in the summer of 1956 before the St. Helens route closure in November that year. To the rear of No.38 stands the pit head gear of Ellesmere Colliery, which last produced coal in 1921. The installation was retained until 1968 for pumping and ventilation. Beyond the colliery were the Walkden workshops of the local NCB railway system.

Photo, Author's collection.

ATHERTON—SWINTON : SWINTON—WALKDEN : WALKDEN—LITTLE HULTON AND FARNWORTH Sections (Trackless Trolley 'Buses)

SUNDAY		am	am	am	am	am	am	am	am	pm	am	pm	pm	pm	pm	
Atherton, Punch Bowl	dep.	...	...	...	9 0	9 30	10 0	1030	11 0	...	1130	...	12 0	...	1230	
Tyldesley, Co-op. Stores ...	„	...	...	...	9 10	9 40	1010	1040	1110	...	1140	...	1210	...	1240	then
Mosley Common	„	...	...	...	9 20	9 50	1020	1050	1120	...	1150	...	1220	...	1250	as
Boothstown, Greyhound ...	„	...	...	...	9 23	9 53	1023	1053	1123	...	1153	...	1223	...	1253	Monday
Worsley, Court House	„	...	8 30	...	9 30	10 0	1030	11 0	1130	...	12 0	...	1230	...	1 0	to
Swinton, Church	arr.	...	8 41	...	9 41	1011	1041	1111	1141	...	1211	...	1241	...	1 11	Friday
Swinton, Church	dep.	8 15	8 45	9 15	9 45	1015	1045	1115	1145	12 0	1215	1230	1245	1 0	1 15	
Walkden, Memorial	„	8 27	8 57	9 27	9 57	1027	1057	1127	1157	1212	1227	1242	1257	1 12	1 27	
Cleggs Lane	„	8 32	9 2	9 32	10 2	1032	11 2	1132	12 2	1217	1232	1247	1 2	1 17	1 32	
Farnworth, Brackley Street ...	arr.	8 42	9 12	9 42	1012	1242	1112	1142	1212	1227	1242	1257	1 12	1 27	1 42	

		am	am	am	am	am	am	am	pm	pm
										1215
Farnworth, Brackley Street ...	dep.	8 45	9 15	9 45	1015	1045	1115	1145	...	1215	
Cleggs Lane	„	8 54	9 24	9 54	1024	1054	1124	1154	...	1224	then
Walkden, Memorial	„	8 59	9 29	9 59	1029	1059	1129	1159	...	1229	as
Swinton, Church	arr.	9 11	9 41	1011	1041	1111	1141	1211	...	1241	Monday
Swinton, Church	dep.	9 14	9 44	1014	1044	1114	1144	1214	1229	1244	to
Worsley, Court House	„	9 25	9 55	1025	1055	1125	1155	1225	1240	1255	Friday
Boothstown, Greyhound ...	„	9 32	10 2	1032	11 2	1132	12 2	1232	1247	1 2	
Mosley Common	„	9 35	10 5	1035	11 5	1135	12 5	1235	1250	1 5	
Tyldesley, Market	„	9 45	1015	1045	1115	1145	1215	1245	1 0	1 15	
Atherton, Punch Bowl	arr.	9 55	1025	1055	1125	1155	1225	1255	1 10	1 25	

The Service between SWINTON and FARNWORTH will be Augmented as follows :—
Sunday ... SWINTON to FARNWORTH 1-53 p.m. and half hourly until 5-23 p.m. then every 15 minutes until 10-23 p.m.
FARNWORTH to SWINTON 2-23 p.m. and half hourly until 5-53 p.m. then every 15 minutes until 10-53 p.m.

Little Hulton

Plate 259. Little Hulton, No.18. Beyond Walkden the trolleybuses travelled just over a mile along the A6 towards Little Hulton past Little Hulton Station, the entrance to which was situated opposite Smith Fold Lane's junction with Manchester Road East. The station was on the ex LNWR Bolton Great Moor St. to Manchester Exchange, via Roe Green junction, line from which passenger services were withdrawn on 27th March 1954. Upon reaching Little Hulton, the trolley wires left Manchester Road East to follow Cleggs Lane into which trolleybus No.18 waits to turn at traffic lights. Behind the trolleybus, which is operating a Saturday afternoon Walkden to Farnworth 'jigger', Roe bodied Guy Arab II 6LW No.297 is operating the basic Atherton to Farnworth service and shows 'TT', an abbreviation for 'Trackless Trolley', on its route number blinds as was usual when motor buses were substituted for trolleys in the last months of operation.

Photo, Author's collection.

Plate 260. Little Hulton, No.4. A policeman's eye is caught by the antique appearance of trolleybus No.4 as it turns from Cleggs Lane into Manchester Road East, Little Hulton on 21st August 1958. By this time, No.4 was the last remaining Guy in service with an unrebuilt front. Beyond the Little Hulton Co-operative building on the corner, the trolleywires in Cleggs Lane were suspended to one side of the road owing to the continued use of former tramway bracket arms. Atherton bound trolleybus drivers travelled this section with care to give the extended booms every chance of staying on the wires!

Photo, P.J.Thompson (Photosales)

Plate 261. Little Hulton. On 4th August 1998, the junction of Cleggs Lane with the A6 is still dominated by a legacy of the Rochdale Pioneers, albeit now divided between a bookmaker's and a discount furnishing store rather than a Co-operative. Even so its former identity remains clear to all, pronounced in the stonework at roof level.

Photo, Author.

Plate 262. Cleggs Lane, No.28. Once Cleggs Lane was reached, the trolley wires reverted to being suspended from former tramway bracket arms resulting in the overhead's alignment being significantly offset to one side of the road. This arrangement made it difficult for Atherton bound trolleybuses to pull into bus stops and drivers expected passengers to take one or two steps in the road when either boarding or alighting from the bus. On 23rd August 1958, the driver of No.28 ensures that he avoids dewiring by pulling up at the trolleybus stop opposite Edward Street a few feet from the pavement causing the lady leaving the bus to step down into the road. Even so, No.28's trolley poles are already exerting some sideways drag on the overhead.

Photo, Roy Brook.

125

Farnworth

Plate 263. Cleggs Lane, No.4. With the housing estates around Buckley Lane in the distance, trolleybus No.4 eases under the bridge carrying the mineral railway serving Sandhole and Brackley Collieries across Cleggs Lane in April 1958. A reducing number of serviceable lowbridge trolleybuses around at this time resulted in trials which successfully demonstrated that there was just sufficient clearance for highbridge trolleybuses to pass under this bridge after which Leylands, Karriers and even the occasional post war Sunbeam were to be seen supplementing the dwindling number of older lowbridge Guys on the Farnworth service. Nevertheless the clearance was so acute that resurfacing of the road, when required, had to be conducted with due regard to the section immediately beneath the bridge to maintain clearance. The overhead wire carriers for Atherton bound trolleybuses are visible under the bridge, offset to the nearside to avoid the trolley booms fouling their parking hooks. Whilst the trolleybuses disappeared in 1958 the bridge remained until closure of the colliery railways around a decade later. *Photo, Author's collection.*

Longcauseway.

Plate 264. Longcauseway, No.5. Trolleybuses continued along Cleggs Lane into Buckley Lane to reach Farnworth, crossing the A575 Bolton to Walkden road, into Longcauseway. When introduced in August 1931, the service originally terminated in a reversing triangle situated in Old Hall Street alongside the *'Bird I'th Hand'* pub at the end of Longcauseway. During the summer of 1936, wiring was erected allowing trolleybuses to follow Manchester Road before turning left to a new terminus in Brackley Street. Departure was via Albert Road meeting the inbound wires at the junction with Longcauseway and Buckley Lane, so completing a rectangular circuit. The original reversing triangle was retained to be used three days each year when Brackley Street was closed for the annual fair. Trolleybus No.5 turns into Manchester Road from Longcauseway with the reversing triangle off to the left of the picture. Whilst maintained by the SLT, the wiring beyond Buckley Lane in Farnworth was owned by Farnworth Corporation. *Photo, C.Carter.*

Plate 265. Old Hall Street reverser, No.42. No.42 disappears out of view on 2nd April 1958, as it turns into Manchester Road from Longcauseway to follow the normal Farnworth circuit. The triangle, seldom used after 1936, required trolleybuses to draw halfway across Manchester Road beyond the *Bird I'th Hand* pub to allow their trolley heads to clear the frog prior to reversing. Traffic levels meant that this arrangement became increasingly inconvenient and the new loop was introduced following representations by Kearsley UDC, the reverser being retained for emergency use only. A typical SLT assortment of fittings supports the overhead including differing types of old 18" spacers on the reverser exit wiring into Longcauseway. Note the hand cart standing in Old Hall Street and the LUT Guy Arab III entering Bolton Road.   *Photo, P.J.Thompson,*
(Photosales)

Plate 266. Old Hall Street reverser, No.31. In 1954, with the normal Farnworth loop closed by the annual fair, the original terminus in Old Hall Street and its reverser, retained for such eventualities, are brought back into temporary use. The appearance of Guy BT No.31 here causes the old gentleman outside the Farnworth and Kearsley Labour Club to pause and recall when he last saw a trolleybus using these wires. As was the practice at the St. Helens route terminus in Lambeth Street Atherton, the driver of No.31 has parked on the offside of Old Hall Street for an easy exit into Longcauseway.

Photo, Author's collection.

Plate 267. Farnworth and Kearsley Labour Club. The Farnworth and Kearsley Labour Club remained on the corner of Longcauseway on 4th August 1998. Could those be the same letters on the wall as seen 44 years before? On the other side of Old Hall Street the lone man seated on the bench marks the spot where the pints were pulled in the long demolished *Bird I'th Hand* pub! One wonders if he knew he was sitting next to the one time location of an infrequently used trolleybus reverser? Meanwhile, beyond the telephone kiosk, traffic in Bolton Road waits for a green light before setting off on earsplitting dashes along Manchester Road and Longcauseway. The thought of reversing trolleybuses here today is chilling!

Photo, Author.

Plate 268. Longcauseway, No.2. Having reversed in the Old Hall Street triangle rather than following the rectangular circuit in 1954, Guy BTX No.2 provides the rare sight of a trolleybus using the westbound wires in Longcauseway. No.2, on its way to Atherton followed by a pair of Ford vans, will rejoin the usual route on crossing into Buckley Lane. This trolleybus in grey roof livery was to receive a final repaint into all red with a single cream band although it was withdrawn on closure of the St. Helens route in November 1956. It remained in substantially original condition with bulbous front panel until withdrawn when it went for scrap. What a pity the preservation movement had not taken off at the time.

Photo, Author's collection.

Plate 269. Manchester Road, No.42 .The *Bird I'th Hand* pub and the Farnworth and Kearsley Labour Club provide the backcloth to trolleybus No.42 at the bus stop in Manchester Road having turned from Longcauseway whilst a Standard car heads towards Bolton Road. The driver's attention will be divided between activity around No.42's platform, seen in his nearside mirror and the approaching inspector, visible in his offside mirror. The trolleybus stop sign is mounted on the concrete lighting column whilst a motor bus stop is on the traction pole to the rear of No.42. Discernible, just above the 'Magees Ale' sign is the reverser frog and the head shunt crossing Manchester Road.

Photo, Author's collection.

Plate 270. Manchester Road. Manchester Road as it looked on 4th August 1998. Though further away in order to include the half timbered *Ye Old Three Crowns* pub and some remaining slate roofs to the left, the Farnworth and Kearsley Labour Club remains prominent. As is the case everywhere, the motor car has taken over. Strictly speaking this road carries two names, the boundary between Farnworth and Kearsley running down the centre of the road. The properties to the right of the picture stand on Manchester Road, Farnworth whilst those opposite are on Higher Market Street, Kearsley. Manchester Road is therefore correct when one refers to the route followed by the trolleybuses. The reverser however was entirely in Kearsley.

Photo, Author.

Plate 271. Manchester Road. This interesting early post war view sees the trolleywires following Manchester Road towards Brackley Street with the Farnworth and Kearsley Labour Club behind the photographer. The tarmac in the centre of the road was laid after closure of the last SLT maintained tram routes, operated by Bolton Corporation, from Walkden to Moses Gate and the *Black Horse* to Moses Gate on 12th November 1944. Note *Ye Old Three Crowns* pub on the Higher Market Street side of the road visible just past the Austin van with its single headlight. Directly across the road from the van stands the *Black Horse* with an open window on the extreme right serving as an off licence.

Photo, Author's collection.

Plate 272. Brackley Street, Nos.6 and 12. Trolleybus No.6, with No.12 behind, rest at the Brackley Street terminus in Farnworth some 14¼ route miles from Atherton. Whilst this route length was only exceeded by the 14½ mile route of the Nottinghamshire & Derbyshire Traction Company between Nottingham and Ripley (operated 1933 to 1953) and by London Transport's route 630 from Croydon to 'Near Willesden Junction', 14¾ miles, (1937 to 1960), the actual distance between Atherton and Farnworth was only 4¾ miles! Journey time was about 1hr.10 mins. at a 20 minute frequency, increasing to 15 minutes in the afternoons. For fare purposes the route was considered as two overlapping services, Atherton to Swinton and Worsley to Farnworth. Only the enthusiasts of the day boarded at Atherton to ride on an 'ancient', as the lowbridge Guys were nicknamed, all the way to Farnworth, risking funny looks from the conductor.   *Photo, Author's collection.*

On the way back to Atherton.

Plate 273. Brackley Street, No.19. As with most fleets certain vehicles seemed camera shy, true of SLT No.19 seen departing for Atherton from Farnworth's Brackley Street terminus on 17th September 1954. Today Brackley Street is no longer a thoroughfare, although Farnworth bus station remains in nearby King Street next to Littlewoods Store and a market. Trolleybus No.19 remained in unrebuilt condition retaining its bulbous front cab panel and the nearside extractor type ventilators that were originally fitted to the 11 to 30 batch delivered in 1931. It was withdrawn upon closure of the St. Helens route in November 1956.
Photo, Author's collection.

Plate 274. Albert Road, No. 32.
On a fine day in the Spring of 1958, trolleybus No.32 emerges from Brackley Street to turn left into Albert Road on the return trip to Atherton. This, the final side of the Farnworth circuit rectangle will take No.32 to the junction with Buckley Lane. Travellers today along Albert Road would be hard pressed to locate this position, Brackley Street having been truncated and the area redeveloped. Once in Albert Road No.32 will soon pass the location of the former SLT Farnworth tram depot, to the left, closed in 1906. All other depots, Atherton, Swinton and Platt Bridge survived to become trolleybus depots.

Photo, the late J.Batty.

Plate 275. Albert Road, No.11. With the traffic lights now showing green, trolleybus No.11 can draw forward out of Albert Road to turn right into Buckley Lane. The cigarette advertising is prolific even extending to the sun blinds at the shop windows, adding to the variety. Note the overhead wiring which was positioned very close to the kerb by the traffic lights, a legacy of the period from 1936 to 1944 when the SLT trolleybus wires

had to run parallel with Bolton Corporation's Walkden route tramway overhead in Albert Road before crossing it to rejoin the SLT trolleybus overhead in Buckley Lane .

Photo, the late J.Batty.

Plate 276. Albert Road, No.42. On 2nd April 1958 the only overhead wires in Albert Road are the SLT trolley wires completing the rectangular circuit around Farnworth. No.42 emerges from Albert Road to turn into Buckley Lane, its trolleyheads crossing the inbound wires leading into Longcauseway from which the rarely used west bound wires emerge to join the route to be followed by No.42.

Photo, P.J.Thompson
(Photosales)

Plate 277. Albert Road, No.38. A motorbike and sidecar wait for No.38 to cross into Buckley Lane as it makes its way back to Atherton. Beyond the trolleybus, on 20th June 1954, lies a deserted Worsley Road. The smoking concept, this time in the form of Condor tobacco, is advertised on No.38's offside panels. The trolleybus, with a double platform window, uniquely retained a staircase window until withdrawn. In about 70 minutes No.38 will be back in Atherton after having travelled along probably the most interesting and varied route of the South Lancashire Transport trolleybus system.

Photo, Author's collection.

Duty cards.

3.36 P.M. DUTY No. **260**

TAKE'S. CAR. 4. OVER. AT. 3.46. P.M.

Car 7

		x		Car 7				
ATHERTON	4.25	4.30		7.40	7.45	10.10	10.15	
TYLDESLEY	4.15	4.40		7.30	7.55	10.0	10.25	
MOSLEY. COMMON.	4.6	4.50		7.20	8.5	9.50	10.35	
BOOTHSTOWN.	4.2	4.53		7.17	8.8	9.47	10.38	
WORSLEY. C.H.	3.55	5.0	OFF	7.10	8.15	9.40	10.45	
SWINTON. DEPOT.	3.46 ON	6.16		7.1				
" CHURCH.	5.11	6.11			8.26	9.29	10.56	
" "	5.15	6.14			8.30	9.26	11.0	11.24 TO. GARAGE
WALKDEN.	5.27	5.59			8.42	9.14	11.12	11.12
CLEGG. LANE.	5.32	5.54			8.47	9.9		
FARNWORTH.	5.42	5.45			8.57	9.0		

X LOOK.OUT.FOR. T.T. FROM. LEIGH.

@ 11.0 P.M. WAIT. FOR. 20 BUS. To FARNWORTH. + No.11. To. RAKE. LANE. DUE. AT 10.59 P.M

5.0 A.M. DUTY No. **261**

TAKE'S CAR. 2 OUT. AT 5.10 A.M.

REQUIRE'S. 56 SEATER. BUS.

Car 5

			x		Car 5	x			
ATHERTON	5.55	6.0	8.25	8.30		11.40	11.45		X LOOK.OUT. FOR. T.T BUS. FROM. LEIGH.
TYLDESLEY	5.45	6.10	8.15	8.40		11.30	11.55		
MOSLEY. COMMON	5.35	6.20	8.5	8.50		11.20	12.5		
BOOTHSTOWN	5.32	6.23	8.2	8.53		11.17	12.8		
WORSLEY. C.H.	5.25	6.30	7.55	9.0		11.10	12.15	OFF	
SWINTON. DEPOT.			9.9 OFF		9.54 ON		1.31		
" CHURCH.	5.14	6.41	7.44		9.56	10.59	12.26	1.29	
" "		6.45	7.41		10.0	10.56	12.30	1.26	
WALKDEN		6.57	7.29		10.12	10.44	12.42	1.14	
CLEGG. LANE.		7.2	7.24		10.17	10.39	12.47	1.9	
FARNWORTH.		7.12	7.15		10.27	10.20	12.57	1.0	

ISSUE. WORK'S. RETURN'S. UP. TO. + INCLUDING. BACCA. SHOP.

@ LOOK.OUT FOR. BUS. FROM TRAFFORD. PARK.

TROLLEYBUS ABANDONMENT   1955 - 1958

The announcement in August 1955 to abandon the trolleybuses in favour of motor buses came as no real surprise. The electrical infrastructure including the feeder system inherited from the tramways and the overhead were due for renewal and whilst work had been continuing to replace 18" overhead spacing and former tramway bracket arm suspension, many stretches remained to be completed. The fleet, with only six 3-axle Sunbeams of post war manufacture, was old and in urgent need of renewal. Only one trolleybus, the Guy demonstrator No.47 had been withdrawn, whilst the entire lowbridge fleet of 1930 to 1933 remained in service, their lives having already been extended in many cases by a partial rebuilding programme.

Following nationalisation of the electrical supply industry in 1948, the Company, having originally generated its own electrical power as the Lancashire United Transport and Power Co. Ltd., had been forced to buy power from the British Electrical Authority, later the Central Electricity Generating Board. The Atherton depot power station continued to be operated by the Company on behalf of the C.E.G.B. but was latterly retained only as standby capacity.

Housing developments and changing public transport needs in the regions served by the trolleybuses demonstrated only too clearly that the SLT system, merely a legacy of tramway days, provided no basis upon which to develop an integrated transport provision for the area. Apart from the Leigh to Bolton service, the meandering, interurban routes with their infrequent services

could not generate the passenger volumes required to ensure anything like the financial returns required to support a significant investment in the trolleybus network. The 'Green Lobby' was decades away and, as long as the engine house of the industrial north west continued to pump out smoke and noise, would have gone unheard anyway.

Following replacement of the Company operated local services from Bolton to Hulton Lane and Four Lane Ends by municipal motor buses in March 1956, the intention had been to close the Leigh to Bolton route later that same year. The closure of the jointly operated St. Helens route would follow in conjunction with St. Helens Corporation's programme to replace its trolleybuses. Beyond that the plan was to retain the newer trolleybuses, the 6 wartime Karrier Ws, Nos 60 to 65 and the Sunbeam MS2s, Nos.66 to 71 which still had a useful life, and operate them from Swinton depot on a retained section of the Atherton to Farnworth route between Swinton and Farnworth until 1964/5.

In the event, a lengthy dispute developed involving Leigh Corporation who applied for a Road Service Licence to operate the Leigh to Bolton service, opposing the joint application that had been submitted by SLT and Bolton Corporation. An agreement, which included Leigh's participation in the provision of this service jointly with Lancashire United Transport, was eventually reached, thus permitting final arrangements to be made for closure of the remaining trolleybus routes.

The South Lancashire Transport act of 23rd July

Plate 278. Wiring at Hindley South Station.

The overhead on the St. Helens and Farnworth routes was originally constructed with 18" spacing. A combination of splicing ears, a mixture of fittings and both 18" and 24" spacing was to be seen in Liverpool Road near Hindley South Station, until the overhead wiring was dismantled in 1957. Elsewhere many stretches of 18" spacing remained along with former tramway bracket arm suspension.

Photo, the late J. Batty.

1958 provided for the abandonment of the trolleybus system and for the S.L.T. company to be dissolved on 31st October 1958, or on such earlier date at the discretion of the directors. The 31st. August was selected for final closure, including, by this time, the whole of the Farnworth route. An attempt, later to prove abortive, would be made to sell the newer vehicles for use elsewhere. A ceremonial run for civic dignitaries and invited guests would take place on 1st September from Atherton depot to Leigh using the newest Sunbeam trolleybus No.71 which was to be specially repainted for the occasion.

Trolleybus withdrawals of 1955.

Plate 279. Atherton motor bus depot, No.21. Following the closure announcement, plans to rebuild any further trolleybuses were abandoned. The repainting programme ceased and maintenance was reduced to the minimum compatible with safe operation. The emergence of trolleybus No.24 with a rebuilt front early in 1955 proved to be the last and rather than overhaul No.21, which had survived over the years with little modification, it was withdrawn in mid 1955 and stored in the motor bus depot where it is pictured. Later that year it was joined by No.26, the last Guy BTX to remain in the early post war livery. In November 1955, rebuilt No.25 was withdrawn following collision with a traction pole in Manchester Road, Tyldesley. These vehicles were not disposed of until the following year when they were sold, along with others which had become unserviceable, to a dealer in Farnworth.

Photo, Author's collection.

Replacement of trolleybuses on Bolton local services, 25th March 1956.

The acquisition by Bolton Corporation of four Leyland TTB trolleybuses in 1936 for service to Hulton Lane and Four Lane Ends heralded what was seen as the beginning of Bolton's association with the trolleybus in its pursuit of the abandonment of tram services. The four Leylands, maintained at Atherton depot and painted in SLT livery with SLT legal ownership lettering, turned out to be Bolton's first and last trolleybus purchases following the post war decision not to introduce trolleybuses to Dunscar and along Chorley Old Road together with Deane, Moses Gate and Walkden in spite of conversion having been sanctioned.

Bolton's local service trolleybuses to Hulton Lane and Four Lane Ends, operating in red SLT livery, last ran on 24th March 1956, being replaced the following day by diesel buses in the maroon livery

of Bolton Corporation. Whilst Leylands, numbered 48 to 51 in the SLT fleet, had been purchased by Bolton for these services, they shared the duties with the SLT owned Leylands, Nos.52 to 59. Whilst not unknown, it was uncommon to see other makes of trolleybus operating these services.

After 24th March 1956, trolleybuses continued to operate to Bolton on the SLT service from Leigh, the only overhead dismantled being the turning loop in Hulton Lane which was quickly removed. The reverser in Back Manchester Road, Four Lane Ends, in SLT territory, remained to be used for short workings and learner trips from Atherton.

The Bolton owned trolleybuses were despatched to Bolton's Bridgeman Street depot from where, following sale for scrap, they were eventually towed to Birds at Stratford upon Avon.

Plate 281. Hulton Lane. The partly dismantled turning circle this time viewed looking towards Hulton Lane. Enthusiasts of the day took some comfort that the turning circle was the only wiring removed and that it was still possible to travel to Bolton on a trolleybus on the service from Leigh.

Photo, the late J.Batty.

Plate 282. Birds, No.50. After spending some weeks in the yard of Bolton's Bridgeman Street depot, the four Bolton owned trolleybuses, Nos.48 to 51, were towed to Birds at Stratford upon Avon for scrap. Having reached the end of the road, No.50, standing alongside No.49, displays a destination on the St. Helens route along which it never operated. Had it not been for the rigours of book keeping, the prospect of the SLT retaining these four trolleybuses in place of some older lowbridge buses might have seemed an attractive proposition. Apart from Guy demonstrator No.47, which was withdrawn in 1951, these were the first trolleybuses to be disposed of, a number of withdrawn lowbridge trolleys remaining stored in Atherton motor bus depot.

Photo, Author's collection.

135

Plate 283. Howell Croft, Bolton, Crossley No.256. The motor buses provided by Bolton Corporation to replace the trolleybuses on the local services to Hulton Lane and Four Lane Ends were usually Crossley DD42/3s or Leyland PD2s of which Bolton operated large numbers. Craven bodied Crossley No.256 in spotless condition awaits departure from Howell Croft on service 17 to Four Lane Ends at 4.35 p.m. whilst trolleybus No.59, on a short working to Atherton, loads in the background under the gaze of Bolton's Town Hall clock. *Photo, Author's collection.*

Plate 284. Four Lane Ends, No.58. Trolleybus No.58 on service from Bolton to Leigh departs from the lay-by at Four Lane Ends leaving the driver of a Bolton Corporation Leyland PD2/4, parked under the trolleybus reverser in Back Manchester Road alongside the *Hulton Arms*, to discuss the relative merits of the Ford cars parked outside Hulton Service Station before departure back to Bolton with trolleybus replacement service 17. An LUT Massey bodied Guy Arab II leaves St. Helens Road to cross the A6 in the background on a Saturday short working to Atherton, by this time mostly motor bus operated, leaving the trolleys to operate the basic Leigh to Bolton service only. *Photo, Author's collection.*

The Omnibus Society Tour. June 1956.

Plate 285. Swinton Depot, No.1. On Sunday 24th June 1956, rebuilt trolleybus No.1 based at Platt Bridge was hired by the Omnibus Society for a tour of the whole of the SLT system together with those wires owned by St. Helens beyond Haydock on the Atherton to St. Helens route. The tour started at 12.30 p.m. in St. Helens and ran to Atherton, Leigh, Bolton and back to Atherton to join the Farnworth route. All the depots were visited and the tour ended at Farnworth at 5.30 p.m. Timings allowed for the trip were far too easy and Swinton depot, where No.1 is seen, was arrived at 17 minutes ahead of schedule. Apart from following the normal route wiring, No.1 would have had to use the wires leading from Wigan Road into Mealhouse Lane, Atherton, normally only used to transfer trolleybuses from Platt Bridge to Atherton depot. *Photo, J.Fozard.*

Disposal of the first lowbridge trolleys, summer 1956.

Plate 286. Cubbins Yard, No.8. By the summer of 1956, the number of lowbridge trolleybuses stored at Atherton had risen to 7, the long withdrawn Nos.21 and 26 having been joined by Nos.3, 8, 25, 36 and 38. The last two were due for overhaul whilst others were taken out of service having become defective, the repair costs being beyond the minimal budget allocated to holding the system together for a couple of years. Having been stripped of useful spares, the buses were sold for scrap, most going to Cubbins, a Farnworth dealer, in whose yard No.8 is seen mingling with withdrawn Manchester Corporation buses and trolleybuses along with SLT No.21 in the background. The author well remembers his surprise on seeing trolleybus No.8 in the final livery, and to which a new front had been fitted around 1950, being towed up New Brook Road, obviously on its last journey, having sacrificed its front cab panels, head lamps, half shafts and both trolley booms to keep others in the fleet running. This trolleybus carried various versions of the 'S.O.S' Swales Oatmeal Stout advertisement, the abbreviation bearing a particular poignancy in this scrap yard view. *Photo, Author's collection.*

Plate 287. Cubbins Yard, No.36. Guy BT trolleybus No.36 had been out of service for some three months when photographed in Cubbins Yard on 22nd July 1956. Partly visible to its right is the nearside of No.25 whilst another Guy BTX No.8 stands behind No.36 and the Manchester Corporation motor bus to its left. The abandonment announcement of August 1955 meant that rather than being overhauled, No.36 and No.38, also in the yard, were early withdrawals some seven months before the closure of the St. Helens route. They were the first Guy BTs to be taken out of service. No.36 still retains its trolleys and appears complete although a hole has been cut into the front panel for towing on its last journey.

Plate 288. Cubbins Yard, No.21. This offside view of No.21 which had survived in the early post war livery serves to emphasise the dated appearance of this first trolleybus to be withdrawn after the 1955 announcement. Noteworthy is the recessed rather than flush panelled former staircase window and the remains of the front cab panel which was of a somewhat different design immediately beneath the cab windscreen from other Guys where a flat replacement had been provided for the original bulbous variety. No.21 has sacrificed its trolleys, front mudguards and lights and, unlike No.3 visible immediately behind in the final livery, its axle half shafts.

Plate 289. Cubbins Yard, No.3. Apart from No.25, withdrawn prematurely after an accident in November 1955, the first trolleybus in the final livery to be withdrawn was No.3 in April 1956. By this time these unrebuilt trolleybuses had a decidedly outdated appearance about them and No.3 gives the impression that all its energies are spent even though it carries the final livery and a later four leg trolley gantry, unlike No.21 as in *plate 288.* The survival until final closure of the system over two years later of the next bus in the fleet, No.4, which was in similar condition to No.3, seems ironical, although in the final years the ingenuity of the depot staff was tested in keeping all serviceable trolleybuses on the road.

Photos, C.B.Golding.

The closure of the St. Helens route, 11th November 1956.

For many years, travel by electric public transport from Liverpool's Pier Head to the foothills of the Pennines had been made possible by a combination of tramway and trolleybus services. Liverpool Corporation trams on service 10 and 9A inward bound short workings, had run as far east as Prescot, terminating in St. Helens Road along which the St. Helens trolleybuses ran on the circular route via Rainhill. The first link in electric transport, to the west of the SLT network, was lost on 26th June 1949 when the Liverpool tram services were cut back by just over a mile to Long View Lane, the stretch of track beyond to Prescot being abandoned.

Another 14 miles of electric traction along this east - west route was to succumb towards the end of 1956. St. Helens Corporation had begun to implement a trolleybus replacement programme in 1952 and the withdrawal of trolleybuses on the No. 1 route to Atherton, jointly worked with SLT, would be undertaken in conjunction with abandonment by St. Helens of the local trolleybus service No.3 to Haydock.

The last trolleybuses ran between Atherton and St. Helens on Sunday 11th November being replaced the following day by a joint motor bus service on which Weymann bodied Daimler CVG5Ks delivered to the SLT in January 1956 shared duties with Leyland PD2s from St. Helens and the occasional RT type AEC Regent. St. Helens' newly delivered AEC Regent Vs also became regular performers on this route following their introduction during August 1957.

The St. Helens route closure meant the end of SLT trolleybus operation from Platt Bridge depot. The normal trolleybus allocation was 15, although 14 were there at the time of closure, Nos. 1,4,6,7,9,11,14,17 and 39 - 44. All were driven during the late evening of 11th November to Atherton. Rather than enter the depot upon arrival, their booms were lowered and they were towed, away from the overhead, onto land used as an employees' car park adjacent to the motor bus depot where they were lined up awaiting disposal. The exceptions were the completely rebuilt Nos.1 and 7 which would automatically see further service elsewhere on the system.

A warm welcome for the new Daimlers.

Plate 291. Daimler CVG5K. Whilst nostalgic reflection might suggest otherwise, the diesel buses were warmly welcomed as replacements for the long serving but ramshackle trolleybuses. Lancashire United acquired 24 Weymann Orion bodied Daimlers, Nos.570 to 593 during 1956, the initial 12 being allocated to Platt Bridge depot for use on the St. Helens route. These were amongst 55 motor buses purchased after the trolleybus abandonment announcement of 1955 which, for accountancy reasons, were the property of the wholly owned subsidiary SLT company. Whilst carrying the LUT fleet name, legal ownership was shown as the SLT. With the trolley wires still in place, Daimler No.574 passes through Platt Bridge on its way to St. Helens. These Daimlers with their Manchester style destination layouts and rear wheel discs bore an uncanny resemblance to MCTD's own Metro Cammell Orion Daimlers, CVG6Ks Nos.4480 - 4489 and CVG5Ks Nos.4490 - 4509. LUT No.574 would not have looked out of place alongside contemporaries from Manchester's Princess Road garage. *Photo, Author's collection.*

The following motor buses numbered in the LUT fleet and carrying the Lancashire United name were the property of the SLT.

Nos.542 - 551	WTB 41 - 50	1956 Guy Arab IV	Northern Counties H61R
552 - 561	WTB 61 - 70	1955 Atkinson Alpha	Roe DP40F
562 & 563	WTB 71 & 72	1956 Leyland PSUC1	Weymann B44F
570 - 593	YTD 871 - 894	1956 Daimler CVG5K	Weymann H61R
594 - 602	311-319 ATC	1957 Guy Arab IV	Northern Counties H64R

The Daimlers were the first LUT buses with Manchester style destination layouts.

The Suez crisis of 1957 and a stay of execution.

The abandonment of the St. Helens route trolleybuses coincided with the Suez crisis which, with petrol and fuel oil rationing, introduced the possibility of a resumption of trolleybus operations. For some eight months the overhead was left intact and none of the withdrawn trolleybuses disposed of. This stay of execution resulted in some of the stored trolleybuses being reinstated in place of others which had become unserviceable.

Plate 292. Atherton. As if waiting for the next trolleybus to arrive, the St. Helens route wiring in Wigan Road Atherton remained intact on 24th April 1957. However it was dead, the electrical feeder from the Bolton route wires on the right having been cut and tied back onto the span wire in an 'S' shape. Just visible in Lambeth Street under the reverser wiring, awaiting departure time, is a St. Helens Leyland PD2 operating the joint replacement No.1 service. Since November 11th 1956, the only wiring in use in Wigan Road had been that leading into Mealhouse Lane to the right, used by trolleybuses on the Bolton and Farnworth route services.
Photo, P.J.Thompson,
(Photosales)

A line up of withdrawn trolleybuses and a reprieve for a few.

Plate 293. Atherton depot. For those travelling past the SLT/LUT head offices and depots at Howe Bridge, the row of trolleybuses parked alongside the motor bus depot remained a familiar sight well into 1957 as the Suez crisis ran its course. Not apparent to all were the changed identities of some of the trolleybuses whenever those remaining in service that developed faults requiring more than minimal expenditure were replaced by others out of service but in better condition. The line up of withdrawn trolleybuses is seen from in front of the SLT/LUT head offices and trolleybus depot. With No.17 closest, the order of the line up was:- 17,46,42,39,41,14,5,6,40,34,9 and 43. By this time, three trolleybuses, Nos.4,11 and 44 had been recovered and replaced in the line up by 5,34 and 46. Sometime later Nos.42, 41 and 6 were replaced by 30, 15 and 22. It is interesting to note that of the trolleybuses transferred from Platt Bridge at the time of the St. Helens route closure, Nos.1,4, 6,7,11,42 and 44 survived until the final day of trolleybus operation in August 1958.
Photo, the late J.Batty.

Plate 294. Atherton depot. With the cooling tower of Atherton depot power station visible to the right and the Leigh bound trolley wires off to the left, the same group of trolleybuses as in the previous photograph is seen facing the motor bus depot. Note the mixture of liveries and the rebuilding of all visible rear platform windows irrespective of whether new fronts had been received.

Photo, the late J.Batty.

Overhead dismantling commences and trolleybuses sold.

Plate 295. Wigan Road dewiring. By the spring of 1957, the Suez crisis had been resolved removing any possibility of trolleybus operation being resumed on the St. Helens route. Dismantling of the overhead, begun in June, was completed by November and the trolleybuses finally sold. Lowton Metals were contracted to remove the wiring, tackling the straight runs and leaving the complicated layouts associated with reversers and junctions to the SLT overhead linesmen for removal at a later date. By 21st September, only one running wire remained on the Wigan Road bend towards Collier Brook bridge. *Photo, P.J.Thompson (Photosales)*

Plate 296. Atherton depot line up. With the overhead along the St. Helens route being dismantled, the days were now numbered for the redundant trolleybuses which, for some eight months, had become a familiar sight lined up outside the motor bus depot at Atherton. On a cloudless summer's day, the trolleybuses, with their fate sealed, wait to be towed away. The final line up pictured just prior to disposal comprised 15 as follows from the left Nos. 17, 46, 30, 39, 15, 14, 5, 22 ,40 ,34, 43 ,9 and three late additions Nos.31, 19 and 2. *Photo, the late J.Batty.*

South Lancashire Transport Company

TELEGRAMS
"TRAMWAYS, ATHERTON"
TELEPHONE: 36 (3 LINES)

GENERAL MANAGER
C. C. OAKHAM, B.Sc., M.I.R.T.E.

SECRETARY
J. W. MORLEY, F.I.A.C.

Howe Bridge,

Atherton, Lancs.

JRH/JJ.

23rd. August, 1957.

Mr. J. Batty,
  10, Crescent Avenue,
    Over Hulton,
      Nr. Bolton.

Dear Sir,

      Further to your letter of the 17th. ultimo regarding the purchasing of various items of overhead equipment. I should be pleased if you would call to see me some time during the next week, preferably between 10 a.m. and 5 p.m.

      Yours faithfully,

J.R. Hurst.

      John R. Hurst.
    Station Superintendent

Plate 297. Atherton Depot line up. With the wires of the Leigh to Atherton route in the distance, the withdrawn trolleybuses facing the motor bus depot display a variety of liveries and front profiles. By this time it had become impossible to reach St. Helens by trolleybus, the wires from Atherton having been removed beyond Ashton by June 1957. Fortunately some of the salvagable overhead fittings were saved for what is today the National Tramway Museum at Crich. Trolleybus No.2 stands nearest the camera; this, and No.19 standing alongside, retaining the original bulbous front cab panel, the last BTXs to do so. A few BTs remained in service with this feature. *Photo, the late J. Batty.*

143

Plate 298. Colbro's scrap yard. No.39. Those trolleybuses withdrawn following the closure of the St. Helens route were towed many miles from their native SLT system to the premises of Colbro, of Rothwell, a scrap dealer near Leeds. When photographed there alongside FR 6904, a former Blackpool tower wagon converted from 1925 Leyland C7 bus No.13 in 1933, No.39 had already had much of its external panelling removed from its Roe body revealing the teak framed structure beneath. Ruling scrap metal prices dictated the speed with which vehicles were dealt with. Non ferrous metal such as copper and aluminium was stripped from the vehicles and the steel chassis and running gear cut up whilst the worthless wood and leather upholstery was amassed into funeral pyres for burning ; a sad finale which should not be allowed to dull fond memories. *Photo, Author's collection.*

Plate 299. Wigan Road. Well into the Autumn of 1957, little appears to have changed in Wigan Road Atherton as Guy BT No.37, in the first post war livery, waits to depart for Farnworth on 2nd November. However all is not as it seems. It is almost one year since trolleybuses last ran to St. Helens and the wires in Wigan Road beyond the disused reverser have been removed. One of LUT's Daimler CVG5Ks is leaving Lambeth Street on service No.1 to St. Helens. Later that month the reverser overhead was dismantled leaving only the wires being used by No.37 leading into Mealhouse Lane. By this time No.37 was one of only two trolleybuses to remain in service in this livery, the other being another Guy BT No.45.

Photo, P.J.Thompson (Photosales).

More trolleybus withdrawals and an unexpected casualty.

Like the lull before the storm, a quiet period ensued between completion of overhead removal from the St. Helens route in November 1957 and final closure on 31st August 1958. The last year of operation dawned with 44 out of the original fleet total of 71 trolleybuses remaining available for service. Of the original batch of 10 lowbridge Guy BTXs of 1930, no less than 5 were still in service including totally rebuilt No.1 and fundamentally unrebuilt No.4.

By 1958 the effect of minimal maintenance was beginning to show. The SLT management no doubt wished the last months away with fingers crossed in the hope that the electrical infrastructure would see them through without major expense. Meanwhile the remaining trolleybuses were expected to struggle on until the end of August by which time new Leyland PD3s and Guy Arab IVs would have arrived in sufficient numbers to replace them. Nicotine stained upper decks and rear domes darkened by carbon deposits from trolley heads only served to emphasise shabby paintwork whilst in some cases smooth hums from motors and transmissions gave way to growls of protest.

There was nevertheless some cheer in these last months particularly when a trolleybus emerged from Atherton depot having been granted some expenditure such as new cab panelling and side mounted headlamps, rubber mounted windscreens or attention to rear platform panels and a lick of red paint. Unseen by the travelling public would have been the ongoing commitment and ingenuity shown by the SLT engineering staff in keeping the fleet operational within a limited budget.

It came as no surprise when some of the older trolleybuses succumbed to either electrical defects or other maladies resulting in their withdrawal some months before the end. By February 1958, Guy BTXs Nos.13 and 23 and BTs Nos.33 and 35 had carried their last passengers and were dumped alongside the motor bus depot awaiting disposal. Another Guy BTX No.29 was withdrawn the following month leaving 39 trolleybuses available for traffic. Basic services excluding 'extras' required 28 and there was increasing use of motor buses on certain services to supplement the available trolleybuses. The fleet was dealt another blow in April 1958 when Sunbeam No.67 collided with a traction pole near Howe Bridge, wrecking the nearside of the cab. Ironically this trolleybus had received repairs to the rear platform during 1957. Whilst the necessary repairs were doubtlessly within the scope of the SLT bodybuilders, expenditure was considered unjustified and No.67 was to spend its last months gathering dust, parked over a pit in Atherton depot.

Plate 300. Atherton depot.
A forlorn trio of withdrawn trolleybuses stands dumped alongside the motor bus depot in February 1958. Guy BT No.33 sustained the damage to its cab on 22nd January following collision with a lorry in Manchester Road Walkden. Alongside 33 stands BTX No.23 and another BT No.35. Useful items were recovered from these trolleybuses before disposal. The trolley booms were taken from No.35 and certain light units removed from all three. No.23 was later towed out and repositioned well to the right of 35 after which its half shafts were extracted to be stored as spares for other Guys still in service.
Photo, Roy Marshall.

145

Plate 301. No.67 .The collision of No.67 with a traction pole in April 1958 would have come as particularly bad news to the SLT Traffic Superintendent since the shortage of trolleybuses available for service was becoming acute forcing the use of motor buses onto some basic services particularly on the Farnworth route. Apart from being expected to see the system out, the 10 year old Sunbeams were to be put up for sale for use elsewhere after closure. Nobody had demonstrated better than the SLT that more than ten years service could be expected from a trolleybus. Repairs to No.67 were not to be carried out so late in the day. (Whilst the other Sunbeams and the Karrier Ws were stored for possible re-sale after closure, No.67 was sold with the other trolleybuses, and was towed to a scrap yard in Butley where it was photographed with its damaged cab on 20th September 1958 alongside No.28, some 3 weeks after closure of the SLT system.)

Photo, P.J.Thompson,
(Photosales).

Motor buses operating on trolleybus services at trolleybus fares!

Plate 302. (below) Five more Guy trolleybuses, Nos.12,20,37,41 and 45 were withdrawn a month or so before the end of trolleybus operation. Nos.37 and 45 had been the last to carry the first post war livery of red with a grey roof and two white bands. In addition to the occasional appearance of highbridge trolleybuses on the Farnworth route, the dwindling number of serviceable Guy trolleybuses, in the final months of operation, saw the increasing use of motor buses operating basic duties, even though rush hour extras continued to be trolleybus operated. All types of LUT double deckers were used including wartime Guy Arabs such as Weymann bodied Arab II, No.305 pictured in Worsley, Atherton bound, crossing into Worsley Brow from Worsley Road with the Court House off to the right. The motor buses showed 'TT', for Trackless Trolley, on their route number blinds. Public awareness that these buses were substituting for trolleybuses was further clarified by a poster affixed to the front nearside window proclaiming; "Operating on Trolleybus Service at Trolleybus Fares". *Photo, Author's collection.*

Plate 303. Whilst the poster in the nearside front window suggested the equivalent of a trolleybus service, passengers travelling on the wartime Guys would have been left in no doubt that they had boarded something other than a trolleybus such were the noise and vibrations emanating from the solid mounted, rough but rugged Gardner engines. The cacophony was augmented by orchestrations from constant mesh gearboxes, a quite pleasant accompaniment in the right hands! The reliability of these wartime Guys was to bear great influence on Lancashire United's post war fleet policy.
Photo, Author's collection.

The last day, Sunday, 31st August 1958.

Apart from posters displayed inside the buses, the last day of trolleybus operation was much as usual with little to suggest that the dissolution of the South Lancashire Transport Company was less than 24 hours away. Being a fine summer Sunday, some took the opportunity for a stroll in the sun and perhaps a last trolley ride home, whilst a small band of enthusiasts gathered to savour and record the last hours of trolleybus operation.

Those plucky enough to seek a glimpse inside Atherton depot would have seen a gleaming Sunbeam MS2 No.71, taken out of service some time before the end and repainted for ceremonial duties on 1st September. Elsewhere within the depot stood No.4, the only Guy still available for service to retain its original angular front. Those opting for a final ride from Leigh to Mosley Common and back might well have come across Guy BT No.42 which was operating on that service, the last in the fleet to retain grey roof livery. Much that contributed to the atmosphere and variety of the SLT was still there right up to the very end.

By 31st August, 34 trolleybuses remained in stock including eleven of the 1930/1 batch of Guy BTXs, Nos.1,4,6,7,10,11,16,18, 24,27 and 28, and three of the smaller BTs, Nos. 32,42 and 44.

Inevitably the time approached when final duties were being operated. Wreaths and suitable inscriptions chalked on front and rear panels adorned the last runners and whilst the general public did not appear en masse around the hour before midnight, the flash cameras of a few enthusiasts ensured that the events were recorded for posterity.

As midnight approached trolleybuses coming off service made for either Swinton or Atherton depots. The last in service was No.28 which ran into Swinton depot after completion of the 11.15 p.m. Farnworth to Swinton service. By the time it reached Swinton depot all other trolleybuses had completed their duties.

As the trolleybuses entered the depots the excise licences were removed to obtain refunds. Those returning to Swinton were immediately 'ferried' on trade plates to Atherton depot. The Swinton depot staff attached a poster to the cab panels of the last one, No.28, which read:- "The Last: To Atherton with the Compliments of Swinton". Whilst the newest trolleybus, Sunbeam No.71, would make a ceremonial trip the following day, No.28's run from Swinton to Atherton really marked the end of the SLT in both spirit and reality, the Company having been wound up at midnight shortly before No.28's final departure.

Plate 304. Worsley Court House, No.1. Passengers step down at Worsley Court House from trolleybus No.1 on service from Farnworth to Atherton whilst others seem happy to view proceedings from the nearby bench seat in the summer sun. The day is Sunday 31st August and there is little clue as to this being the final day of trolleybus operation. The driver, sporting his summer jacket, has his windscreen open on first notch, just sufficient to allow a cool air flow through No1's cab. It is fitting to include this photograph of the earliest trolleybus in the fleet in service on the last day, since by this time it had provided sterling service to the SLT for 28 years, albeit with a major rebuild. This bore testimony to the SLT's ingenuity in organising life extension programmes for the fleet, in some cases undertaking significant body rebuilding themselves, although No.1 was rebuilt by Bond.

Photo, E. Gray.

Plate 305. Spinning Jenny Street, No.70. A group of photographers intent on capturing the final hours of SLT trolleybus operation pause to chat in front of Sunbeam No.70 as it waits, facing the *Royal Oak* Inn, at Leigh's Spinning Jenny Street terminus, prior to its departure to Bolton. It would be another decade before motor buses such as Bolton's Leyland PD2 No 435 on service 16 to Horwich started to become a rarity.

Photo, Walter E. Amos.

Plate 306. Atherton depot, No.71. Walter Amos was fortunate enough to gain access to the trolleybus depot at Atherton during the final day. The reward for his visit was a glimpse of No.71, to which the final touches were being put in readiness for its role as the ceremonial last trolleybus the day following abandonment. Staff at Atherton depot had made a splendid job of No.71, which involved a complete repaint and significant attention to detail. Fitters admire the gleaming trolleybus standing in stark contrast to its rather forlorn sister No.67 alongside, which had remained in the depot, out of service following its collision in April. Note the typical Weymann outward flare to the bottom of No.71's rear platform panels, lost by No.67 following repairs after an earlier accident. The 'Esso for Extra' advertisement was somewhat strangely reinstated on No.71 following repainting and lettering for the sombre duty spelled out in its destination box. *Photo, Walter E. Amos.*

Plate 307. Outside Atherton depot, No.71. Many photographs exist of No.71 outside Atherton depot on 1st September waiting to depart with invited guests on 'The Last' journey. What makes this photograph so interesting is that it was taken the day before. The depot fitters were initially reluctant to let anybody near No.71 for fear of interference with the carefully prepared trolleybus. Eventually they mellowed to the well meaning enthusiasts, and finally acquiesced to requests to draw it out of the depot for an opportunity to photograph the painters handiwork, after which it was hastily but carefully reversed back in before too many people got to know about it! No.71, soon to become the first and last Lancashire United trolleybus, makes a splendid sight as it poses with a 'guard of honour' displaying legal lettering appropriate to its forthcoming star role under LUT ownership. *Photo, Walter E. Amos.*

149

Plate 308. Leigh Spinning Jenny Street, Nos.42 and 52. Later that evening, with just hours of service remaining, a valedictory view of trolleybuses at Spinning Jenny Street Leigh finds Guy No.42 bound for Mosley Common and Leyland No.52 destined for Bolton awaiting departure under a blaze of street lighting for final runs before returning to the depot for the last time. Come the dawn and motor buses would be in charge of all services. No.42 valiantly saw service out still sporting a grey roof. Neither trolleybus has many takers for a last ride, indeed the crowds that saw the trams off 25 years previously were absent to bid farewell to the trolleybuses.

Photo, J.C.Gillham.

Plate 309. Bolton, No.68. The last trolleybus to leave Bolton was No.68 which departed for Atherton at 10.58 p.m. Amongst this group of passengers having a final ride on a trolleybus are at least two who ensured some photographic record of the SLT remained. Seated on the extreme left of the picture is Walter Amos who was photographing during this final day of SLT operation. SLT Chief Inspector, Mr.T.Boothroyd, with more than 50 years service sits alongside, presiding over the final trolleybus duties. Behind the left shoulder of the conductor stands Jack Batty who had been active recording the SLT on both colour transparencies and cine film just prior to the St. Helens route closure and whilst Bolton local services to Hulton Lane were still trolleybus operated.

Photo, Bolton Evening News.

150

Plate 310. Atherton Punch Bowl. No.11. SLT crews and the odd bystander gather in front of No.11 outside the SLT offices at Atherton Punch Bowl at 11.40 p.m. after the trolleybus had completed the last run from Farnworth. Third from the left in the group is off-duty inspector F. Wilson whose father had driven the last tram from Four Lane Ends 25 years previously. After pausing for this photograph, No.11 ran down Leigh Road to Atherton depot for the last time. Just prior to No.11's arrival, No.69, the last trolleybus from Four Lane Ends appeared with a wreath

draped across the front carrying the message;- "After much suffering patiently borne". Before that No.68 had arrived from Bolton whilst Nos.44 and 53 were the last to turn back to Atherton from Mosley Common and Tyldesley respectively. Whilst No.11 had been the last to run to Atherton on service, the last workings of all were to Swinton depot. The final Atherton to Farnworth duty, terminating at Swinton on the return, was operated by No.28, timed to depart Farnworth at 11.15 p.m. and to arrive at Swinton at 11.41 p.m., exactly the same time as the last Atherton to Swinton service on which No.16 was running. No.16 had left Atherton at 11.00 p.m. bearing the chalk inscription ;- 'Roll up for your last chance' on the front panels and in typical SLT and Lancashire humour;- 'Too late you've missed it' on the rear ! In the event, No.16 arrived at Swinton just ahead of No.28 ensuring that the latter was the last SLT trolleybus in public service. The period around midnight saw all Swinton's trolleybuses pass through Atherton on trade plates as they made their final journeys to Howe Bridge depot. Trolleybus 28, bearing trade plate No. 0310 B and the poster reading 'The last; to Atherton with the compliments of Swinton', departed Swinton shortly after midnight arriving at Atherton at 12.40 a.m. on 1st September thus closing an unequalled chapter in the history of public transport service in this country.

Photo, The late R. Boardman.

Lancashire United's first and last trolleybus, 1st September 1958.

The final run of SLT trolleybus No.28 in public service on 31st August 1958 had brought to an end not only the South Lancashire Transport Company and its trolleybus system dating from 1930 but also a whole era of electric traction spawned by the South Lancashire Tramways Act of 1900. The trolleybuses had been the electrical heritage of General Manager Mr E.H. Edwardes who had been with the SLT since 1902 and had managed the undertaking from 1911 until his retirement in March 1955 at the age of 81, in all probability a unique reign in public transport. The repainting of Sunbeam trolleybus No.71 complete with lettering to commemorate the SLT's 58 year period was a fitting tribute to both Mr. Edwardes and to the passing of a mode of transport which, in 1958, was not regretted perhaps as much as it later came to be in this age of pollution and congestion. The renaissance of electric public transport in the guise of modern tramway or light rail systems is adequate evidence that what was a good idea at the beginning of the twentieth century could, in modern form, provide sensible solutions to the

challenges of public transportation into the next century. However, in 1958, the powerful oil lobby ruled the day and by the end of December 1966, even the more modern Manchester and Ashton trolleybus systems had run for the last time, bringing to an end electric road traction in Lancashire apart from the Blackpool trams. Trolleybus No.71 did the honours for the SLT in fine style on Monday 1st September 1958.

After cocktails served in the offices and the presentation of souvenir booklets and tickets, invited guests boarded No.71 for the journey to Leigh, departing Atherton depot around mid-day. The trolleybus was accompanied by a new Northern Counties bodied Guy Arab IV No.639, delivered the previous Thursday. Upon arrival at Leigh Spinning Jenny Street, the guests transferred to the Guy which whisked them away to a luncheon in Wigan. No.71 returned to Atherton depot, loaded to the limit with passengers who took the opportunity for one last trolleybus ride. After a brief pause for photographs at the depot entrance No.71 was driven inside to be parked up for the last time.

Plate 311. Atherton depot, No.71. Sunbeam No.71, specially repainted for the occasion, makes a fine sight in Atherton depot yard on 1st September 1958. Officials at the rear of the trolleybus discuss arrangements and check watches prior to departure just before noon for the final trip to Leigh with civic dignitaries aboard together with others of local prominence. The invited guests included representatives of the transport industry and of local authorities through whose areas the trams and trolleybuses had run for over half a century.

Photo, Jim Saunders.

SOUVENIR

Last S. L. T. Journey
Monday, 1st September, 1958
DEPARTED ATHERTON AT 12-0 Noon

TICKET

The souvenir card ticket issued on 1st September 1958, reverse side. For obverse side see front inside leaf of jacket.

Ticket, courtesy Brian Hughes.

Plate 312. Atherton depot, No.71 and driver. The melancholy but honourable responsibility for the safe handling of No.71 with its distinguished passengers on this last trolleybus duty fell to driver Mr. Len Hasler of Atherton and his conductor Mr. Jack Henry of Swinton. Mr. Hasler stands alongside No.71 in Atherton depot yard just prior to departure, both trolleybus and driver smartly turned out in the best traditions of the SLT. *Photo, The late R. Boardman.*

Plate 313. Leigh, Spinning Jenny Street, No. 71. The attention of two small boys standing alongside the bus shelter at the Leigh Spinning Jenny Street terminus is caught by the arrival of No.71 which is using the Mosley Common route wiring through the terminus. One wonders whether they later recalled the significance of this 'The Last' trolleybus. Were they lucky enough to be able to board for one last ride to Atherton depot? Many children were amongst No.71's passengers on the return to the depot, in some cases the older ones travelling alone being given the bus fare for the return motor bus to Leigh. No.71 departed from Spinning Jenny Street fully loaded with 15 passengers standing on the lower deck and the stairs fully occupied. Without doubt the rule forbidding upper deck standees was waived for this one last trip. The route back to Atherton was lined with those wishing to bid farewell as No.71 passed quietly along in a silent and dignified manner that could never be emulated by the replacing motor buses.

Photo, Wigan Heritage Services.

Plate 314. Atherton depot , No. 71. Fitters and garage staff gather around driver Len Hasler and conductor Jack Henry following No.71's return to Atherton depot. Perhaps it is a chance for them to browse through the souvenir booklet and ponder the passing of the SLT which had been both their livelihood and their way of life for many years. In the murk of the depot stand the withdrawn trolleybuses, Leyland No.54 visible in front of Karrier W No.63. Soon, all that will be left will be for No.71 to make its final entrance into the depot to join them.

Photo, The late R.Boardman.

Plate 315. Atherton Savoy, Guy No.467. Just days after final closure of the trolleybus system Northern Counties bodied Guy Arab IV No.467 of 1952, operating on the Atherton to Farnworth via Swinton replacement trolleybus service No.83 turns right from Atherton's Market Street to the loading point in Wigan Road. The trolley wires still remain and everything appears unchanged. Judging by the apparel, the days are still warm even though the lady standing beneath the canopy of the Savoy cinema has her raincoat on just in case the recent showers return, unlike the trolleybuses which never will. Leyland PD3s, along with new 30ft.long Guy Arabs were ultimately to dominate the replacement services, but, until they had all been delivered, the new buses were were supplemented by older stock, some of which was of older vintage than this relatively modern 27ft 6ins long Guy which was not all that far removed from the brand new vehicles as far as the travelling public were concerned.

Photo, Author's collection.

Plate 316. Mealhouse Lane, No.332. Lancashire United possessed quite a varied motor bus fleet at the time of trolleybus abandonment including wartime and early post war stock together with some survivors from pre war days. Deliveries of successive batches of Guy Arabs (until 1968 when they were no longer available) were eventually to oust the older stock such as No.332, an all Leyland PD1 of 1946 which lasted until 1963. On 13th September 1958 it was employed on the Leigh to Mosley Common trolleybus replacement service 84. The bus still appeared well cared for and up to the job as it turned into Mealhouse Lane Atherton having left the Wigan Road loading point. In the background a St. Helens AEC Regent V waits in Lambeth Street on another trolleybus replacement service, this time the jointly operated route 1 to St. Helens. Whilst, at this time, the overhead remained intact in Mealhouse Lane, the splicing ears visible next to the bracket arm twin line hanger bear witness to the removal of the junction wiring from the St. Helens route some 10 months earlier.

Photo, P.J.Thompson, (Photosales).

Plate 317. Wigan Road, No.448.
Whilst the two previous photographs showed motor bus replacements on services 83 to Swinton and 84 to Mosley Common, the other arterial route replacment was the 82 Leigh to Bolton service. This time the variety is provided by No.448, one of LUT's fleet of 5 Foden PVD6Gs of 1951, bodied by Northern Counties in similar fashion to the Guy Arabs. Standing behind the Foden on service 84 is No.657, the last of 14 newly delivered Leyland PD3s carrying the highest LUT fleet number, subsequent deliveries commencing a new numbering sequence. Note the different destination layouts, the Manchester style carried by the PD3 having been introduced with the Daimlers which had replaced the St. Helens route trolleys in 1956.

Photo, Author's collection.

Plate 318. Atherton Savoy, No.324. Leyland PD1 No.324 of 1946 standing outside the LUT Atherton booking office next to the Savoy cinema, on service 84 to Leigh provides a visual reminder of some of the trolleybuses it replaced, the outward flares to its lower panels, the deep sliding windows and front window louvres of its Weymann body being shared by the Sunbeam MS2s delivered two years later in 1948. This batch of 4 buses survived the trolleybuses by some 5 years. The route numbers had initially been used on 14th July 1957 when the rebuilding of the railway bridge at Howe Bridge resulted in the temporary replacement of the entire Leigh to Bolton service and the Leigh to Atherton section of the Mosley Common service by motor bus services numbered 82 and 84 respectively.

Photo, Author's collection.

Plate 319. Atherton, Wigan Road, Guys 605 and 636. The true inheritors of the last SLT trolleybus routes were the 73 seat 30 ft Guy Arab IVs and Leyland PD3s which eventually assumed total command of these services, (in conjunction with Leigh Corporation Dennis Lolines on service 82 to Bolton), once they had arrived in sufficient numbers. The Guy Arabs were splendid machines and became a benchmark of reliabilty with their rugged and reliable Gardner engines and solid but elegant Northern Counties bodies. No.605 from the first 30ft. batch of 16 delivered in 1958 awaits departure on service 83 to Farnworth via Swinton whilst No.636 of a later batch of 14 delivered later the same year waits behind on service 84 to Mosley Common. The forerunner of these 30ft Guys and many others that followed was No.603, exhibited at the Commercial Motor Show in 1956. It is heartening to know that one or two of these Guys survive today in the hands of responsible preservationists, having found a place in transport museums where they can be maintained in working order and appreciated. *Photo, Author's collection.*

Plate 320. Bolton, Howell Croft, Leyland PD3 No.646. LUT took delivery during 1958 of 14 Metro Cammell bodied Leyland PD3s which were quite distinctive in a fleet which was becoming dominated by Northern Counties bodywork. The brief departure from the Guy chassis to the Leyland PD3, (a 30 ft version of the ultra reliable Leyland PD2) marked the return of the exposed radiator and black front mudguards in place of the Birmingham style new look front worn by all LUT Guys delivered since 1951 and the St. Helens route Daimlers of 1956 . If their somewhat 'Manchester' appearance, length apart, was not distinctive enough, these buses possessed, when delivered, exhaust systems that created audible effects akin to 'ripping linoleum', most impressive when pulling away with anything like a load on! They turned out to be the only PD3s purchased by LUT. No.646 pictured at Howell Croft, Bolton, displays the undeniably handsome good looks of a batch of double deckers that provided reliability and touch of variety to the LUT fleet.
Photo, Author's collection.

Plate 321. Bolton, Howell Croft. Leigh Dennis Loline. The agreement following the application by Leigh Corporation for a Road Service Licence to operate the Leigh to Bolton trolleybus replacement service in opposition to the joint application by LUT and Bolton resulted in Leigh's provision of a vehicle for this service. Bolton, who did not operate on the route save for a couple of school children's journeys, shared a proportion of LUT's revenue. Leigh purchased four 72 seat East Lancashire bodied Dennis Loline Mk1 buses from which to operate one duty on this route. Being of low height and in the blue livery of Leigh Corporation they were quite distinctive. With the trolleybus overhead still intact, Leigh No.60 is seen leaving Bolton Howell Croft with a light load for the return journey to its home town. Behind the Dennis Loline is another lowbridge Dennis, this time an LUT Weymann bodied Lance operating a short working, yet another example of Lancashire United's varied early post war fleet.

Photo, Author's collection.

The trolleybus overhead.

Plate 322. Atherton. On 13th September, twelve days after No.71 had made its ceremonial last run, the wires at the junction of Wigan Road and Market Street Atherton are still intact. Furthermore they are still energised! Power continued to be fed into the wiring between Leigh and Atherton for several weeks until the lighting in the waiting rooms and offices at Atherton *Punch Bowl* and Leigh Spinning Jenny Street could be converted from the 600 volt DC traction supply to the public electricity supply! The feeder to the Atherton offices can be seen routed along the second span wire. For many years, the SLT had been responsible for the provision of street lighting along their routes resulting in these roads being plunged into darkness when the traction supply was switched off at night! Lighting, often gas, provided in side roads by local authorities meanwhile remained on!

Photo, P.J.Thompson, (Photosales).

Plate 323. Bacca shop. By the end of September work was well under way to dismantle the trolleybus overhead. Lowton Metals who had removed the St. Helens route wiring were once again awarded the contract. By the 28th of the month, the Bolton route wiring past the Bacca Shop at Atherton had been reduced to just one running wire whilst only the traction pole and its bracket arm remain at the start of the Farnworth route in Bolton Old Road. Fortunately some of the overhead fittings were again salvaged for use at the Crich Tramway Museum.

Plate 324. Mealhouse Lane. By 28th September the wiring in Mealhouse Lane, Atherton had been removed, although the street lanterns ensured that these redundant traction poles would survive a little longer as lighting columns. The bracket arms, however, would disappear before long. An eerie sensation existed without the trolleybus wires and it took a while to get used to their absence. There did seem to be more light at junctions without the relatively heavy overhead fittings of the sort used by the SLT. In the distance an LUT Daimler CVG5K rests in Lambeth Street before returning on service No.1 to St. Helens. An eagle eye will see that some of the wiring leading into Mealhouse Lane from Wigan Road still dangles overhead.

Plate 325. Atherleigh. The work to dismantle the overhead had yet to reach Atherleigh on 28th September. This view of the road works at Atherleigh bend looking towards Atherton on that date shows the position of the disused trolleybus overhead relative to the revised road alignment which, during the last weeks of operation, has made the passage of trolleybuses decidedly difficult. Bolton Corporation Leyland PD2 No.435 bound for Leigh on service 16 from Horwich sweeps unimpeded around the bend followed in the distance by an LUT Guy. During the last few weeks of operation, trolleybuses had had to pass at dead slow speed, those Leigh bound having to negotiate their way in the centre of the road against the oncoming traffic. Note the lack of 'cordoning off' of the road works and the minimalistic warnings just beyond the car.

Photos, P.J.Thompson (Photosales)

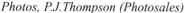

Disposal of the trolleybuses.

By the time No.71 was making its final ceremonial run, all the pre-war trolleybuses together with the collision damaged Sunbeam No. 67 had already been sold to a scrap merchant in Butley near Macclesfield Cheshire. The Karrier W trolleybuses, Nos.60 to 65 and Sunbeams 66 and 68 to 71, were retained in the hope of selling them to another undertaking. Sadly, there were no takers and, at the end of the year, these trolleybuses were finally sold to the same dealer. At the time, other systems such as Huddersfield and Bournemouth were still operating Sunbeam MS2s whilst Bradford, destined to be the last British trolleybus operator, had become a refuge for redundant trolleybuses from other systems. Eight BUT 9611T trolleybuses had been acquired by Bradford from St. Helens following closure of that system on 30th June 1958 and many other second hand acquisitions had been rejuvenated by rebodying to see years of further service. Perhaps in the case of the SLT it was just too late in the day. Had things been different, a few years extra service with another operator, especially for the Sunbeams, which were far from life expired, might have eventually seen one of these fine vehicles secured by the preservation movement for restoration into SLT livery and future safe keeping. However, it was not to be, although Lancashire's association with the trolleybus is remembered by way of a preserved St. Helens BUT 9611T that survived another thirteen years with Bradford and examples of BUT 9612Ts from Manchester and Ashton together with Crossley Empire and Dominion 2 and 3 axle trolleybuses from Ashton and Manchester respectively.

Plate 326. Butley, Cheshire, Nos.53,44,7 & 1. Less than one month after closure of the system, these pre-war SLT trolleybuses were photographed on 20th September 1958, having made their final journeys to J.C.Broadhead's scrap yard near Butley Cheshire. Visible from left to right are Leyland No.53, Guy BT No.44 and the rebuilt BTXs Nos.7 and 1. They were joined just over three months later by the Karrier and Sunbeam trolleybuses. The destination blinds had been specially set with No.53's showing Hulton Lane, a service which had run for the last time some two and a half years earlier, whilst Haydock, on the St. Helens route, had not seen a trolleybus for almost two years. St. Helens Corporation bye-laws had required all trolleybuses operating into the borough to be licensed as Hackney carriages, SLT trolleybuses Nos.1 to 18 and 39 to 46, which were at various times allocated to the route, carrying St. Helens licence lettering on the rear platform panel. No.1's , still visible, denotes its St. Helens licence number as 115 whilst No.7's, formerly licence No.121, has been over painted. No.44 carried licence No.114.

Photo, P.J.Thompson (Photosales).

Plate 327. Brinksway, Stockport, No.6. Whilst most of the SLT trolleybuses towed to Butley were broken up there, a few later appeared in other scrap yards. On 1st November 1959, some 13 months after it first arrived at Butley, one of the original batch of ten Guy BTXs, No.6, was to be found in a yard at Brinksway, Stockport, in use as a store. The remnants of a 'Players Weights Cigarettes' advertisement are just discernible and the trolleybus appears to be intact. Though not visible, the front destination blind was still in situ with 'Swinton' displayed. Booms up and we could be on our way, Farnworth bound! Alas, not the case. Visible beyond No.6 through the frame of a shattered cab door window is the roof of another trolleybus, Karrier No.61 which was in the process of being stripped of panelling. The cab door in the foreground belongs to Sunbeam No.67 which, having suffered two collisions in service, was finally to fall victim to a fire in the yard at Brinksway reducing this once elegant trolleybus to a twisted skeleton.

Photo, P.J.Thompson (Photosales).

Plate 328. Macclesfield, Moss Lane, No.71. Some three years after the closure of the SLT system, one trolleybus, No.71 still survived, having been moved from Butley to a breaker's yard in Moss Lane Macclesfield for use as a store. Those who had turned out on 1st September 1958 to bid farewell to the SLT and witness No.71's valedictory journey would have been saddened to learn of its plight, languishing in this scrap yard on 24th September 1961. The commemorative lettering and the 'Esso for Extra' advertisement still remain though it has lost its trolley heads and rear destination blind. Interestingly, it rests between two former SLT service vehicles; tower wagon BTF 882, a rare torque converter fitted Leyland Badger TSA 5 model and Commer Service Van FTE 703. At this late hour the rescue and restoration of these vehicles would have provided a fitting memento to the SLT. However the full swing of the preservation movement was a few years away and the service vehicles were broken up shortly after whilst No.71 continued to fulfil its role as a store until 1963.

Photo, P.J.Thompson (Photoslaes)

160

COLOUR OF THE SLT, THE WAY THINGS WERE IN 1956, A TRIBUTE TO THE LATE JACK BATTY

Plate 329. A rare visit to Bolton by lowbridge Guy No.15 on a short working to Atherton. The trolleybus, its paintwork gleaming, stands under the gaze of the town hall clock alongside an equally smart Bolton Corporation Leyland PD2/4 in Howell Croft bus station.

Plate 330. Leyland trolleybus No.53 waits on the setts in Ashburner Street, Bolton, alongside the junior library for the last passengers to clear the platform before moving empty into Howell Croft bus station prior to loading for the return to Leigh.

Plate 331. A forward facing interior view of the lower saloon of Leyland trolleybus No.59. Note the rearward facing front bulkhead seat for five persons. Wood and moquette featured extensively in the interior trim of these Roe bodied vehicles which were also of teak framed construction.

Plate 332. The turning circle at Hulton Lane is host to Leyland trolleybuses Nos.54 and 56, operating the Bolton local services in the last week before replacement by Bolton Corporation motor buses, after which the turning circle wiring was quickly removed and the four Bolton owned trolleybuses, Nos.48-51, withdrawn. The remaining Leylands, Nos.52-59 remained in service until final closure of the system.

Plate 333. The shapely Weymann bodywork of the Sunbeam MS2s, with the characteristic outward flare to the lower panels, is shown to good effect by No.69 standing just within the Bolton boundary in St. Helens Road, Four Lane Ends, operating on the Leigh to Bolton service.

Plate 334. Leyland trolleybus No.51 stands at Four Lane Ends awaiting departure to Leigh. Having crossed from Bolton Corporation to SLT wires the conductor will change ticket machines prior to working through the vehicle afresh issuing new tickets for the onward journey. Whilst No.51, in SLT livery, was the property of Bolton Corporation, it was not confined to the Bolton local services. It was however, withdrawn upon their replacement by motor buses.

Plate 335. (right) No.57, operating the Bolton to Four Lane Ends service, stands under the reverser in Back Manchester Road on the right hand side in order to make an easier left hand exit onto New Brook Road. Note the lighting provided by the SLT in the form of a lamp suspended by, and powered from the overhead to the rear of No.57's trolley heads.

Plate 336. (below) Leyland No.55 stands at Four Lane Ends in immaculate condition. The trolleybus positively gleams and carries new power cables to its trolley gantry plus a smart set of black mudguards. It is believed that No.55, an early repaint into the final livery with small fleet numerals was one of just a few trolleybuses to receive a subsequent repaint in this livery together with larger Gill Sans fleet numbers just prior to final overhauls in 1955.

Plate 337. A rare view of a Guy BT on the Leigh to Bolton route. Originally intended for the Bolton service, these small capacity trolleybuses were soon displaced to appear only occasionally on extras such as short workings to Atherton on Saturdays. No.45, standing at Four Lane Ends with Sunbeam No.67, still looks smart in the first post war livery with large shaded numerals and was the last trolleybus to remain in service with this paint scheme.

Plate 338. Karrier W No.61 rests in the sun at Four Lane Ends on a service to Leigh. The trolleybus still retains its panel mounted headlamps although the side lamps have already been replaced by the SLT bracket mounted variety on the panel corners.

Plate 339. Turning into the gloom of Mealhouse Lane, Atherton, from Wigan Road is Guy BT No.44, rebuilt with a new front and deepened lower panelling. This trolleybus was unique and thus immediately identifiable with the all over red livery and large shaded fleet numbers. The Lambeth Street reverser used by trolleybuses on the St. Helens route is visible behind No.44 which is about to pass the junction wiring that provided a connection between the St. Helens route and the rest of the system.

Plate 340. Karrier W No.64 on the Leigh to Bolton service stands alongside the SLT booking office by the Atherton Savoy Picture House awaiting departure to Leigh. Apart from the replacement of the upper deck offside drop window with a sliding vent and the fitting of bracket mounted sidelights, the trolleybus was much as delivered. It was the only SLT trolleybus to carry the Dulux advertisement.

Plate 341. (right) Guy BT No.41, with a rebuilt front showing destination Swinton, stands in a damp Wigan Road, Atherton, at the Farnworth route loading point with no apparent rush to board. Whilst No.41 was licensed to operate on the St. Helens route, (as were Nos.1-18 and 39-46) those surplus to service requirements were employed on the rest of the system operating either from Swinton or Howe Bridge depot, Atherton.

Plate 342. (below) With its blind already changed for return to St. Helens, an immaculate trolleybus No.9 prepares to reverse into Lambeth Street, Atherton, on 27th February 1956. In this evocative scene, the absence of garish road markings, the polished black car, the corner shop with the Wills Capstan cigarette advertisement above the canopy and a venerable red trolleybus on an otherwise empty road combine to capture the essence of the 1950s, now but a bygone age.

165

Plate 343. Trolleybus No.4 is about to reverse from Wigan Road into Lambeth Street. This trolleybus survived until final closure as the only remaining Guy in unrebuilt condition, its antique appearance making it quite an eye catcher. Note the shallow side panels and the angular front profile as well as the unusual overhead wiring layout.

Plate 344. The jointly operated St. Helens route provided an extra splash of colour with the red and cream livery of the St. Helens Corporation trolleybuses. SLT Guy No.14 is followed over the railway bridge at Hindley South station towards Atherton by St. Helens Sunbeam No.306. The St. Helens trolleybus displays route number 1, unlike those of the SLT which showed destinations only.

Plate 345. We will never know if this man's rush to cross in front of trolleybus No.34 at Atherton was to board another trolleybus in Wigan Road. At 2.20 p.m. by the clock in the SLT booking office he was probably too late for a pint in either the *Letters Inn* or the *Punch Bowl.* Whilst he has the attention of the lady seated in No.34's lower saloon, the driver is preoccupied with activity around the rear platform as seen in his nearside mirror prior to departing to Leigh on the service from Mosley Common.

Plate 346. Sunbeam MS2 No.71 stands outside Atherton depot whilst visible just inside the far door is Guy No.43, still in the early post war livery and normally allocated to Platt Bridge to work the St. Helens route.

Trolleybuses entered the depot using the furthest set of wires, these running onto the turntable at the far end of the depot.

Plate 347. No.24, the last trolleybus to be rebuilt with a new front in 1955, stands in Partington Lane, Swinton, on the Atherton service from Farnworth and has a Salford City Transport Metro Cammell bodied Daimler CVG6 as distant company. The spacious grassed area between the buses lay in front of Swinton Town Hall, off to the right of the picture.

Plate 348. Trolleybus No.1, the pioneer of the fleet, stands in Brackley Street, Farnworth, before returning to Atherton via Swinton, a little over 14 miles. Whilst the modern appearance of No.1 bestowed upon it during a thorough rebuild in 1953 belies its age, the two letter registration, TF 2072, suggests otherwise.

Plate 349. Karrier W No.60, on the way to Leigh, has just passed under the railway bridge at Howe Bridge, the station being visible beyond the telegraph pole behind the trolleybus. All the panel mounted front lights have been replaced by the standard SLT bracket mounted variety.

Plate 350. Leigh's Spinning Jenny Street terminus is host to Sunbeam No.69 in the final single cream band livery operating on the Bolton service and Guy No.23, retaining the earlier grey roof livery, awaiting departure to Mosley Common. One could smell the atmosphere generated by the relentless output from factory chimneys such as that behind No.69.

Plate 351. Two late repaints into the final red livery, Leyland No.53 on the Bolton service and lowbridge Guy No.33 on the service to Mosley Common, stand together at Spinning Jenny Street alongside a Bolton Corporation Leyland PD2/4 on service 16 to Horwich.

TROLLEYBUS FLEET HISTORY

Trolleybus fleet list.

GUY BTX 3 Axle Trolleybus

Fleet No.	Registration	St. Helens Licence No.	Chassis No.	Into Service	Withdrawn	Notes
1	TF 2072	115	23532	7/30	8/58	R
2	TF 2073	116	23531	8/30	11/56	
3	TF 2074	117	23557	8/30	4/56	
4	TF 2075	118	23555	8/30	8/58	
5	TF 2076	119	23553	8/30	11/56	F1
6	TF 2077	120	23554	8/30	8/58	F2
7	TF 2078	121	23534	8/30	8/58	R
8	TF 2079	122	23556	8/30	8/56*	F1
9	TF 2080	123	23533	8/30	11/56	
10	TF 2081	124	23547	8/30	8/58	F1,A
11	TF 5792	1	23704	8/31	8/58	F1
12	TF 5793	2	23705	8/31	6/58*	F2
13	TF 5240	125	23712	7/31	2/58	
14	TF 5794	3	23713	8/31	11/56	F1
15	TF 5795	4	23719	8.31	11/56	
16	TF 5796	5	23720	8/31	8/58	F1
17	TF 5241	126	23722	7/31	11/56	F1,B
18	TF 5797	6	23723	8/31	8/58	F1
19	TF 5798	-	23714	8/31	11/56	
20	TF 5799	-	23699	8/31	6/58*	F1
21	TF 5800	-	23725	8/31	8/55*	
22	TF 5801	-	23736	8/31	11/56	F1
23	TF 5802	-	23744	8/31	2/58	F1
24	TF 5803	-	23738	8/31	8/58	F2
25	TF 5804	-	23739	8/31	11/55	F1
26	TF 5805	-	23740	8/31	10/55*	
27	TF 5806	-	23741	8/31	8/58	F2
28	TF 5807	-	23742	8/31	8/58	F2
29	TF 5808	-	23743	8/31	3/58*	F1
30	TF 6951	-	23737	11/31*	11/56	F1

GUY BT 2 Axle Trolleybus

Fleet No.	Registration	St. Helens Licence No.	Chassis No.	Into Service	Withdrawn	Notes
31	TJ 3320	-	23932	12/33	11/56	F2
32	TJ 3321	-	23933	12/33	8/58	F2
33	TJ 3322	-	23934	12/33	2/58	
34	TJ 3323	-	23935	12/33	11/56	
35	TJ 3324	-	23936	12/33	2/58	
36	TJ 3325	-	23937	12/33	4/56*	
37	TJ 3326	-	23938	12/33	6/58*	
38	TJ 3327	-	23939	12/33	-/56	
39	TJ 3328	30	23940	12/33	11/56	
40	TJ 3329	31	23941	12/33	11/56	F2
41	TJ 3330	32	23942	12/33	6/58*	F2
42	TJ 2969	33	23943	12/33	8/58	F1
43	TJ 3331	34	23947	12/33	11/56	
44	TJ 3332	114	23945	12/33	8/58	F1
45	TJ 3334	35	23946	12/33	6/58	
46	TJ 3335	36	23944	12/33	11/56	

GUY BTX 3 Axle Trolleybus

Fleet No.	Registration	St. Helens Licence No.	Chassis No.	Into Service	Withdrawn	Notes
47	JW 5370	-	23637	-/35	-/51	

LEYLAND TTB 3 Axle Trolleybus

Fleet No.	Registration	St. Helens Licence No.	Chassis No.	Into Service	Withdrawn	Notes		
48	ATE 792	-	8111	3/36	3/56	G F2,	C	
49	ATE 793	-	8112	3/36	3/56	G	C	
50	ATE 794	-	8113	3/36	3/56	G	C	
51	ATE 795	-	8114	3/36	3/56	G	C	
52	BTE 951	-	12179	-/37	8/58	G		
53	BTE 952	-	12180	-/37	8/58	G		
54	DTC 261	-	16856	-/38	8/58			
55	DTC 262	-	16857	-/38	8/58			
56	DTC 263	-	16858	-/38	8/58			
57	DTC 264	-	16859	-/38	8/58			
58	DTC 265	-	16860	-/38	8/58			
59	DTC 266	-	16861	-/38	8/58			

KARRIER W 2 Axle Trolleybus

Fleet No.	Registration	St. Helens Licence No.	Chassis No.	Into Service	Withdrawn	Notes
60	FTD 452	-	50034	11/43	8/58	
61	FTD 453	-	50035	11/43	8/58	
62	FTD 454	-	50036	11/43	8/58	D
63	FTD 455	-	50037	11/43	8/58	
64	FTE 152	-	50063	-/44	8/58	
65	FTE 153	-	50064	-/44	8/58	

SUNBEAM MS2 3 Axle Trolleybus

Fleet No.	Registration	St. Helens Licence No.	Chassis No.	Into Service	Withdrawn	Notes
66	HTD 863	-	60001	10/48	8/58	
67	HTD 864	-	60002	10/48	4/58	
68	HTD 865	-	60003	10/48	8/58	
69	HTD 866	-	60004	10/48	8/58	
70	HTD 867	-	60005	10/48	8/58	
71	HTD 868	-	60006	10/48	8/58	

Notes

A - Carried St. Helens licence No.3 in error for some time.
B - Latterly carried St. Helens licence No.125 in error.
C - Property of Bolton Corporation though in SLT livery.
D - Ran briefly, in 1956, after front panel and headlight replacement, carrying registration plate FDT 454 in error.
F1 - Rebuilt with new front and deeper skirt panels all round.
F2 - Later rebuild, with new front only.

R - Body extensively rebuilt.
G - At time of delivery described as Leyland 'TB' 3 - axle trolleybus.
* - Approximate date; may be a month earlier or later.

The fleet in detail.

Much of the fascination of the SLT trolleybus system, apart from the overhead wiring weaving its way through terraced urban back streets and beyond into wooded suburbia with occasional interludes of open spaces, was generated by the elderly and varied fleet of 71 trolleybuses. Only the last 6, the Sunbeam MS2s, were of post war manufacture. Many of the original Guy lowbridge trolleybuses delivered between 1930 and 1933 remained in service at the time of abandonment in 1958, by which time they had, for some time, been the oldest vehicles in regular public service in the country.

The longevity of the fleet had been achieved through modification and partial rebuilding. Only two vehicles could be considered as completely rebuilt and even these retained much of their original framework. Alterations, particularly to the older vehicles, had been so numerous that hardly any two were alike with varying arrangements of opening windows, trolley bases, external beading and panelling. The final rebuilds to re-enter service before the abandonment announcement emerged having received new fronts with rubber mounted windows. Passengers were faced with a variety of seating arrangements and upholstery augmented by some trolleybuses still carrying earlier versions of the basic red livery with various applications of grey roofs and white or cream bands. Whilst alterations to the newer vehicles were less numerous, even these carried detailed differences in most cases.

Nos. 1 - 30 Guy BTX

Chassis were 3 axle BTX by Guy Motors of Wolverhampton, with lowbridge bodies by Charles H. Roe of Leeds. Electrical equipment was by The Electric Construction Co., Ltd. with Metropolitan Vickers 90 h.p. motors. Unladen weight was 8 tons 7 cwt. The first ten were delivered in 1930 for the initial Atherton to Ashton stage of the St. Helens route conversion to trolleybuses, Nos.11 to 30 following in 1931. No.1 was in use for driver training from early July 1930. Externally the later deliveries differed from the first ten by the presence of ventilators above the nearside lower deck windows and headlamps which were carried, like the initial ten, at the side of the cab panelling, but in a slightly lower position towards the base of the front mudguards.

The initial seating capacity of the first batch was upper deck 29, lower deck 31, however this was modified within a year to 25 upstairs by shortening the first, third and fifth seats to seat three rather than four and the first seat forward of the rear seat to take two rather than three. Following this modification the total capacity for both batches was 56. The longitudinal seats over the rear wheel arches of the first ten seated five, ahead of which were four rows of forward facing double seats and a rearward facing front bulkhead seat for five. This gave a lower saloon capacity of 31. The later batch had only three rows of forward facing double seats with seating for six longitudinally over the rear wheel arches providing instant recognition from a side view as to which batch the trolleybus belonged. A nett loss of 2 in lower saloon capacity in the later buses was made up for with an upper deck seating arrangement in rows from front to back of 4,4,3,4,3,4,3,2 giving a total of 27, whilst the arrangement in the first ten was; 3,4,3,4,3,4,2,2. totalling 25. Some vehicles, Nos.11,16,18,20,23 & 29 have been noted as having a seating arrangement of 4,4,4,4,4,3,2,2, on the upper deck whilst No.30 was unique in having an arrangement of 3,4,3,3,3,3,3,3,2 i.e:- one extra row.

The first modification occurred from 1943 when roller blinds were introduced to replace the original illuminated stencil route indicators. To accommodate the mechanism, the original 'piano lid' front destination panel was replaced by a flatter profile. No.27 was the first to be altered but this and one or two others retained the rear route stencil for a while. Rear destination stencils placed at the top of the upper deck windows were replaced with

roller blinds in the rear panel between saloons, although that on No.9 was uniquely placed just above the platform window for some years.

Commencing in the immediate post war period, the extractor type ventilators fitted to the nearside of Nos.11 - 30 were removed on all except No.19 which retained them until withdrawal. Drop windows, which, on the upper deck were only fitted to the nearside, began to be replaced by sliding ventilators which were generally, but by no means universally, fitted to alternate windows on both sides of both decks.

From about 1948, the bulging front cab panels, so often prone to damage, began to be replaced with flat panels. At the same time the location of the bamboo pole used for manoeuvring the trolley booms was altered so that it was stowed and accessed from the rear rather than the front of the vehicle, presumably for easier access by the conductor. The replacement flat front panels had a slot cut in at the base, to the offside of the number plate, in the shape of an inverted 'U' to provide clearance for the steering drag link when fully forward on full lock, necessary by virtue of the reduced clearance behind the flat panels. At this time, modifications to the rear platform windows were undertaken with the double window being replaced with a single window of about three quarters the width of those replaced. Only Nos.2 and 19 remained unaltered in these aspects until withdrawn. All vehicles had the rear offside lower deck window replaced by a flush aluminium panel, except Nos.2,19 and 21 where it was inset like the previous glazing. Other modifications took place, such as four leg trolley gantries replacing the original eight leg pattern and removal of drainage tubes when the guttering above the upper deck windows was replaced by beading.

There commenced, in 1950, a series of alterations which was to bestow a much younger look to many of these trolleybuses, the youngest of which were already 19 years old! As if taking a styling cue from the new Crossley trolleybuses being introduced by Manchester Corporation for the Hyde Road services, a programme of rebuilding commenced involving the fitting of a completely new smooth profiled front with chromium plated surrounds to curved based windscreens. At the same time the framing was straightened below the lower deck windows and deeper panels with a single life rail fitted in place of shallow curved panels and multiple life rails. The end result was of a much more modern appearance, especially from the front where the only clue to the venerable age of the trolleybuses was the two letter registration plates. Trolleybuses so treated were Nos.. 5,8,10,11,14,16,17,18,20,22,23,25,29 and 30. Some were rebuilt by the SLT, others by S.H.Bond of Wythenshawe in whose workshops, according to a body maker, they proved most awkward to manoeuvre without power. Most, if not all, re entered service in the second post war livery, all red with a grey roof. All, except Nos.5,22, 23 and 30, eventually received the final livery of all over red with a single cream band.

An even more extensive rebuilding programme was carried out during the summer of 1953 when Nos.1 and 7 were completely reconstructed with new external and internal panelling on the original frames. All the windows were mounted in rubber and the square upper deck rear dome was replaced by a modern curved profile. To the ordinary passenger these two trolleybuses must have appeared as new vehicles. During rebuilding, the upperdeck seating was re arranged on both trolleybuses so that the layout from the front to rear on No.1 became; 3,4,4,3,4,3,2,2, whilst that on No. 7 became ; 4,4,4,4,4,3,2, one row less providing much more leg room, both arrangements still retaining an upper deck capacity of 25. Both re entered service in the final single cream band livery. Upon overhaul, seating arrangements may have been altered and No.7 has been noted as having eight upperdeck rows of seats.

From 1952, a rather more cost conscious rebuilding plan commenced with trolleybuses Nos. 6,12,24,27 and 28 receiving only new fronts, the remainder of the bus behind the cab remaining unaltered. All, apart from No.12, received rubber mounted windows, 27 being a hybrid with rubber mounted windows except the windscreen which had chromium plated screen surrounds. The new fronts on this group of trolleybuses appeared somewhat incongruous being grafted onto otherwise unaltered 1930's style bodywork. Abandonment plans halted the rebuilding programme, the last two to be rebuilt being Nos.28

and 24, the latter being the final one to re enter service early in 1955. Rather than receive an overhaul and a new front No.21 was withdrawn in the late summer of 1955, the first trolleybus apart from Guy demonstrator No.47 to be withdrawn. No.26 followed in the autumn, both buses still retaining the first post war livery.

Around this time Nos.10 and 11, the subjects of earlier rebuilding, re-appeared having had the upper deck windows in the rebuilt portion remounted in rubber surrounds.

In the following 12 months further withdrawals took place with Nos.3,8 and 25 being taken out of service, all in the final livery. Whilst No.25 had been involved in a collision and No.3 was unrebuilt, the withdrawal of rebuilt No.8 in the summer of 1956 before the closure of the St. Helens route was somewhat surprising. That closure in November 1956 heralded larger scale withdrawals resulting in Nos.2,5,9,14,15,17,19,22 and 30 being taken out of service. Nos.4,6 and 11, also withdrawn initially, were immediately reinstated as replacements for other defective trolleybuses, and remained in service until the end. Others may have had temporary reprieves such as No.15, brought back into service for a few days and seen by Peter Thompson operating on the Farnworth route on 24th April 1957. No.23, withdrawn in February 1958, was the last BTX to survive with a grey roof livery. At the time of final closure in August 1958, Nos.1,4,6,7 and 10 of the first batch and Nos. 11,16,18,24,27 and 28 of the later batch were still in service. Of these, No.4 was particularly remarkable being the only Guy to remain in service right to the end in fundamentally unrebuilt condition. By 1958 its venerable appearance had become something of a spectacle.

Apart from the St. Helens route, the Guy BTXs, along with the 4 wheel BTs will always be associated with the Atherton to Farnworth route, Whilst sharing the Leigh to Mosley Common service with all other classes, except the post-war Sunbeams, they occasionally appeared on weekend short workings from Atherton to Bolton, but after 1956 were seldom seen in Bolton.

Modifications to Guy BTX trolleybuses Nos 1-30.

Plate 352, No.30 . No.30, the last of the second batch, displays the original condition of the class as it passes along Tyldesley Road Atherton with the pit head gear of Chanters Colliery in the background. Note the ornate original livery with the SLT monogram carried on the front cab panelling and the piano front destination panel with stencil indicator. This 3/4 nearside view allows the extractor ventilators above the lower deck windows to be seen as fitted only to Nos.11 to 30. These were gradually replaced as sliding ventilators were fitted, No.19 being the only BTX to retain this feature until withdrawal.

Photo, A. Ingram.

Plate 353, No.26. A very early post-war view in Bolton sees No.26 little altered from original condition. The livery has been simplified and the fitting of a roller blind indicator has necessitated modification to the front destination panel. Only the fleet number is now carried on the front cab panel either side of which the standard SLT lighting arrangements have appeared. Note the glazed rear staircase window.

Photo, Author's collection.

Plate 354, No.2. No.2, at Atherton Savoy about 1953, ran until withdrawn in this condition although it was later repainted in the final livery. Although the trolleybus has received sliding ventilators, the staircase window, whilst panelled over, remains inset. The lower panelling with beading below the windows and with a bulbous cab panel remain original. An eight leg trolley gantry is still carried.

Photo, Author's collection.

173

Plate 355. No.3. Although still carrying the first post-war livery, No.3, at the St. Helens terminus, represents the final condition of those BTX trolleybuses which remained in the fundamentally unrebuilt condition. A flat front panel to the cab has replaced the original bulbous design and all beading below the windows has disappeared. The staircase window has received flush panelling and a four leg trolley gantry has replaced the original. Note the inverted 'U' shaped aperture at the bottom of the front panel to accommodate the forward travel of the steering drag link on full lock. The trolley pole retriever is now accessed from under the rear of the trolleybus.

Photo, C. Carter.

Plate 356. Manchester Trolleybuses Nos.1212&1245, Piccadilly. Concurrent with the rebuilding programme begun in 1950, which displaced the last vestiges of piano front styling from many of the venerable SLT trolleybuses, was the introduction by Manchester of new trolleybuses in conjunction with commencement of trolleybus operation along Hyde Road to Gee Cross. The superb driver visibility afforded by these modern trolleybuses was not lost on the SLT who incorporated similar curved based windscreens into their replacement front end design. It should be noted that the rebuilding programme was applied to those vehicles where age was taking its toll of the body structure ahead of the front bulkhead, modern styling and improved visibility being desirable by-products. Pictured in Portland Street, Piccadilly, the driver of Manchester, three axle Crossley Dominion trolleybus No.1245 operating a 210x Hyde Road rush hour extra leans across the nearside cab to exchange a few words with the driver of two axle Crossley Empire No.1212 operating to Gee Cross via Hyde, Belle Vue and Denton. Visible in the background, with similar bodywork, is Ashton-under-Lyne Crossley Empire No.81 operating service 219 to Ashton via Guide Bridge. It is heartning to know that a Manchester Crossley Dominion, No.1250 and Ashton Empire No.80 survived to be preserved and well cared for in the Boyle Street museum of the Greater Manchester Transport Society.

Photo, J.Fozard.

Plate 357. No.5. No.5 was one of the first trolleybuses to receive a new front and deepened side panelling. As it waits, Atherton bound, at Swinton in 1951, it presents quite a contrast to the appearance of the class as delivered. No.5 was one of the few rebuilds to retain, until withdrawal, the grey roof livery.

Photo, the late Reg Wilson.

Plate 358. No.7. Trolleybuses Nos.1 and 7 were subject to major rebuilding in 1953. New bodywork was built around the original framing and all windows were rubber mounted. Considerably modernising their appearance were new, smooth curved rear domes. No.7 stands at Swinton around 1957 with a couple of Manchester Leyland PD2s in the distance. Manchester Corporation Transport and Salford City Transport operated a joint service between Reddish and Swinton, service No.57 reaching Swinton via Manchester Road from Irlams O'Th' Height whilst the 77 reached Swinton via Station Road having travelled via Bolton Road, Pendlebury. The two services returned towards Manchester via each others outward bound routes.

Photo, C. W. Routh.

Plate 359. No.27. From around 1952, the final trolleybuses to be rebuilt re-entered service with new fronts only, the bodywork rearwards from the cab remaining unaltered. No.27 stands at Atherton Savoy in front of LUT Dennis and Guy single deckers, its new front sitting rather incongruously on otherwise unaltered 1930s bodywork. No.27 was the only one to retain the beading along shallow lower deck panels and, together with No.12, an eight leg trolley gantry. The last trolleybuses to be rebuilt, Nos.24 and 28, re-entered service early in 1955 and had a large radius to the top outer corners of the upper deck windows similar to the totally rebuilt No.7.

Photo, Author's collection.

Plate 360. No.28 Interior. The start of the former trolleybus route to St. Helens, can be seen through the rebuilt front upperdeck rubber mounted windows of trolleybus No.28 as it stands at the Farnworth loading point in Wigan Road Atherton on 31st August 1958. Note the radiused window top outer corners as fitted to this and No 24, the last two trolleybuses to be rebuilt along with the offset gangway and seating arrangement, standard features of the lowbridge trolleybuses. The seating arrangement follows the normal pattern i.e:- 4,4,3,4, 3,4,3,2 from the front. A single skin roof reveals the steel frame spanning the upper deck whilst to the left of the fleet number the centre dividing member supporting the front dome and housing the power cables is visible.

Photo, J.C.Gillham.

Nos. 31- 46 Guy BT

Entering service in December 1933, were 16 Guy BT 2 axle trolleybuses with 48 seat Roe lowbridge bodywork. Seating for 22 was provided on the upper deck and 26 on the lower with 5 forward facing rows and seating for 3 over each wheel arch. The upper deck seating arrangement was somewhat cramped with eight rows; six seats for three ahead of two seats for two. Unlike the BTXs, there was no rearward facing bulkhead seat. Each was powered by a GEC 80 hp motor. Electrical equipment was provided on some by Metropolitan Vickers whilst others had Electric Construction Co. Ltd. equipment. Unladen weight was 7 tons 2 cwt 1 qtr.

These trolleybuses were originally intended for the Leigh to Bolton service but, owing to insufficient seating capacity, were soon replaced by BTXs and the first 3 axle Leylands delivered in 1936.

Curved rear domes and front destination panels suitable for roller blinds gave these buses a less angular appearance than the BTXs. Extractor ventilators originally fitted and similar to those fitted to the 11 - 30 class were removed on all but 35, 38 and 45 when sliding ventilators replaced drop windows after the war.

Modifications were made in a similar manner to the 1 - 30 class. A flat cab front panel replaced the original bulging variety on all except Nos. 33,34,35,38 and 45 which ran all their lives unaltered in this respect. New fronts were fitted to Nos. 31,32,40,41,42 and 44 but only Nos. 42 and 44 had the side and rear panels deepened. None had rubber mounted windows. The original double windows at the back of the platforms were modified in a similar way to the BTXs except on Nos.38 & 40. The latter was unique amongst the rebuilds in retaining its unmodified rear end. No.44 was of interest being probably the first of all the Guys to be rebuilt by Bond around 1950. At this time, photographs of an unrebuilt BTX were 'treated' to demonstrate a 'before and after' effect for advertising purposes. Although initially repainted in grey roof livery, No.44 re entered service in a unique 'all red' livery with no cream bands which it retained until withdrawal upon closure of the system. The first to be taken out of service was No. 36 in April 1956, soon followed by No.38, both buses retaining the first post war livery. Nos.31,34,39,40,43 and 46 followed when the St. Helens route closed at which time Nos. 31,34 and 40 carried the final livery whilst Nos.39 and 43 retained the early two white band livery. No.46 was in 'all red with a grey roof' livery. A collision in February 1958 resulted in the withdrawal of No.33. No.35 also succumbed around the same time, both in the final livery. Another trio, Nos.37,41 and 45, was withdrawn around June 1958, Nos.37 and 45 having been the last trolleybuses still carrying the first post war livery. By this time, No.45 had become something of a spectacle retaining a bulging front cab panel, extractor ventilators, 8-leg trolley gantry and the first post war livery complete with large shaded fleet numerals. By 31st August 1958 only Nos.32, 42 and 44 remained in service. No.42 had the distinction of being the only trolleybus to survive to the end with a grey roof livery.

Modifications to Guy BT trolleybuses Nos. 31 - 46.

Plate 361. No. 41. No.41, new in 1933, stands in Atherton depot in pristine condition. As delivered the Guy BTs were easily distinguishable from the BTXs, apart from being 2-axle, by the destination panel shaped to house roller blind indicators subsequently fitted and the pronounced 'V' shape to the upper deck front windows; those of the BTXs being flat. This nearside view shows the extractor type ventilators above the lower deck windows, later lost by most trolleybuses as sliding ventilators replaced drop windows.

Photo, Author's collection.

WELL KNOWN TROLLEYBUS FLEETS

1. South Lancashire

One of the earliest authorities to run a trolleybus service was the South Lancashire Transport Co. This Company has placed 5 repeat orders for—

METROVICK TROLLEYBUS EQUIPMENT

and now has a fleet which includes 41 Trolleybuses so equipped.

METROPOLITAN Vickers

ELECTRICAL CO., LTD.
TRAFFORD PARK ··· MANCHESTER 17.

K/V 901

COSMOS LAMPS *burn brighter longer*

Plate 362. No.34. No.34, little altered from original condition apart from the fitting of sliding ventilators and a panel in place of the staircase window, stands at Atherton alongside the SLT offices next to the Savoy cinema. Whilst some BTs which did not receive new fronts had the bulging cab front panel replaced by a flat panel, others, including No.34, survived until withdrawn in this condition. No 34 later received the all red livery but retained the eight leg trolley gantry. *Photo, Author's collection.*

Plate 363. No.44. Of those BTs to receive new fronts, only Nos.42 and 44 received deepened side and rear panelling in addition to the new fronts which, in these two cases, were identical in style to the early BTX rebuilds. Later rebuilds received fabricated domes with a centre seam as opposed to the single pressing as carried by No.44 seen outside Atherton depot. The traditional Roe waist rail moulding was replaced on No.44 by curved beading, the only trolleybus so treated. The all red livery applied to No.44 was best considered as the second post-war scheme albeit with a red rather than a grey roof, as opposed to the final livery without the single cream band. Around the time of No.44's re-entry into service, use of the large fleet numbers was discontinued in favour of smaller numerals, No.44 being one of just a few rebuilds to receive the earlier numerals, another example being Guy BTX No.29. *Photo, J. Fozard.*

Plate 364. No.32 Bolton. The appearance of a Guy BT in Bolton was uncommon in later days. With No.64 in the background on service to Leigh, No.32 on a short working to Atherton shows off its 1933 vintage rearwards of the cab with twin life guards below shallow panels which still retain the beading under the waist rail. Note the centre seam on the new front dome.

Photo, Photobus.

No.47 Guy BTX

Originally a Guy demonstrator, hence the Wolverhampton registration JW 5370, No.47 entered service with the SLT in 1935 although its construction predated this by some 5 years. It had General Electric equipment. Strangely its registration dates from around 1934 adding to the belief that this vehicle, chassis No.23637, was originally sent to South Africa.

It was the first highbridge trolleybus on the SLT and with a seating capacity of only 56 its Guy built body would have seemed capacious within. The lower deck, with seating for 29, was arranged as for the 11 to 30 class whilst upstairs boasted rows of double seats ahead of a strange glass vestibule at the head of the stairs.

The front of the trolleybus was extremely angular in shape with a raked windscreen as favoured by Birmingham inset below a pronounced piano front. The original cab front panel was a curvaceous affair bulging forwards in a single sweep from below the windscreen. This was replaced around 1938 with a panel identical to those originally fitted to the 1 - 30 and 31 - 46 classes.

Roller blind destination indicators were fitted from new and the bus was equipped with battery lighting. For a while after delivery the bus ran in green livery. No 47 left the SLT briefly during 1939 for a period of trial service in Southend on Sea.

On the SLT its use was usually restricted to rush hour 'jiggers' between Leigh, Atherton, Tyldesley and Worsley. It occasionally appeared in Bolton but never operated beyond Worsley or on the St. Helens route. Very much the odd man out in the fleet, it was the first trolleybus to be withdrawn in 1951, some years ahead of the abandonment plans.

Modifications to Guy BTX No.47.

Plate 365. No.47. A wartime view of No.47 approaching Atherton Punch Bowl from Leigh on a short working to Tyldesley. Note the replacement front panel fitted a few years earlier in the style of the lowbridge Guys as delivered. This compares with the view of No 47 in the line up outside Atherton depot when still fitted with the original cab front panel. The vehicle has a cumbersome look about it. However within a few years smooth front profiles had evolved eliminating the angular shapes and perhaps some of the character associated with vehicles of the early thirties. *Photo, A.N.Porter.*

Nos. 48 to 59 Leyland TTB

Within this batch of Leyland trolleybuses were two groups of vehicles of generally similar specification but with the later vehicles Nos.54 to 59 built with a somewhat more modern appearance. The highbridge Roe bodies seated 64 passengers, with 29 seats on the lower deck arranged in the same manner as the lowbridge Guy BTX trolleybuses.

Electrical equipment was by Metropolitan Vickers though No.51 alone had GEC equipment. Most had 90 h.p. motors although there were at least two 115 h.p. motors latterly fitted to Nos.52 and 53. The unladen weight ranged between 8 tons 13 cwt 2 qrs. to 8 tons 15 cwt 3 qrs.

Nos.48 to 51 were delivered in 1936 and were purchased on behalf of Bolton Corporation who paid the loan charges and running expenses. After eight years when fully depreciated, the buses became the nominal property of Bolton Corporation although they always carried SLT livery and legal lettering. Two similar vehicles, Nos.52 and 53, were delivered in 1937 but were the property of the SLT. These six trolleybuses were virtually indistinguishable. One minor difference was the position of the front upperdeck hand rail, positioned centrally across the front windows on 48 to 51 but a little lower on the later two.

Nos.54 to 59, delivered in 1938, presented a much more modern appearance with a smooth sloping front replacing the angular profile of the earlier trolleybuses. The rear domes were rounder with a larger radius to the upper deck rear windows and the lower deck side panels were slightly deeper and straighter. The somewhat cramped upper deck seating remained unaltered resulting in the extra length at floor level associated with the streamlined front leaving a vast space ahead of the front seats.

Whilst Nos.48 to 53 had luggage shelves above the lower deck longitudinal seats, Nos.54 to 59 did not.

Modifications were made in similar fashion to the lowbridge trolleybuses with roller blinds replacing stencil indicators just after the war. Half drop windows were replaced by sliding ventilators and extractor ventilators removed from above the lower deck windows. Around 1950, the double windows to the rear platforms were replaced, except on No. 55, by narrower single windows offset to the nearside and the lower deck staircase windows were replaced by panels in similar fashion to the earlier trolleybuses.

From about 1951, the bulging front cab panel fitted to Nos.48 to 53 was replaced with a flat panel, whilst on the later vehicles, with the exception of No.55, the depth of the front panel was reduced to permit tow bar access from beneath rather than through a panel aperture. No.57 varied in several respects, retaining deep front panels but without the tow bar aperture and, along with No.53, having replacement sliding windows fitted in the same place as the original drop windows. All the other Leylands received sliding ventilators to alternate windows starting from the front bulkhead rearwards.

In the spring of 1954, No.48, which had survived without many of the modifications, emerged from Atherton depot after overhaul fitted with a completely new front. The upperdeck windows were mounted in rubber in a flush profile whilst the cab front windows sported chromium plated surrounds with a curved baseline in a similar style to the lowbridge rebuilt fronts. No.48 was the sole highbridge trolleybus so treated and presented a most modern appearance in comparison with the other early Leylands.

Nos.48 to 51 were withdrawn in March 1956 upon replacement of the Bolton local trolleybus services. They were returned to Bolton Corporation for disposal, eventually to be towed from Bridgeman Street depot Bolton to Bird's in Stratford upon Avon for scrap. All the others, including 52 and 53 with the earlier style bodywork, remained in service until the end of trolleybus operation.

Late in the day, No.54 received rubber mounted glazing to the cab door.

As was the case with all highbridge trolleybuses, they never worked the St. Helens route and only began to operate beyond Worsley to Farnworth during 1957. They were regulars on the Leigh to Bolton service, however the later batch seemed to appear more frequently on the Bolton locals.

Modifications to Leyland TTB trolleybuses Nos. 48 to 53.

Plate 366. No.49. No.49 stands in the yard at Atherton depot when only a few weeks old. From new, the fleet numerals were placed centrally on the cab front panel unlike the earlier lowbridge trolleybuses which originally carried the SLT monogram in this position only to have it replaced at a later date by the fleet number. Note the aperture for the tow bar and the 'V' profile of the upperdeck front window layout, a carry over from the earlier Roe bodied Guy BTs with which these highbridge Leylands bore many similarities.

Photo, Author's collection.

Plate 367. No.48. By the early 1950s most of the Leylands had received flat cab front panels, panelling in place of the staircase window and had lost the extractor ventilators upon receipt of sliding ventilators. The original rear platform double window was also replaced by a single unit. No. 48, seen at Howell Croft Bolton about 1952, had, at that time, managed to avoid many of the modifications and, apart from sliding ventilators, is in virtually original condition, even to the extent of retaining somewhat jaded lining out along the raised moulding below the lower deck windows, so characteristic of Roe bodywork.

Photo, C.Carter.

Plate 368. No.50. Although still carrying the grey roof livery, No.50 is seen behind Sunbeam No.70 at Howell Croft Bolton in its final condition having had the bulbous front cab panel replaced with a flat panel, sliding ventilators in place of half drop windows and extractor ventilators removed, together with replacement of the staircase window with panelling. The trolleybus later received a final repaint into the red roof livery as did all the highbridge trolleybuses except Guy demonstrator No.47 withdrawn in 1951.

Photo, Roy Marshall.

Plate 369. No. 48. In the spring of 1954, No 48, which had run for so long in unaltered condition, emerged from overhaul having received a new front with rubber mounted upperdeck front windows and a curved base line to chromium plated windscreen surrounds in a style generally similar to the last lowbridge rebuilds. This trolleybus provides a modern appearance seen at Four Lane Ends with its rebuilt front and was something of a sensation, being the only highbridge trolleybus so treated. Photographs of it are rare since it disappeared from service along with 49 to 51 upon replacement of the Bolton local services in March 1956.

Photo, the late J.Batty.

Plate 370. No.52 Interior.
The shelves fitted above the longitudinal rear seats on trolleybuses Nos.48 to 53 provided useful additional space for luggage. This rearward view inside No.52, on 31st August 1958, also shows the platform space taken up by the protruding half turn staircase and the single window to the rear of the platform which replaced the original wider double window. One of the stickers in the offside rear window will advertise the trolleybus abandonment plans, a copy of which appears earlier in the book.

Photo, J.C. Gilham.

Modifications to Leyland TTB trolleybuses Nos. 54 to 59.

Plate 371. No.57. Number 57, seen at the Ashburner Street unloading point in Bolton, is in original condition save for the loss of the glazed louvre above the rear lower deck drop window. Note the lower waist rail beading, the staircase window, extractor ventilators above the lower deck windows and the tow bar aperture. All the Leyland trolleybuses were delivered with four leg trolley gantries which they retained throughout their lives.

Photo, Author's collection.

Plate 372. No. 59. Number 59, still carrying the first post war livery in this view at Howell Croft Bolton, has received all the modifications applied to the Leylands. Note the position of the sliding ventilators in relation to the original location of the half drop windows. This arrangement was generally, although not always, adopted as standard when sliding windows were fitted. Most trolleybuses also lost the beading below the waist rail during the overhauls in the early 1950s.

Photo, Author's collection.

Plate 373. No.57. Only two of the Leylands, Nos.53 and 57, had the sliding ventilators fitted in the same place as the original drop windows they replaced. Both retained some of the beading below the waist rail. No.57, seen passing a Weymann bodied lowbridge Guy Arab III outside Atherton motorbus depot, retained deep front panelling below the cab windows although it lost the tow bar aperture. One Leyland, No.55, uniquely retained the double window to the rear of the platform as well as the tow bar aperture and deep cab panels. These details are clearly visible in the photographs of 55 at Spinning Jenny Street Leigh and Hulton Lane elsewhere in the book.

Photo, Author's collection.

184

TRANSPORT WORLD

THE FIRST TRANSPORT PAPER — ESTABLISHED 1892

Editor:
JAMES FINLAY

Advertisement Manager
J. M. WING

Publishers:
TRAMWAY AND RAILWAY WORLD PUBLISHING CO. LTD.
82 Tankerville Road, London, S.W.16
Telephone : Pollards 4153
Telegrams : Tramigro, Streath, London.

Directors :
A. M. WILLCOX (*Chairman*)
J. FINLAY (*Managing*)
H. E. TOWNELL
W. M. WILLCOX

NOVEMBER 11, 1943

No. 3019 (Vol. XCIV)

New Trolleybus for South Lancashire

METROPOLITAN-CAMMELL BODY ON KARRIER "W" CHASSIS

The accompanying illustration shows a new double-deck trolleybus which has just been completed for the South Lancashire Transport Company. The chassis is the Karrier "W" type which was described and illustrated in our issue of October 14; it has G.E.C. electrical equipment. The body has been built by a well known Surrey firm within the Metropolitan-Cammell-Weymann organisation, according to the standard wartime specification for composite construction.

There is seating capacity for 56 passengers- 26 in the lower saloon and 30 in the upper saloon. While wartime requirements provide for timber slatted seats, in this case the seats are of the upholstered type from stock materials.

Again, for the floor boards of both saloons and the platform vestibule, slats have been provided by the manufacturers from stock. The upper saloon floor is covered with lino and the lower with lino substitute.

The upper saloon roof is panelled with

Karrier "W" type trolleybus, with Metropolitan-Cammell-Weymann body, recently completed for the South Lancashire Transport Company.

20-gauge steel sheet, the front and rear ends being shaped, but beaten panels are eliminated. All exterior panels are of 20-gauge S.W.G. steel.

The wartime specification provides that no interior side casing panels are to be fitted, but the interiors of the exterior panels between the window rail and the seat rail are painted to match the upholstery. In both saloons, from seat rail to floor, cove panels are fitted and the floor lino is continued to the seat rail. Lining panels are fitted to the front bulkhead in both saloons and covered with lino from the waist to the floor level.

All interior mouldings, cappings, pillars, etc., are finished in natural grain, the use of mouldings and cappings being restricted to essential requirements. The ceiling of the lower saloon consists of 22-24 gauge steel side covering panels with the centre rails of pressed board.

Rails and grab handles

Tubular steel grab handles are provided on each side of the entrance platform, and a centre stanchion extends from the platform to the canopy. Commodes, stanchions and handpoles are covered with white cellulose acetate, as are the staircase rails.

The staircase has timber treads and steel risers, each tread being fitted with the same type of Ferodo tread plates as fitted to saloon and vestibule floors, and supplied from the customer's "frozen" stocks. There is a small landing about halfway up the staircase.

The driver's cab is of the full type built integral with the body. The metal frame windscreen is fitted only to the top half off side. The windscreen and the other front glasses are glazed with laminated plate safety glass. The bucket seat is adjustable both horizontally and vertically, and two spring roller blinds are provided across the front bulkhead.

There are five main windows of plate glass on each side of both saloons, only one on each side being of the half-drop type. Continuous metal louvres are fitted above the windows on each side.

Extractor type ventilators with fixed undergrids are provided in the upper saloon roof, two forward and two rear of the overhead gantry. Ventilation of electrical equipment has also been provided as necessary.

Provision is made for destination indicator to be accommodated, but no rear or side indicators are fitted.

For lighting, ten interior fittings are provided in the lower and twelve in the upper saloon. These consist of white reflectors without glass and are fitted with A.R.P. shades. A further lamp is on the platform.

The gantry to accommodate the trolley bases and booms, is the normal Metropolitan-Cammell-Weymann patented type. It has been modified to meet certain local conditions.

Painting has been carried out in accordance with wartime requirements, but it is understood that the exterior painting will be finished by the South Lancashire Transport Company from their own stocks.

The unladen weight of the complete vehicle is 7 tons 15 cwt.

The overall length is 26ft.; width, 7ft. 6in.; and unladen height, 15ft. 1½in

Automobile Research
IMPORTANT WORK BY I.A.E.

The twelfth annual report of the automobile research committee of the Institution of Automobile Engineers has just been issued. This contains a record of the committee's work for the year 1942-3, and shows its resources have been fully utilised on work of national importance.

Experiments have been made in the filtration of used lubrication oil. The Committee is working to determine the extent to which oil cleaning must be carried in order to remove all particles likely to cause wear in the engine bearings. Tests are also being made on oil filter performance.

Another important set of investigations has been concerned with producer gas vehicles. This has included the determination of the power loss due to conversion and the amount of power that may be regained by increasing the compression ratio. Work has started on the conversion of a compression-ignition engine to run on producer gas.

In the course of these investigations a new gas-air mixer was developed, since the type of mixer used for converted petrol engines was found unsuitable for the compression-ignition engine. The mixer, with a modification to the injection pump control gear, has provided a satisfactory solution for the conversion of the vehicle engine chosen.

Nos. 60 - 65 Karrier W

Six wartime 'utility' trolleybuses were delivered to the SLT during late 1943 and early 1944. The vehicles were designated as 'Karriers' although the Rootes Group also supplied similar chassis under the name Sunbeam. Where the operator had not previously taken delivery of either Karrier or Sunbeam trolleybuses, deliveries were designated as 'Sunbeams'. In this case it seems the SLT was an exception to this rule. The 56 seat bodies were built by Weymann to a relaxed 'austerity' specification, passengers thus benefiting from upholstered seats in otherwise starkly equipped interiors. Externally, the typical wartime bodywork did away for the need of expensive press tools and was purely functional. There were few curves, even the rear domes being fabricated rather than pressed. The quoted unladen weight was 7tons 18cwt 3 qrs.

There were differences with regard to the electrical equipment. All had 80 h.p.. motors but Nos. 60 to 63 had GEC equipment whilst that of 64 and 65 was supplied by English Electric. The first four had battery lighting, whilst the other two had lighting fed from the traction current.

These were the first SLT trolleybuses to have the conventional upper deck rear window emergency exit. As delivered, a label in the platform window served to display the registration number. Rear destination indicators were fitted after the war.

The half drop windows originally fitted were replaced by sliding ventilators at which time most trolleybuses lost the louvres above the windows. The exceptions were No.63 which retained a louvre above the front upper deck windows only and Nos. 64 and 65 which retained all the upper deck louvres. Uniquely, No.64 retained its half drop windows with the exception of a single sliding ventilator fitted on the upper deck offside.

Around 1955, Nos.61, 62 and 64 had their original fabricated rear domes replaced with smooth contour pressed domes. On an ad hoc basis from about 1950, the sidelamps, originally fitted into the front cab panel, were removed and replaced by the standard SLT fitments projecting from the cab sides. Nos.60 to 63 received the standard SLT headlamps around 1956, numbers 64 and 65 retaining their headlamps in the original position. When so treated in 1956, number 62 emerged from Atherton workshops carrying the incorrect registration FDT 454. This was quickly corrected to FTD 454. The headlamps fitted to SLT trolleybuses provided only low levels of illumination and did not need to be dipped. However a single fog lamp was fitted to aid progress in poor visibility.

Late in its career No.63 emerged from Atherton workshops having received new cab front panels with side mounted headlamps, probably the last to be so treated. At the same time the trolleybus received a rubber mounted nearside windscreen and cab side windows.

These trolleybuses were regular performers on the Leigh to Bolton and Mosley Common services. They made occasional appearances in Farnworth in the last year or so of operation and all remained available for service until the system's closure.

Modifications to Karrier W trolleybuses Nos.60 to 65.

Plate 374. Not to be confused with a latter-day No.64 which survived in exactly this condition, is No.65, in almost original condition seen at Spinning Jenny Street, Leigh, in mid 1950. The sidelamps have already been transferred to cab side brackets. The panel mounted headlamps were however to survive on this trolleybus and No. 64.
Photo, the late Reg Wilson.

Plate 375. No.63. Seen in the second post war livery around 1952, No.63 stands in a deserted Howell Croft bus station under the gaze of Bolton's town hall clock. Whilst the half drop windows have been replaced and all but the front window louvre have gone, the bus still retains panel mounted head, side and fog lamps.

Photo, East Pennine Transport Group.

Plate 376. No.65. Waiting to depart Spinning Jenny Street Leigh for Mosley Common, No.65 is seen in its final condition having retained its upper deck window louvres and the panel mounted headlamps and foglamp.

Photo, Roy Marshall.

Plate 377. No.63. Trolley wires and a street lamp reflect in the recently fitted rubber mounted nearside cab window of No.63 on 8th March 1958 as it stands outside Atherton Savoy cinema. The emergence of No.63 with its modified headlamp arrangement and attention around the cab area with a lick of paint on its new panels provided a brighter note to an otherwise ageing trolleybus system.

Photo, P.J. Thompson, (Photosales).

Nos. 66 - 71 Sunbeam MS2

The last trolleybuses purchased by the SLT in 1948 were, without doubt, the flagships of the fleet. These were 6 Weymann bodied Sunbeam MS2s which, when acquired, were seen as the first of a second generation of trolleybuses for possible operation in conjunction with Bolton Corporation over an extended network and perhaps, ultimately, to replace the Guy BTX fleet by then some 18 years old. They turned out, however, to be the last additions to the fleet and SLT's only post war trolleybuses.

Although badged as 'Karrier' they were always licensed and described as Sunbeams. Karrier Motors Ltd. and Sunbeam Commercial Vehicles Ltd. had been, for some time, part of the Rootes Group and trolleybus chassis had been marketed under both names. Not long after the delivery of these MS2s, Rootes sold the Sunbeam works after which no new trolleybuses were to carry the Karrier name.

Electrical equipment was by Metropolitan Vickers with 115 h.p. motors. The 64 seat bodies were built by Weymann at Addlestone and had capacity for 34 on the upper deck. Battery lighting, roller blind destination indicators and sliding ventilators were fitted from new. They were without doubt stylish vehicles whose appearance was enhanced by the characteristic Weymann outward flare to the base of the lower deck panels. They carried the SLT first post war livery well which, together with their 30 ft. length on 3 axles, gave them an imposing whilst refined appearance. Their unladen weight was 9 tons 16 cwt 2 qrs.

Whilst most of the modifications to the earlier vehicles followed the patterns set by these trolleybuses, they underwent few alterations themselves. Following collision damage, the platform of No.67 was rebuilt, during which the outward flare to the base of the rear panels was lost, without doubt a panel beaters nightmare to replicate. Some months before it was withdrawn for repainting as 'The Last' ceremonial trolleybus for the system's closure, No.71 lost an offside upper deck sliding ventilator, the window aperture receiving a plain glass replacement.

These trolleybuses were always associated with the Leigh to Bolton service although they made occasional appearances in Farnworth in the final months of trolleybus operation.

All were available for service until the end except for No.67, withdrawn prematurely after a second accident in April 1958, and No.71 which was being repainted for its ceremonial duties on 1st September.

Modifications to Sunbeam MS2s Nos.66-71.

Plate 378. No.68. When almost new, No.68 stands at Howell Croft bus station Bolton on a Bolton to Four Lane Ends local service. The trolleybus is in unaltered form and was to remain so for its 10 year service life. *Photo, C. Carter.*

Plate 379. No.71. On a damp day early in 1958, No.71 approaches Four Lane Ends along St. Helens Road from Bolton. By this time it had lost the second upper deck sliding ventilator which was never replaced. These trolleybuses always retained their original side and headlamp arrangement as if the SLT did not dare meddle with the pedigree Weymann design of these fine vehicles.   *Photo, C.W. Routh.*

Plate 380. Sunbeam MS2 Lower Saloon. Functional and somehow less lavish than the Roe bodied pre war trolleybuses were the impressions gained upon entering the lower saloon of an SLT Sunbeam MS2. Their Weymann bodies were metal framed as opposed to the wooden frames of all pre war and wartime SLT trolleybuses, whilst apparent to the passengers were the much slimmer wood finishers around the windows and the restricted use of wood on the bulkhead. Most significant was the provision of five forward facing pairs of seats and the absence of the rearward facing front bulkhead seat as provided on all earlier SLT three axle trolleybuses, thus exposing a vast expanse of unrelieved panelling. Being a trolleybus there was no contoured cover for a clutch and bell housing creating a false impression of finish having come second to functionality. In truth the Weymann bodies were of the highest quality and the equal of anything that had gone before. Indeed, as with other SLT trolleybuses, there was that sense of warmth upon climbing aboard bestowed by the attractive leather trimmed, red patterned moquette seat upholstery whilst the wooden top rails to the seat frames were warm to the touch, unlike chromed steel, as one countered the sprightly acceleration of the trolleybus whilst moving along the gangway towards a vacant seat. As with all trolleybuses in the fleet the stanchions and handrails were originally cellulose acetate coated and latterly taped thus ensuring that the travelling public were never exposed to sensations from earth leakage!

Photo, the late R.Boardman.

SLT MISCELLANY

Destination Indicators

All trolleybuses were eventually equipped with roller blind destination indicators, had they not been from new. With the exception of No.47, the layout was the same and always in upper case letters, with a white blank at each end as follows:

LEIGH
BOLTON
HULTON LANE
FOUR LANE ENDS
DEPOT
ATHERTON
FARNWORTH
WALKDEN
SWINTON
WORSLEY
MOSLEY COMMON
BOOTHSTOWN
TYLDESLEY
DEPOT
ATHERTON
ST. HELENS
HUNTSMAN
HAYDOCK
ASHTON
HINDLEY
LEIGH ROAD

Some blinds showed 'HULTON LANE', 'FOUR LANE ENDS' and 'MOSLEY COMMON' in the same style as 'LEIGH ROAD' with mixed letter sizes. Others had equal sized lettering for all destinations. Of interest is that the motor bus replacements for the trolleybuses showed 'Hulton Lane Ends' rather than 'Four Lane Ends' on both their intermediate and ultimate destination indicators.

Plate 381. Black lettering on a yellow background was standard for trolleybus stops. This particular example standing at Spinning Jenny Street terminus Leigh was ironically positioned since the trolleybuses actually loaded on the other side of the shelter, to the left of the picture.
Photo, W. Ryan.

Bus Stops

Until the end of the war, stopping places had been indicated by a white band painted half way up the traction poles supporting the trolleybus overhead and the wiring for the trams that preceded them. A good example can be seen earlier in the book in Elliott Street Tyldesley. The location of a banded pole served to indicate the stopping place for travel in both directions and were generally observed by motor buses travelling along trolleybus routes. Where there were separate stops these were indicated by signs reading 'Petrol Bus Stop' and 'Trolley Bus Stop'. On routes not served by either trams or trolleybuses, the LUT generally used red painted stop signs with white lettering. In the pre war period, timetables proclaimed that 'In rural places buses will stop anywhere in reason'!

The legacy of petrol fuelled motor buses was to last until the end of the trolleybus era by which time the buses pulling up at these stopping points had been diesel powered for many years! Even so, 'petrol bus' was to remain in local parlance for many years.

There was one oddity at Howe Bridge School where trolleybuses would stop at certain times only. A hand painted sign was erected reading 'Trackless Trolley Bus Stop'.

Visitors on Trial

The SLT, with its relative proximity to the factory of Leyland Motors, was occasionally host to new trolleybuses making trial runs. The section between Atherton and Four Lane Ends was normally used, but it was not unknown for 'strangers' to venture as far as Bolton or even to Farnworth.

Whilst the trolleybus was always a silent mode of transport, some of these new vehicles seemed even more so and the author well remembers being taken by surprise as a green double decker destined for Colombo glided silently by, down New Brook Road from Four Lane Ends whilst on trial.

It was not always complete trolleybuses that took to the road. In the earlier years 'chassis only' were run on test under the wires using temporary wooden structures to support the trolley gantry. As far as is known, only one, the unique twin steering trolley, destined to become London trolleybus class X7, No.1671, ran in revenue earning service between Leigh and Bolton. More conventional trolleybuses destined for London Transport including Class D1 No.384 designed to LT specification, ran on the SLT before delivery for service, in 384's case, to London Transport's Bexleyheath depot.

Plate 382. Travelling from Spinning Jenny Street along Market Street, Leigh, trolleybuses passed this 'Petrol Bus Stop' with white letters on a red background. These bus stops did their bit to ensure that the very 'British' trait of queue discipline was never compromised !   *Photo, W. Ryan.*

Strangers Under SLT Wires.

Plate 383. In September 1933, the Leyland single deck TBS1 demonstrator trolleybus runs over the cobbles and tarred over tram tracks in Manchester Road East, Little Hulton, having turned from Cleggs Lane on the return trip from Farnworth to Atherton. This right hand drive trolleybus was also demonstrated in Chesterfield and was, whilst visiting the SLT system, also photographed for continental publicity purposes outside Worsley's Mill Brow cafe on the wrong side of the road and on the wrong wires. The design around the cab area is very evocative of London Transport styling.

*Photo, Ribble
Enthusiasts Club.*

Plate 384. In February 1935, a most futuristic three axle double deck trolleybus appeared on the SLT. Bodywork was by Massey and featured a two door low height layout and a seating capacity of 63 with 34 on the upper deck. It stands outside the *Stocks Hotel*, Swinton bound, with Walkden Memorial behind, to its right. Its smooth outline was most modernistic and at the time was, without doubt, seen as the trolleybus of the future. However nothing came of it and it is believed to have been dismantled by Leyland.

Photo, Ribble Enthusiasts Club.

Plate 385. One of the most significant trolleybuses ever to have operated under SLT wires was the unique twin steering trolleybus which was later to become London Transport's sole X7 class No.1671. Built in 1939, it bore a Lancashire registration DTD 649 and is known to have run in revenue earning service between Leigh and Bolton. Of characteristic London appearance, it was destined to remain a one-off. Noteworthy was its chassisless construction similar to London's 'L' classes. In the capital it initially operated from Fulwell depot, mainly on the 667, but was later transferred to Hanwell, principally operating, as photographed, on service 607 to Shepherds Bush. It was withdrawn in May 1955. Ironically, it was to encounter SLT trolleybuses for the second time, being despatched for scrap to Birds at Stratford upon Avon, soon to meet SLT Leylands Nos.48 to 51, also sold to Birds after cessation of trolleybus operation on the Bolton local services. *Photo, Author's collection.*

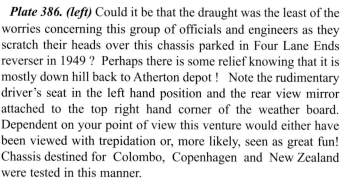

Plate 386. (left) Could it be that the draught was the least of the worries concerning this group of officials and engineers as they scratch their heads over this chassis parked in Four Lane Ends reverser in 1949 ? Perhaps there is some relief knowing that it is mostly down hill back to Atherton depot ! Note the rudimentary driver's seat in the left hand position and the rear view mirror attached to the top right hand corner of the weather board. Dependent on your point of view this venture would either have been viewed with trepidation or, more likely, seen as great fun! Chassis destined for Colombo, Copenhagen and New Zealand were tested in this manner.

Photo, the late J. Batty.

Plate 387. (right) Around 1954, a green double deck trolleybus sits in the reverser at Four Lane Ends about to return to Atherton. This was one of several batches of double deckers to run under trial on the SLT before shipment to the Ceylonese capital Colombo. Further Colombo trolleybuses appeared on trial again in 1957 though none operated in public service.

Photo, the late J. Batty.

Plate 388. Most trials on the SLT saw trolleybuses reversing at Four Lane Ends, the Bolton boundary, to return to Atherton. An exception was Glasgow BUT RETB1 dual entrance single decker TB 35 which travelled, on trial, through to Bolton on 16th January 1951. BUT was an amalgamation of Leyland's and AEC's trolleybus interests. Its Weymann body was internally laid out for high capacity standee operation. TB 35 turns a few heads as it departs Howell Croft bus station and no doubt has the undivided attention of the driver of the following Leyland TTB. His trolleybus has just received the all over red livery with a grey roof.

Photo, Ribble Enthusiasts Club.

Plate 389. The most modern trolleybuses to operate on the SLT system were several Sunbeam MF2B single deckers destined for Colombo which, in 1957, were to be seen on proving runs after completion of their bodywork by East Lancashire Coachbuilders of Blackburn. Of modern appearance, they were quite striking in their green livery and were to be seen, sometimes three together, on test between Leigh and Bolton prior to being towed to Birkenhead docks to await the long sea journey to Ceylon. Capturing infrequent and unscheduled trial runs as these was a matter of luck but Cyril Golding was fortunate enough to be in the right place with his camera to take this photograph of No.55 as it passed along King Street, Leigh, towards Spinning Jenny Street terminus on a wet 12th July 1957. These trolleybuses bore a remarkable resemblance to Glasgow BUT TB35 which had operated on the SLT some six years earlier in January 1951. *Photo, C.B.Golding.*

Plate 390. The Colombo single deckers were produced in two different lengths, an initial batch of 20 at 30ft long, of which No.55 pictured in Spinning Jenny Street terminus was the last, followed by a further batch of 6 at a length of 35ft. The shorter trolleybuses possessed a bulky appearance, a side on view belying their 30ft length. Their trolley bases were mounted amidships, the combined effect of being single deckers with trolley poles which were not overly long resulting in quite an acute angle being presented to the overhead. One effect of this was a somewhat reduced ability to deviate from the line of the overhead by virtue of a restricted outward reach by the trolley poles. *Photo, C.B.Golding.*

195

Plate 391. Reg Wilson managed to photograph some of the Colombo single deckers on 27th June 1957 at Bidston Dock, Birkenhead, about to depart these shores, including No.50 awaiting shipment with trolleys removed for safe transit. Note the bodybuilder's sign positioned in the centre bay window. The raked driver's windscreen was an anti glare measure, similar in style to that adopted post war by Birmingham City Transport. The neat proportions of these single deckers was enhanced by the smart green and cream livery.

Photo, the late Reg Wilson.

Plate 392. Manchester BUT 9612 trolleybus No.1302. Whilst Manchester's BUT 9612T trolleybuses never operated on the SLT, inclusion of a photograph of one of these fine vehicles is wholly appropriate in a section entitled *Strangers under SLT wires.* Earlier mention was made of their being towed brand new in groups of three or four from bodybuilders H.V.Burlingham of Blackpool in 1955/56, passing along the A6, firstly under the Leigh to Bolton wires at Four Lane Ends and then between Little Hulton and Swinton beneath the wires of the Atherton to Farnworth route. The first, No.1302 delivered in the summer of 1955, arrived just in time to operate on service 211 to Moston along Oldham Road before closure and is seen in Stevenson Square, in the company of an English Electric bodied Leyland TB5, awaiting departure on a 211x short working to the *Ben Brierley* on Moston Lane. Fortunately one of these BUT trolleybuses, No.1344, is preserved in fine order at the St.Helens Transport Museum, ironically just yards from another route once followed by SLT trolleybuses, namely the joint service with St. Helens Corporation from Atherton.

Photo, Author's collection,

Service Vehicles

A comprehensive record of service and support vehicles owned over the life of the South Lancashire trolleybus system is difficult to assemble bearing in mind that many would have operated in support of Lancashire United Transport. Some were dedicated to overhead line repairs whilst others were of a more general utility nature. However a complete listing of service vehicles owned at the time of dissolution of the SLT is as follows:-

TJ 5739   Leyland TS6 tower wagon, ex LUT bus No 241, new in 1934
CTJ 57   Leyland Badger tower wagon
CTJ 889   Leyland Badger tower wagon
BTF 882   Leyland Badger tower wagon
XTD 126   Bedford CA general purpose van
XTE 509   Bedford general purpose van
FTE 703   Commer service van
TC 3780   Bristol tower wagon, ex LUT bus No 67, new in 1923
RTJ 47   Ford service van
FTJ 796   Bedford utility service lorry
346 CTF   Bedford service lorry
TTF 516   Ford service van
225 CTC   Publicity van
BTF 576   Leyland TS7 breakdown crane, ex LUT bus No 23, new in 1937
TE 7074   Leyland LT1 pole carrier, ex LUT bus No 173, new in 1929
CTJ 168   Bedford lorry with collapsible platform on cab roof and equipped to tow buses.

For those who lived on the SLT system the vehicles that quickly became familiar and caught the eye when in action were tower wagons with their collapsible staging. One was often left to ponder as they seemingly took up whatever position was required, often at junctions, at will amidst the traffic, to attend to errant overhead wiring or the trolley heads of disabled trolleybuses.

Plate 393. TJ 5739 and its crew take a break in Atherton with the Savoy cinema and SLT booking office in the background. Its bus origins from 1934 are obvious and it became a familiar sight around the system, often found parked up between tasks as seen here in Atherton. The ladders on the side of the staging seem none too secure!   *Photo, R.C.Jackson.*

Plate 394. The Leyland Badger tower wagon BTF 882 was a purpose built overhead line repair vehicle. The front 'alpine' lights permitted an unobstructed view of the overhead without the crew members having to crane their necks forward. Seen here the crew attend to the wiring in Chaddock Lane, Boothstown.

Photo, East Pennine Transport Group.

Tickets

In the early days of the South Lancashire Tramways, Bell Punch tickets were issued which gave precise travel details i.e:- starting point and destination, the punch holes indicating the extent of travel. These were later simplified and coded to represent start and end of journeys. By 1930, at the time of the South Lancashire Transport Company's inception, Bell Punches were still in operation, and irrespective of journey, all tickets were white with the fare value overprinted in red. Coloured tickets reappeared in the mid 1930s denoting different values. An 'A', 'S' or 'PB' printed at the foot indicated from which depot the service was operated from. Day returns were available, overprinted 'R' and 'W' denoted a workman's ticket.

Whilst Lancashire United converted to TIM (Ticket Issuing Machines Ltd.) ticket machines in the late 1930s, the SLT persisted with Bell Punches until 1948 although the machines used by LUT were lettered for use by both companies and are known to have seen occasional use on trolleybuses well before their general introduction by the SLT. Tickets issued on SLT trolleybuses operating the Bolton local services continued to be of the Bell Punch type for some time after until Bolton converted to TIM machines. Until then conductors on trolleybuses working to Four Lane Ends from Atherton depot to take up Bolton local duties continued to issue Bell Punch tickets in order to avoid TIM machines lying idle whilst working for the rest of the day wholly within Bolton territory.

There were no through bookings at Four Lane Ends, passengers paid as far as Four Lane Ends after which the conductor would work through the trolleybus once more, issuing fresh tickets. Until 1952, when Bolton converted to TIM machines, conductors would issue TIM tickets on the SLT side of Four Lane Ends, changing over to Bell Punch tickets for fares collected within the Bolton boundary. After 1952 conductors found themselves swapping over identical TIM ticket machines at Four Lane Ends. To avoid confusion, the Bolton TIM machines had a large 'BC' painted on the machine and the tickets issued had a green stripe on both edges. The green stripe tickets alone were also valid for onward travel to Trinity Street Railway station.

A special card ticket was issued to the invited guests travelling on trolleybus No.71 on 1st September, the ceremonial last trolleybus which travelled from Atherton depot to Spinning Jenny Street Leigh. No tickets were issued on the return to Atherton depot since the public were allowed to travel free on this final return journey.

ABBREVIATIONS

AA......................Automobile Association.
BICC..................British Insulated Callender's Cables.
BUT...................British United Traction
B32F..................Single deck 32 seats, front entrance.
B44F.................. Single deck 44 seats, front entrance.
CEGB.................Central Electricity Generating Board.
DP40F................Dual Purpose 40 seats, front entrance
FC35F.................Full Front Coach 35 seats, front entrance
GCR...................Great Central Railway
GEC...................General Electric Company.
GPO...................General Post Office.
H61R..................Highbridge 61 seats, rear entrance
H64R..................Highbridge 64 seats, rear entrance
LMSR.................London Midland & Scottish Railway.
LNWR.................London & North Western Railway
LUT....................Lancashire United Transport.
L&Y...................Lancashire & Yorkshire Railway
MTMS...............Manchester Transport Museum Society.
NCB...................National Coal Board.
PTE....................Passenger Transport Executive
RAC...................Royal Automobile Club
SLT....................South Lancashire Transport.
TIM...................Ticket Issuing Machine
UDC..................Urban District Council.
UL24/26R..........Utility Lowbridge 24 seats upper deck 26 lower, rear entrance.

BIBILOGRAPHY

South Lancashire Tramways. E.K.Stretch, Manchester Transport Museum Society, 1972.

Lancashire United.   Eric Ogden, Transport Publishing Company, 1974.

Lancashire United/SLT.   Eric Ogden, Transport Publishing Company, 1985.

Trolleybus Trails.   J.Joyce, Ian Allan, 1963.

British Trolleybuses 1911 - 1972. Geoff Lumb, Ian Allan, 1995.

The Trolleybuses of St. Helens. Geoffrey Sandford, Reading Transport Society.

Local Transport in St. Helens.   T.B.Maund & M.J.Ashton, Venture   Publications 1995.

Manchester's Trolleybuses.   D.M.Eyre, C.W.Heaps, C.Taylor, Manchester Transport Museum Society, 1967.

Roads and Rails of Manchester 1900 to 1950. J.Joyce, Ian Allan, 1982.

British Trolleybus Systems.   J.Joyce, J.S.King, A.G.Newman, Ian Allan, 1986.

London's Trolleybuses.   PSV Circle, 1969.

Liverpool Transport. J.B.Horne & T.B.Maund, Transport Publishing Company, 1989.

Roads and Rails of Liverpool. J.Joyce, Ian Allan, 1983.

British Railways Maps and Gazetteer, C.J.Wignall, Oxford Publishing Co. 1983.

A Lancashire Triangle. Part One, D.J.Sweeney, Triangle Publishing, 1996.

A Lancashire Triangle. Part Two, D.J.Sweeney, Triangle Publishing, 1997

The Bridgewater Canal.   Ron & Marlene Freethy, Aurora Publishing.

The Worsley Village.   Ann Monaghan & C.Carson, City of Salford Education and Leisure.

Four Centuries of Lancashire Cotton. Geoffrey Timmins, Lancashire County Books, 1996.